KNOWLEDGE
AND SOCIETY

'T.K. Oommen...addresses conceptual, methodological, and substantive issues with clarity and critical acumen. The essays highlight his deep concern with the enterprise of living in a multicultural society. His emphasis on contextualization in sociological research, his readiness to disagree with prevailing perspectives, and his determination to provide alternatives are defining features of his work... This stimulating volume should interest both the learners and the mature practitioners of the craft of sociology.'

—**T.N. Madan**
Honorary Professor (Sociology), Institute of Economic Growth, Delhi

T.K. Oommen

KNOWLEDGE AND SOCIETY

Revised Edition

SITUATING SOCIOLOGY AND SOCIAL ANTHROPOLOGY

OXFORD
UNIVERSITY PRESS

OXFORD
UNIVERSITY PRESS

Oxford University Press is a department of the University of Oxford.
It furthers the University's objective of excellence in research, scholarship,
and education by publishing worldwide. Oxford is a registered trademark of
Oxford University Press in the UK and in certain other countries

Published in India by
Oxford University Press
YMCA Library Building, 1 Jai Singh Road, New Delhi 110 001, India

© Oxford University Press 2007

The moral rights of the author have been asserted

First Edition published in 2007
Revised Edition 2013

ISBN-13: 978-0-19-809046-5
ISBN-10: 0-19-809046-3

Typeset in Nebraska 10/12
by The Graphics Solution, New Delhi 110 092
Printed in India by G.H. Prints Pvt Ltd, New Delhi 110 020

To
Professors Ramakrishna Mukherjee & Yogendra Singh.
Scholars who analysed Indian sociology from
the perspective of sociology of knowledge.

Contents

Preface and Acknowledgements

The 12 chapters of this book were written during the course of half-a-century spanning the professional career of its author. The three chapters of Part III, added to this revised edition, were delivered as memorial lectures in honour of three distinguished sociologists/social anthropologists of India. These lectures are printed in this volume in the order in which they were delivered. Independently and collectively, the book addresses some of the issues relating to the impact of society and polity in producing and disseminating knowledge in the two cognate disciplines of sociology and social anthropology.

The major part of Chapter 2 was the first to be published. It appeared in *Economic and Political Weekly*, 4 (19), 1969, pp. 809–15 under the title 'Data Collection Techniques: The Case of Sociology and Social Anthropology'. A small part is added to the chapter to update it and, thus, Chapter 2 is an amalgam and is published for the first time in this form but reproduced here with the permission of the editor of *Economic and Political Weekly*.

Chapters 1, 3, 7, 9, 11, and 12 were published in *Sociological Bulletin*, the official journal of the Indian Sociological Society. Chapter 1 was published with the same title in 1983, vol. 32 (2), pp. 111–36; Chapter 3 was published with the title 'Theoretical Framework and Empirical Research: Their Interaction in the Analysis of Two Social Movements' in 1987, vol. 36 (2), pp. 57–75 and Chapter 7 was published in 1991, vol. 39 (1 & 2), pp. 128–41 with the title 'Sociology for One World: A Plea for an Authentic Sociology'. This is a revised version of the presentation made in the concluding plenary session of the XIIth World Congress of Sociology, held in Madrid (Spain) during 9–13 July 1990, the theme of which was 'Sociology for One World: Unity and Diversity'. Chapter 9 in the earlier edition is replaced by the present version, which is a revised and enlarged one. Chapters 11 and 12 are M.N. Srinivas and G.S. Ghurye memorial lectures published in *Sociological Bulletin* in 2008 and 2011, respectively. These six chapters are reproduced in this volume with the permission of the managing editor of *Sociological Bulletin*.

Chapter 4 was published in *Eastern Anthropologist*, the official journal of Ethnographic and Folk Culture Society, Lucknow, under the title 'On the Craft of Studying Social Movements: Two Illustrations', vol. 40 (3), 1987, pp. 185–202. It is reproduced here with the permission of the editors.

Chapter 5 was published with the title 'Civil Society and the Deprived: The Relevance of Perspective from Below', in T.K. Oommen (2004), *Nation, Civil Society and Social Movements: Essays in Political Sociology*, New Delhi: Sage Publications, pp. 161–78. It is reproduced here with the permission of the publishers.

Chapter 6 was first published in *Current Sociology*, an official journal of the International Sociological Association, with the title 'Internationalization of Sociology: A View from Developing Countries', vol. 39 (1), 1991, pp. 67–84. It is reproduced here with the permission of the editor.

Chapter 8 is an amalgam of two research papers: 'Changing Modes of Conceptualizing the World: Implications for Social Research', published in Partha Nath Mukherji (ed.) (2000), *Methodology in Social Research*, New Delhi: Sage Publications, pp. 153–70, and a paper presented in the first plenary session of the 36th World Congress of the International Institute of Sociology, held at Beijing on 7–11 July 2004, the theme of which was 'Social Change in the Age of Globalization'. It is reproduced here with the necessary permissions.

Chapter 10 is being published for the first time. This is an edited version of the first Y.B. Damle memorial lecture delivered in 2007 at the Department of Sociology, University of Pune.

I thank all the editors, publishers, and organizers of seminars and congresses for permission to reproduce these research papers in this volume.

NEW DELHI   T.K. OOMMEN
May 2012

Abbreviations

CDP	Community Development Programme
CPC	Council of the People's Commission
CPI	Communist Party of India
CPI (M)	Communist Party of India (Marxist)
CPI (R)	Communist Party of India (Right)
EU	European Union
FAO	Food and Agriculture Organization
IADP	Intensive Agricultural Development Program
ICSSR	Indian Council of Social Science Research
ISS	Indian Sociological Society
OBC	Other Backward Class
RSP	Revolutionary Socialist Party
SAP	Structural Adjustment Programme
SC	Scheduled Caste
ST	Scheduled Tribe
TAT	Thematic Apperception Test
TISS	Tata Institute of Social Sciences
UNESCO	United Nations Educational, Scientific and Cultural Organization

Introduction
Sociology and Social Anthropology
Persisting Tensions

There are several persisting tensions in sociology; I shall identify three of them for attention in this introduction. One of these tensions emanates from its ambiguous identity vis-à-vis social anthropology. But this tension is peculiar to post-colonial Old World societies of Asia and Africa. It is absent in the other set of post-colonial societies of the New World—the Americas, Australia, and New Zealand—as well as in Europe. The second tension under reference is based on sociology's claim for 'scientificity' along with material and life sciences. Sociology shares this tension with political science and economics too, although economics has been more successful in staking its claim for a scientific status. The third tension in sociology is to be located in the appropriateness regarding the units of analyses—society, nation-state, and civilization. I shall discuss these tensions in the order in which they are listed. An attempt will also be made to understand the sources of tensions between sociology and social anthropology which is peculiar to Asia and Africa.

Asian sociologists are of two types: those who are sociologists everywhere, at home as well in the West and those who are sociologists at home but are labelled as social anthropologists in the West, both by themselves and by their western colleagues. This has precious little to do with the initial training of these scholars; there are many instances of those who were trained as social anthropologists but metamorphosed into sociologists through their academic activities. The reverse too is true but their number is much smaller. Those who have dual identities—sociologists in South Asia and social anthropologists in the West—are offered/take up assignments in the departments of social/cultural anthropology while in the West on visiting assignments. This is an important source of ambiguity in South Asian sociology.

The source of this ambiguity, however, is to be located in the origins of sociology and social anthropology in the West and their transplantation in the colonies. First, the circumstances which gave birth to these disciplines in the West are dramatically different. In the West, anthropology and colonialism were inextricably intertwined; anthropology was perceived as the child of colonialism. In contrast, sociology is cognized as the offspring of modernity. Pursuantly, anthropologists studied 'other cultures' which were 'pre-modern' and sociologists investigated their own societies which are designated as modern.

Second, conventionally anthropologists studied small-scale societies and situations: tribes initially, peasants subsequently, segments of urban settlements latterly. Sociologists, in contrast, invariably studied modern, complex societies. Third, the themes which engaged the attention of anthropologists initially were social structure and social institutions such as family, kinship, caste, religion, and the like in village settings, that is, microstructures. Sociologists, in addition to these themes, also studied modern organizations, professions, social movements, that is, structures and processes considered to be contemporary and macro and/or micro depending upon the contexts. Finally, given the locales, themes, and the nature of the units studied, participant observation was found to be the most suitable 'method' to collect qualitative data by social anthropologists. In contrast, a multiplicity of 'methods' were/are employed by sociologists; they also give substantial importance to quantitative data.

The exit of colonizers, transformation of erstwhile colonies into sovereign states, the study by social anthropologists of their own societies and their new inclination to analyse a multiplicity of themes which were/are connected with 'nation-building' and policy formulation, the need to collect and analyse quantitative data, the transformation of pre-literate societies into societies in which a substantial segment of the population is literate were all factors which contributed to bring about a paradigm shift in social anthropology in post-colonial countries. Instead of acknowledging this change in the 'historicity of context' and recognizing their 'trained incapacity', some social anthropologists started privileging their discipline vis-à-vis sociology. In fact, sociology was stigmatized by British social anthropologists (see, for example, Homans 1962: 113–19).

The termination of colonialism affected western social anthropology irreversibly. Stigmatized labelling such as 'savage', 'primitive', 'black', 'oriental', and the like have been rejected by non-western social anthropologists. The western anthropologists were also compelled to replace these terms with a new encapsulating term wherein the content of their 'field' shifted from culture to development. Thus the term 'Third World' came into vogue in which three geographical spaces—Africa, Asia, and Latin America—which shared little in cultural terms were bundled together (see Chapter 8). And yet, some western social anthropologists (for example, Claude Lévi-Strauss) insisted that the discipline should keep its focus on 'savage societies'; others (for example, Louis Dumont) argued that sociological understanding is advanced better by social anthropologists' study of foreign societies; and still others like J.A. Barnes suggested that the social anthropological method is better equipped to understand sociological processes (see Chapter 2). There are also western sociologists such as Alain Touraine who suggest that sociology can develop only in modern western societies.

However, the above claims of western social anthropologists have been rejected by non-western social anthropologists (for example, M.N. Srinivas) and sociologists (for example, S.N. Eisenstadt). The argument that sociology can develop only in the 'programmed societies' of the West too has been rebutted (see Oommen 1996: 111–25). In the mean time many social anthropologists have shifted their interest to the study of complex societies, even civilizations. This shift also necessitated the demystification of participant observation as the only authentic method of social anthropology.

Those who ineluctably associate sociology with modernity also had to reckon with two implications of their position. One, non-modern societies will not witness the birth and flowering of sociology, a highly contestable proposition. This is so because a historical conjunction between modernity and the rise of sociology in the West need not hold good elsewhere. Two, sociology will wither away as modernity recedes into the background and the Global Age assumes greater significance. A particular discipline may emerge in specific historical conditions but its demise need not occur with the disappearance of those conditions; witness the persistence of anthropology.

The sane route to cope with these irrelevant controversies is to recast the discipline so as to transcend particular historical contexts. Thus, one can legitimately think of sociologies of 'pre-modern', 'modern', and 'post-modern' societies. However, this did not happen in Indian sociology/social anthropology. If in the 1930s and 1940s an indological approach and exegetical analyses were preferred, during the 1950s and 1960s the 'field view' and participant observation were privileged to study villages, family and kinship, caste and religion. Instead of recognizing the fact that themes of study and techniques of data collection are complementary, the 'deviants' who took up new themes and 'methods' were invariably stigmatized. In Chapter 1, I emphasize the importance of contextualization and in Chapter 2, I discuss the puerile controversy regarding data collection techniques among sociologists and social anthropologists. I have argued that there is an organic relationship between the nature of (1) the themes studied and the methods invoked, (2) the nature and characteristics of the universe studied and the methods employed, and (3) that no method is inherently superior or inferior but they are contextually relevant or irrelevant.

All social science data are elicited through/from three sources: (1) oral/verbal responses, (2) observation, and (3) records. The appropriateness of the sources of data would depend upon the type of information required. If frequency distribution is the type of information required, the best technique for data collection is enumeration and/or studying samples. If it is necessary and feasible to enumerate the entire universe of study, the researcher should conduct census. If only a representative sample needs to be enumerated then sampling should be resorted to; in both cases, census and sampling, survey research is required and it is the most efficient and the best form of data collection technique.

In contrast, if the researcher wants to find out institutionalized statuses and norms prevalent in the society, interviewing informants is the most efficient. Informants are different from respondents in that they speak on behalf of the social segments to which they belong. On the other hand, respondents speak for themselves in their individual capacity. Finally, if data are to be collected about incidents and events, participant observation is the best technique because researchers can participate in them if it is feasible. But in order to decipher the meaning of incidents, researchers have to engage in conversations with informants. Thus, in practice, participant observation and informant interviewing are invariably undertaken together. But if written records exist in a society one can comb them also for relevant information. Instead of recognizing the fact that all techniques of data collection are contextually relevant, participant observation and survey technique have been mystified and often juxtaposed by their advocates. This has been a bane rather than a boon for social research everywhere, including in India.

Most sociologists and social anthropologists of India were happy with what is designated as 'raw empiricism' by R.K. Merton and rarely did they invoke an explicit theoretical framework while undertaking field research. The prescription to go to the field with an 'open mind' was the refrain among social anthropologists. If sociologists attempted to undertake fieldwork equipped with a theoretical framework and conceptual tools, not only was it discouraged, it was also instantly dismissed as foolhardy. Chapter 3 addresses the advantages and disadvantages of having a preconceived theoretical framework and a conceptual kit in the study of ongoing social movements, a theme not studied until the 1960s by Indian sociologists.

This gap is filled through a narration of the specific problems encountered in the study of social movements in Chapter 4. Chapters 3 and 4 conjointly demonstrate as to how theories, concepts, data collection techniques, themes of research, and structure of society are linked. These two chapters also demonstrate how sociology is done in India in a 'sociological' way as against the social anthropological style of doing sociology, which was the dominant pattern in India until recently.

The structure of society deeply impinges on the process of production and consumption of knowledge. All societies are stratified based on age, gender, class, and rural–urban differences. As age groups are distributed across all social categories and those who live long enough pass through different phases of life, age is not considered a disadvantage after the attainment of adulthood in the context of knowledge production. Upward mobility invariably threw up members from lower classes and spatial mobility facilitated those with rural backgrounds into the vocation of knowledge production. But due to deep-rooted persisting prejudices, women did not find a place as producers of knowledge in most societies until the twentieth century. Further, those who are illiterate (in societies with written tradition) are taken to be incapable of even knowledge consumption. By the 1970s women started articulating the need to look at facts and analysing them through the perspective of gender. The demand for representation of women in knowledge production became a 'movement' all over the world and India is not an exception to this.

Most contemporary societies are culturally and racially hetero-geneous. While this fact in itself need not adversely affect the process of knowledge production, reality is otherwise because the collectivities under reference may not have egalitarian relationship thanks to history and tradition, 'ethnic sponsorship', and prevailing prejudices. Thus, community traditions favoured some (for example, Brahmins and Jews) in knowledge production, while others took advantage of their dominant positions in particular societies (for example, Muslim aristocracy, Protestant elites, Buddhist and Catholic clergy). While their near monopoly is gradually changing thanks to modern social forces—industrial urbanization, democratization, secularization—it cannot be asserted confidently that heterogeneous societies have become adequately open and transparent, facilitat-ing all social segments to be equal participants in the process of consumption of knowledge, not to speak of its production.

A third feature of social structure which influences the process of knowledge production may be designated as externalization. There are two variants of the externalized collectivity: those who are actually outsiders to that particular society—immigrants, refugees, exiles—and those who are insiders but are perceived and defined as outsiders by the cultural mainstream. The first category, insofar as they are only a few and do not develop any political ambition, may focus on the production of wealth and knowledge to achieve prominence in the host society. The Jews in diaspora afford the classic example of this type. In contrast are those who are perceived as outsiders, although they are actually insiders, by the dominant group, the cultural main-stream. This seems to be the case of Muslims and Blacks in those societies where they are minorities, which leads to the twin processes of their collective alienation and stigmatization. Consequently, they get excluded from the process of knowledge production.

The fourth and the most crucial element which adversely affects participation in the process of knowledge production is hierarchy, a system which prescribes the task to one group and proscribes other groups from it. This existed in the classical Greek city states vis-à-vis patricians and plebeians, in apartheid South Africa between Whites and Blacks, and traditional India between Brahmins and other castes particularly those who were the 'untouchables'. In the case of India, the principle of hierarchy was legitimized by religion which made the incorporation of the ex-untouchables into the process of knowledge production impossible. Further, the kind of knowledge they produced was undervalued, nay stigmatized (see Chapter 5).

The practice of untouchability has serious implications for the practice of participant observation as a technique of data collection, in that interaction between the researchers who are ritually clean caste Hindus and ritually unclean castes was proscribed. This is particularly debilitating for social anthropology in India which prided in obtaining its data through participant observation. That is, participant observation, the preferred 'method' of data collection by social anthropologists cannot be authentically practised in several contexts in a hierarchical society. Consequently, the knowledge produced about such a society will remain partial and, even partisan, which poses serious methodological issues (see Chapter 5). But those who privilege the 'field view' as against the 'book view' seem to have not taken seriously this methodological issue. Thus, Srinivas: 'Ideally, the anthropologist should be able to empathise with the Brahmin and the untouchable ... ' (2002: 583). Ideally yes, but actually is it possible? Even if the researcher tries, the field situation and social reality in India are not amenable to it (see Chapter 4).

The political circumstances which caused the birth of anthropology and sociology largely explain why the boundaries of the two disciplines are distinct in Europe and why they are ambiguous in post-colonial societies. Whereas the object of anthropological investigation, be it the savage other, the Black other, or the generalized ethnographic other was a distinct and distant other for Europeans, the object of sociological enquiry was one's own society. Therefore, the frontiers of the two disciplines were clearly demarcated. In contrast, in post-colonial societies the situation differed.

In the New World, the Savage or Native Other, the subject matter of anthropological study, initially was distinct but not distant; they formed part of the 'nation-state' and were co-residents in the state territory. Therefore, sociology and anthropology seem to have agreed on a division of labour in the New World; the former focused on society and the latter on culture facilitating a peaceful co-existence.

(It is no accident that the designation in Britain is social anthropology whereas in the US it is cultural anthropology.) In the case of post-colonial societies of Asia where the anthropological focus was on tribes who are distinct, the effort was to 'integrate' them into the national mainstream (see Chapter 9); in Africa the tribes constituted mainstream society. Therefore, it was somewhat incongruous to keep the frontiers of sociology and social anthropology distinct in Asia and Africa. Thus, the historical origins of the two disciplines and the way in which they are practised in different sites are at variance, which explains much of the tension between them in Asia and Africa.

The second tension that I have referred to at the outset of this introduction is the claim made by sociology for scientificity. The conventional position is that scientific laws are universal and they hold true irrespective of time, space, and subject matter. However, even the three founding fathers of social science did not share this view. For Émile Durkheim different social science disciplines are distinct in terms of their subject matter; sociology investigated social facts. But all sciences, according to Durkheim, share unity of method via positivism irrespective of their contents.

Karl Marx also held the view that, irrespective of the nature of the subject matter, all sciences can be studied through a common method, namely, dialectical materialism. In spite of the consensus regarding the unity of methods, although of different types, Durkheim and Marx drastically differed in their ideological dispositions. But that need not detain us here. Max Weber, however, held a different view. According to him, since the subject matter of cultural sciences differed they require a different method. Weber's method may be designated as humanism (see Benton 1977) because it squarely recognized the unique features of human beings and their implications for the methodology to be invoked to study them. To study cultural sciences the researcher needs to develop empathy, an 'understanding' of his/her subject matter. I suggest that it is a good beginning to situate the intricate relationship between the subject matter of a field of enquiry and its implications for methodology.

Viewed in this vein the juxtaposition between universality and indigeneity (see Mukherji and Sengupta 2004) is a misplaced one; like all dichotomies it is simplistic. The fact that no physicist, for example, would argue for indigenization of his discipline should alert us to the reason why such discussions surface in the case of the social sciences. In the case of botany or zoology, indigenization can only mean the study of flora and fauna peculiar to the geographic region scientists study. But such a focus does not alter the germ theory or for that matter the theory of evolution. In contrast, the subject matter of social science is tempered by the context of its existence. I suggest that the context is provided by civilization (see Chapter 7). In this sense, social sciences are already indigenized because social scientists study the empirical reality specific to their contexts.

As I see it, there are three broad fields of knowledge and in each of these there are several disciplines. First, those disciplines which study only matter (material sciences); their subject matter is one-dimensional. Elements in the material universe may react to one another and produce change or disturbance. For example, the interaction between sodium and water or magnet and iron bring about changes in them. Similarly cataclysmic events such as cyclones, earthquakes, and tsunamis are disturbances brought about through interactions in the material universe. But elements in this universe do not have motives or intentions as they do not have agency. They are only capable of *reactivity*. It is relatively easy to understand and explain material phenomena as (1) they are one-dimensional and (2) they do not have agency. This perhaps explains the tremendous progress made in disciplines such as physics, chemistry, geology, and the like.

Second, those disciplines which study matter *and* life, like botany, zoology, physical anthropology, physiology, etc. The subject matter of life sciences is bi-dimensional. That plants and animals respond to music is now well established; they are capable of *responsivity*. However, while plants do not recognize those who nurture them, domesticated animals differentiate between their masters and strangers. They have motives but these are located in their biology—biogenic motives. It is important to note here that progress made in measurement in life sciences is less as compared with progress made in material sciences. In turn, the progress made in botany can be greater as compared with the progress made in zoology as its subject matter is less complex. Plants do not distinguish between friends and foes, they do not have motives. But this is not so in the case of animals. That is, the complexity/simplicity of a discipline determines the advancement it makes.

Third, the subject matter of social/cultural sciences are three-dimensional as it encapsulates matter, life, and culture simultaneously. A paper weight thrown on the floor does not respond to that, but an animal when beaten will respond. But it cannot and will not question why it is beaten up. In contrast, a human being, even a slave or a child (after a certain age) is capable of interrogating those who inflict pain on them and/or appreciate those who treat them with compassion. Human beings are not only capable of reactivity and responsivity but also *reflexivity*. This renders the subject matter of social/cultural sciences enormously complex because of which the progress made in this field is less as compared with material and life sciences.

If matter is the object of study of material sciences and life is the focus of life sciences, culture is the central theme of social sciences; culture being the human capacity to create meanings and symbols which cannot be understood through sense organs. Therefore, the process of verification in social sciences, the route to establish as to whether the facts observed are reliable or not, will have to be different from that of material and life sciences. In social sciences, facts constitute constructed meanings which can only be deciphered with the help of those who construct them, the people.

The proposition can be understood with the help of a few examples. Believers consider certain objects as sacred. For example, believing Hindus consider water from the river Ganga as sacred. But that water according to scientists is merely H_2O. If one uses the same water for nurturing plants or serves it to animals, it would not make any difference to either. But for the believer, holy water is qualitatively different from water that flows out of the tap and the difference cannot be understood through sense organs, by seeing, smelling, or tasting. The difference between the holy water and ordinary water can only be understood through the attributed meaning to the former because it is a symbol and not a mere material object.

The tricolour, India's national flag, is an object of veneration for Indian citizens. But the flag is made of three pieces of cloth of different colours with the Ashok Chakra embossed. The material quality of the flag is exactly the same as the quality of the cloth in the stock out of which it is taken. But its symbolic meaning makes it a qualitatively different object. As a symbolic object which represents the nation, its quality transcends its material attributes. This symbolic quality cannot be verified with the sense organs but it can be discerned on the basis of citizens' attitude to it and their veneration for it.

Finally, the well-established laws of demand and supply in economics cannot be easily applied to the rationale behind buying expensive wedding outfits or the high price that one is prepared to pay for perfumes to please a spouse or lover. The theory of supply and demand based on the rationality of economic transactions cannot account for the arationality which informs such human behaviour. If one ignores these aspects in human behaviour and assumes that it is entirely rational, it is possible to make substantial theoretical advancement as some branches of economics did achieve. In this context *homo economicus* replaces *homo sociologus*. It should be clear by now that I am invoking the notion of culture as constructed meaning which informs all aspects of human behaviour be it religious, political, or economic.

These considerations also prompt a comment on the unwarranted controversy regarding objectivity in social science. Universality presupposes 'objectivity' of a 'generalizing tenor' irrespective of spatio-temporal variations. Such objectivity is untenable in the case of social sciences and hence to pursue it would be a wild goose chase. Does this mean that social scientists should abandon the notion of objectivity? The answer is certainly not in the affirmative. I suggest that social scientists should pursue what may be called 'particularizing objectivity' which is context specific, contextualization being the kernel of sociological enquiry as D.P. Mukherji reminded us (1945).

Objectivity, the sense in which I am invoking the notion, can only mean intrasubjectivity or intersubjectivity. Intrasubjectivity obtains when an investigator gets the same result while analysing the same phenomenon repeatedly provided (1) the phenomenon under investigation has not changed and (2) the investigator holds on to the same value orientation. That is, if the investigator has changed his value orientation and/or the phenomenon under investigation has undergone transformation, it is not possible to get the same results in the process of repeated verification.

Intersubjectivity exists when two persons holding similar value orientations get the same result when they study a phenomenon with similar characteristics at the same point in time. That is, objectivity in social science can only be achieved either as intrasubjectivity or as intersubjectivity and hence my designation of it as 'particularizing objectivity' as against 'generalizing objectivity', the latter being objectivity which obtains irrespective of time and space. Generalizing objectivity is unattainable in the case of the social sciences because in the final analysis their subject matter is cultural in the sense in which I have explained above.

Finally, one should be aware of the perennial possibility of indigenization slipping into hegemonization. What is relevant here is not intention but consequence. Further, that which is taken to be indigenous is not necessarily native, but the dominant, invariably designated as the national. Thus the agenda of indigenization invariably ends up as aggressive nationalism of a pathological orientation. In the South Asian context it will produce Hindu social science in India and Nepal, Buddhist social science in Sri Lanka and Bhutan, Islamic social science in Pakistan and Bangladesh. There is increasing evidence to support this fear (see Chapters 1 and 7).

The above considerations compel one to abandon both universalization (because of the specificity of subject matter of social science and the consequent impossibility of achieving generalizing objectivity) and indigenization (because of the danger of it becoming a tool for pathological nationalism) of social science. Therefore I argue that social science should constantly attempt contextualization both in spatial and temporal terms. I suggest that civilization be the unit of macrosociological analysis, nation (not to be confused with nation-state) be the unit of mesosociological analysis, and structures, institutions, and processes within nations be the units of microsociological analysis. Further, it is also necessary to take into account the social transformation occurring in the world as a whole and in the civilizational and national contexts in particular. Therefore, contextualization is addressed both in spatial and temporal terms (see Chapters 1 and 8).

The third tension relates to appropriate units of analysis in sociology, which also remains a contentious issue. The units of analysis, like the techniques of data collection, are appropriate or inappropriate depending upon the theme of research. Micro units are most appropriate for the study of family and kinship, caste and village, and similar themes. This is not to suggest that these units remain insulated, indeed they are interconnected with the wider macrostructures. Economic, political, educational, and cultural institutions and organizations are mesounits situated between micro and macro units, indeed interconnecting them. And 'society' which constitutes the macro unit of sociological analysis is an extremely ambiguous notion and the problem is common to both sociology and social anthropology. For western sociologists, given the co-terminality between political and cultural boundaries, actual or assumed, the problem is simpler. As Zygmunt Bauman noted, the conflation between society and nation-state is pervasive in western social science.

Both sociologists and social anthropologists refer to 'Indian society' as well as to Tamil, Bengali, Punjabi, Naga, Santali, and Bhil 'societies'. Therefore, the conventional distinction between sociology and social anthropology could have been maintained in the Indian situation. Thus a Punjabi, Tamil, Bengali, or Naga who studies her own society is a sociologist and when she studies a society other than hers, she becomes a social anthropologist! But this is not how 'society' is conceived when we refer to Indian society. Further, the distinction between Indian 'society' and other 'societies' listed above is not sustainable in practice in the Indian subcontinent.

The Punjabi society is divided across India and Pakistan, the Bengali society across India and Bangladesh, the Tamil society between India and Sri Lanka, and the Naga society across India and Myanmar. Can one say that an Indian Bengali sociologist studying Bangladeshi society is studying his own society? Even if the researcher is accepted as a cultural insider by the Bangladeshis among whom s/he does research, s/he is a legal outsider. If boundaries of societies and polities are not co-terminus, it is difficult to maintain the distinction between one's own society and 'other cultures'. For the European anthropologists and sociologists not only did cultural and political boundaries coincide in the entity of nation-state, but the 'primitive', 'savage', 'peasant', 'tribal', or 'oriental' societies he studied were situated far away from his homeland. Therefore, the difference between one's own society and alien society and the distinction anchored to that to distinguish sociology and social anthropology was tenable. To apply that distinction to the situation which obtains in post-colonial societies of the Americas, Australia, Africa, and Asia, particularly South Asia, is certainly not sustainable.

There is a second problem in the case of South Asia where religion is the central element in the formation of states. Thus the Bengali Hindu and the Bengali Muslim or the Punjabi Sikh and the Punjabi Muslim are believed to belong to different 'societies' because of their religious affiliations. Consequently one can speak of Hindu, Muslim, and Sikh societies. But the members of these 'societies' are dispersed all over the world through migrations. This means societies cannot be understood in terms of their spatial locations. Viewed thus, for the Hindus, 'other cultures' would mean cultures of Muslim societies and for Muslims it would mean cultures of Hindu societies, found anywhere in the world.

Third, there are those who are *in* the society but not *of* it, those who are externalized from the society by defining them as 'cultural aliens', the Muslims and Christians in India and Hindus, Sikhs, and Christians in Bangladesh and Pakistan. This makes the societies in the Indian subcontinent 'plural' in the sense in which Furnivall (1948) defined it. Finally, there are those who are accepted as insiders but are treated as congenital inferiors because of their caste affiliation, those who are defined as ritually polluting. This brings in the juxtaposition between the 'society' of the caste Hindus versus that of the 'untouchables'. That is, the notion of society in which all its members share a sense of belonging and have the opportunity to participate in all its activities does not come through easily.

The discussion on the specificities of the South Asian situation prompts two conclusions. First, the distinction between social anthropology as a discipline studying other cultures and sociology as a discipline which studies one's own society is ambiguous and hence the distinction is largely irrelevant. Second, participant observation, the unique selling point of social anthropology, cannot be pressed into service because of two of its distinctive features: plurality and hierarchy. This largely explains the near total absence of the studies of religious minorities and ex-untouchables by caste Hindu social anthropologists through participant observation. These conclusions have serious implications for determining the units of analysis.

If conflation between state and nation is untenable in the South Asian context, the notion of 'internationalization of sociology' as it is understood generally cannot also be easily applied. In Europe, internationalization of sociology refers to the international flows of sociological knowledge, say, between English, French, German, Italian, and similar sociologies. Given the co-terminality between nation, state, and society, sociology became utterly state-centric in Europe. But this is not true in the two post-colonial situations of the New World and Asia and Africa (see Chapter 9).

Conversely, in the case of the multinational state of the former Soviet Union there was only one 'national tradition' of sociology. But with its break up several 'national traditions' emerged. Similarly, if one were to write on the 'national tradition' of sociology in Pakistan during the 1950s or 1960s there would have been only one such tradition. By the 1970s two national traditions emerged; one for Bangladesh and the other for Pakistan. These examples clearly point to the fact that sociology is state-centric everywhere and hence its unit of analysis, namely nation-state remains an artificial entity. It is absolutely necessary to render sociology a society-centric discipline. But the notion of society itself is largely ambiguous as I have shown above and hence this needs to be addressed urgently.

One needs to keep in mind yet another fact in this context. Of the 220 or so member nation-states of the United Nations more than 50 per cent have a population of five million or less. On the other hand, only a dozen of them have a population of one hundred million or more. Needless to say, these 'societies' vary vastly in their cultural and social structural complexities and therefore these societies are not appropriate units for comparative analyses; the birth of authentic comparative sociology thus remains frozen. Keeping these considerations in mind I have argued that the appropriate units for macro sociological analyses are civilizational-societies and not state-societies (see Chapters 7 and 8).

Given the fact that state-societies of the world (invariably referred to as nation-states) are so vastly different in terms of their size, complexity, and power, 'sociology for one world', the advocacy which captures the crystallizing spirit of globalization is a sure invitation for a hegemonic sociology dominated by a dozen countries or so. Hegemonization carries with it the seeds of homogenization. In fact, both globalization at the world level and indigenization at the level of nation-states are homogenizing in their thrust. This combination is a lethal one in that they will impose a cognitive blackout on the rich diversity of cultures and social structures which prevail in the world today. In contrast, civilizational-society recognizes the dignified co-existence of different cultures, lifestyles, religions, and languages within and between societies. Invoking civilizational-society as the unit of analysis is the prerequisite not only for the co-existence but also for the celebration of cultural diversity.

It is true that civilizations rise and fall, but it is a long-term process. In contrast, the rise and fall of state-societies happen within a short span of time (for example, the dismantling of several socialist states; bifurcation and unification of Germany, division of Pakistan, Korea, Ethiopia, Indonesia, etc.). A civilizational-society encapsulates several nations and states and their divisions and unifications do not mean the disintegration of civilization. Within the European civilizational region, nation-states started proliferating in the nineteenth century but by the mid-twentieth century a process of unification started giving birth to a new structure—the European Union (EU). But in spite of these the basic integrity of the European civilization remains intact. This is also true of the South Asian civilization. This provides the rationale for endorsing the civilizational-society as the unit of macro-sociological analysis.

The distinction between nation-state and national state is crucial; nation-states relentlessly pursue the ideal of homogenizing the cultures of minorities through linguistic, religious, and educational standard-ization. Although in the last two centuries the demands for political autonomy based on cultural specificity have increased, only a small proportion of the world's distinctive religious, linguistic, and cultural communities have succeeded in this endeavour (Tilly 1994). Tilly had suggested the notion of the national state because it can foster cultural diversity within its territory. But his definition of national state as ' ... relatively centralized, differentiated and autonomous organizations successfully claiming priority in the use of force within large, contiguous and clearly bounded territories' (Tilly 1990: 43), while accommodating the structure of states, cannot account for the sentiment of nations. Therefore, I suggest that the designation national state should refer to such states which consciously nurture cultural diversity and endorse cultural pluralism as a value.

The emergence of the global age necessitates the transcending of the conventional macro unit of sociological analysis namely 'nation-state' and to extricate sociology from its current state-centrism and render it society-centric. In this new envisioning of sociology, civilization should constitute the macro unit, national societies (not to be confused for nation-states) should be the meso units, and intrasocietal institutions and organizations should be the micro units of analysis.

Given the emphasis I attach to civilization as the unit of macro-sociological analysis and because of the confusing ways in which the notion is conceptualized, it is necessary to provide a few clarifications. The term 'civilization' was first used in 1756 by the French writer Mirabeau according to whom religion was its principal source. But the term 'culture' was invoked by the 1780s to counter the idea of civilization. If civilization meant a cold, calculating, and universalizing mode of thinking as articulated in France and in the Enlightenment idea, culture as enunciated by the German philosopher Herder was rooted in land, blood, and history of the people (folk). Further, if civilization connoted material advancement, culture came to refer to mental and moral dimensions.

Civilization denoted human control of nature and was used in the singular. Technology was the instrument to control nature and the one who possessed it was superior. In contrast, culture referred to the social construction of meaning and was used in the plural; different cultures constructed their specific meaning systems. In this rendition, the West had both civilization and culture; the East had no civilization but only culture, its version of social construction of meaning. Fortunately excavations started in the 1790s although the term 'archaeology' was not coined until 1856. Thanks to archaeological excavations, ancient civilizations of Egypt, Mesopotamia, Babylon, China, India, etc., were discovered. Those who had been hitherto dismissed as barbarians were elevated to the status of the civilized.

Today there are three prominent connotations of the term civilization; one, region-specific civilizations such as African, European, Chinese, South Asian, and the like; two, economy-specific civilizations like agrarian, industrial, and post-industrial; and three, religion-specific civilizations such as Buddhist, Christian, Hindu, Islamic, and similar ones. Religion has been substantially deterritorialized since the sixteenth century and no religion can be exclusively identified with any region. Further, historically viewed, no religious community had the monopoly of knowledge production.

Against this background some scholars revert to the use of the term civilization in singular denoting human control over nature, marked by technological advancement. Civilization in this perspective is viewed as the common heritage of humanity. The problem with this singular notion of civilization based on technology is that a hierarchy of nations, states, and religions anchored to the superiority–inferiority syndrome will necessarily emerge. And this is precisely what Huntington had in mind when he referred to the clash of civilizations. 'To preserve western civilization in the face of declining western power, it is in the interest of the US and European countries ... to maintain western technological and military superiority over other civilizations' (1993: 42).

To conceptualize civilization based on the type of economy is not tenable because no civilization is exclusively agrarian or industrial; all civilizations are invariably anchored to both agriculture and industry. As Francis Boas (1938) observed, the basis of all advanced cultures is agriculture, thereby indicating the interdependence between agriculture and industry. Against this background I suggest that conceptualizing civilization in the singular and/or anchoring civilization to religion or economy is not only unsustainable but also harmful, in that these conceptualizations sow the seeds of disharmony and destruction in the world. But to conceptualize civilization based on their geographical anchorages is to acknowledge their specificities; they are not inferior or superior but different. Their differences need to be recognized and respected. Thus one can speak of African, Asian, European, American, and other similar civilizations.

The preference for civilization as the unit of macrosociological analysis which provides a view from above does not in any way diminish the crucial significance of the bottom-up perspective advocated in Chapter 5. Instead of juxtaposing them into a dichotomy I suggest that a continuum consisting of the macro-meso-micro units should be postulated and accepted.

The nine chapters of Parts I and II directly and indirectly discuss the three tensions which exist in sociology and social anthropology. But the three chapters in Part III unfold the manifestations of these tensions in the practice of these disciplines by three sociologists/ social anthropologists. Interestingly all the three belong to the same academic lineage in that they were attached to/trained at the Department of Sociology, University of Bombay. In fact, both M.N. Srinivas and Y.B. Damle were students of G.S. Ghurye.

Damle was perceived as a sociologist and never as a social anthropologist in spite of his training under Ghurye. He was an enthusiastic advocate of American sociology, particularly the concepts and theories formulated by Talcott Parsons and Robert K. Merton, at a time when Indian social anthropologists and sociologists were wedded to the themes and theories of British social anthropologists. Damle researched and encouraged his students to research on a wide variety of themes usually perceived as 'sociological' rather than social anthropological. His efforts to de-anthropologize sociology at Pune were indeed arduous not only because of the prevailing orientation of the discipline in India in general but also because of the presence of Irawati Karve, a formidable anthropologist, who straddled between social as well as physical anthropology, in the Department of Sociology and Anthropology at Pune (the department was later bifurcated into unidisciplinary ones). Chapter 10 amply illustrates the tensions which existed between sociology and anthropology in India those days.

I have tried to argue and demonstrate that in spite of the perception among Indian sociologists that Damle was a theoretician, he was perhaps more an empirical researcher who contributed to our understanding of social reality in Maharashtra. However, his obsession with an American, particularly Parsonian, theoretical framework often obstructs a deeper understanding of social reality, constricting the possibility of interrogating western theoretical frameworks and conceptual formulations in the light of Indian experience.

Chapter 11 is a critical appraisal of the contributions of M.N. Srinivas, arguably the most illustrious student of G.S. Ghurye, the founder of Indian Sociological Society (ISS) and the one who nurtured the Department of Sociology of the University of Bombay at its formative stage. Srinivas followed a reverse track as compared with Damle; if the latter abandoned social anthropology and took to sociology with great zeal, the former deepened his social anthropological orientation thanks to his academic affinity with A.R. Radicliffe-Brown and E.E. Evans-Pritchard, the two British social anthropologists who were his teachers. On the other hand, Srinivas not only abandoned the indological orientation of his Indian teacher, namely, G.S. Ghurye, but astutely cultivated the method of participant observation, the birthmark of British social anthropology. However, unlike his British teachers Srinivas rescued social anthropology from the study of not only 'primitive' and 'traditional' societies but also from the analysis of other cultures. His academic acumen was unfolded through the study of one's own society through participant observation, the tool British social anthropologists devised to study other cultures.

I argue in Chapter 11 that this academic mutation has led to a serious disjunction between 'field' and method. However, Indian sociology/social anthropology should be eternally indebted to Srinivas for abandoning the obsession with texts (read Hindu texts) to apprehend Indian social reality. But Srinivas created a counter obsession with 'field', diminishing the importance of texts. It is my submission that there is an organic link between the text and the field and for a comprehensive understanding of social reality, social researchers need to take both on board. Further, in a hierarchical society such as that of India the field needs to be observed from bottom up also (see Chapter 5), lest the researcher falls into the trap of a one-sided understanding of social reality, because (1) those placed at the bottom in a hierarchical society are usually subjected to cognitive blackout from texts and (2) if indeed they surface in them, the references are invariably disparaging to them, both of which profoundly obstruct knowledge production.

Not only that the disjunction that I am referring to a la Srinivas is confined to the method and the field, but between these two, vis-à-vis 'concepts' such as dominant caste (see Oommen 1970a: 73–83) and *sanskritization* he enunciated for which he is famous; his 'field' (village, tribe) and method (participant observation) are micro but his concepts are posited as applicable not simply to macro society but to a whole civilization. This micro–macro disjunction sits uneasily in the onward march of sociology in India although it fits well with the practice of traditional social anthropology.

I have suggested that unless a concerted effort is made to study the bottom rung of society it will remain un-researched, particularly in a hierarchical society. This is amply illustrated in the practice of sociology by G.S. Ghurye as is evident in Chapter 12. In spite of his voluminous writings on caste in India, the 'Scheduled Castes' remain barely researched. Further, the 'Scheduled Tribes' who are distinctly different and outside the pale of 'Hindu civilization' came to be designated as 'backward Hindus' by Ghurye. These two groups, together constituting one-fourth of Indian population, were indeed an object of cognitive blackout and conceptual mutilation at the hands of Ghurye. However, since the conventional 'field' of social anthropologists was tribe, many of them were well researched by others. Here one can discern the complementarity between the cognate disciplines of sociology and social anthropology, although this division of labour is scarcely maintained in India.

It is necessary to recall a slice of Ghurye's academic biography here. He was sent to England by the University of Bombay in 1920 to do a PhD in sociology but he opted to do a PhD in social anthropology and this initial inclination certainly contributed to substantial anthropologization of Indian sociology (see Savur 2011: 3–28). Indeed, Ghurye maintained very early in his career that 'anthropological approach to sociology is the most appropriate' (1973: 45) and yet he was/is hailed as 'Father of Sociology' in India. This ambivalence has deeply impacted on the practice of sociology in India. There are several Indian practitioners of the discipline who are 'sociologists' in India but in Europe and North America they are labelled (and the label is proudly accepted) as social anthropologists. Both Ghurye and Srinivas belong to this category. Damle, however, remained a sociologist both in India and elsewhere. I am not suggesting that this dual pattern of labeling is positive or negative but it is indeed worth understanding because it has implications for both disciplines (see Chapter 9).

The 12 chapters in this book singly and in combination address the tensions between sociology and social anthropology with special reference to India. Those who practise these disciplines and are getting training in them need to understand the causes and consequences of these tensions.

PART I

1

Sociology in India
A Plea for Contextualization

Academic sociology[1] has existed in India for hardly a century, although sociological thinking and empirical research did exist since the nineteenth century (see Duttagupta 1972). And since the 1950s discussions on sociology *in*, *of*, and *for* India have been taking place.[2] While sociology in India deals with the academic output of sociologists, the state of the art in the country, discussion on sociology of India concerns itself with approaches to the study of Indian society, as a space-time chunk. In the case of sociology for India, the effort seems to be one of postulating a set of concepts and theories suitable to study Indian social reality. A perusal of the writings on Indian sociology in the three contexts would unfold that the leading questions posed have been the following:

1. The central concerns of sociology being with order and change, which of these have had predominance in Indian sociology and why?
2. Is the concern for change, as and when it surfaced, buttressed with a preference for the directionality of change?
3. What are the appropriate units of analysis for sociological investigations in India?
4. What are the techniques of data collection preferred and employed?
5. How far did Indian sociologists succeed in developing a conceptual baggage and a set of theoretical propositions which are relevant for India?
6. Did Indian sociology give adequate attention to the specificity (historicity) of Indian social reality?
7. To what extent Indian sociologists are victims of academic colonialism?

8. Is it that Indian sociologists invariably accepted state patronage and played second fiddle to the establishment?
9. Why is it that sociologists in India failed to investigate some of the substantive themes?
10. How can we explain the predominance of studies in certain substantive areas?

The above questions, and perhaps many more, have been 'answered' several rounds over by several sociologists and I have no intention to attempt answers to these questions. However, as a starting point it is necessary to note, *how* are these questions answered?

Broadly speaking, one or more of these questions have been answered by sociologists in terms of their understanding of sociology in India as a nation-specific or transnational enterprise. Presently, let me recognize the broad strands of thinking involved.

1. Those who look at India as a unique society, culture, or civilization, thereby emphasizing the need to focus on the specificity of Indian society. Pursuantly, they advocate the need to study Indian society as a whole and this entails delving deep into India's hoary past through Indology and ancient history—the 'traditionists'.
2. Those who do not consider Indian society as unique but recognize that, as in other cases, it has a specificity of its own and argue that this specificity can be understood only through an analysis of Indian history and tradition. This orientation calls for the need to emancipate ourselves from the constricting influence of outsiders (academic colonialism was the catch phrase in the 1970s and 1980s) and to reject the international reference model to render ourselves nationally relevant—the 'nationalists'.
3. Those who argue for the use of native concepts and categories so as to reconstruct social reality as people perceive it. This perspective implies that there are as many versions of social reality as there are sociocultural variations and hence what is emphasized is local history and traditions—the 'nativists'.
4. Those who consider Indian society as essentially the same as anywhere else and hence believe that concepts, theories, techniques, and methods are universally applicable in spite of the variations in the contexts of their origins. Emphasizing the need to focus on the general and the present, they tend to be nomothetic in orientation—the 'cosmopolitans'.
5. Those who attest the position that transformation of societies everywhere falls into a grand evolutionary schema to be accelerated through conscious human intervention. The advocacy of intervention

inevitably calls for an understanding of past experiences and the need to take clear value positions, a prerequisite to pursue desired goals. Those who pursue this strand of thinking also call for a selective rejection of external influences, particularly those of the capitalist first world—the 'radicals'.

The ongoing debate in Indian sociology discerned both in terms of the questions posed and perspectives postulated points not simply to the multiplicity of orientations of its practitioners, but a real identity crisis of the discipline. The fact that Indian sociologists have been discussing the problems that beset the discipline for the past several decades is a healthy sign. To recall the pertinent words of the Review Committee of the Indian Council of Social Science Research (ICSSR): 'Much of the current research effort has *no relevance* to contemporary social and national problems ... It is not yet emancipated to develop research tools, designs and models of its own *appropriate to the Indian situation*' (ICSSR 1973: 9, italics added). I submit that in order to get out of this impasse, we need to *contextualize* sociology in India.

The problematic involved in contextualization of sociology in India may be viewed as a series of tensions. The first of these is articulated through the differential emphases accorded to the study of past and present, indology and sociology, tradition and change. Notwithstanding D.P. Mukherji's (1958) emphasis on the seminal importance of tradition in the study of Indian society, it is the provocative statement made by Dumont that '... a sociology of India lies at the point of confluence of sociology and indology' (1957: 7) which triggered off the hitherto unsettled controversy in this context. Those who emphasize the study of indology suggest that this is the surest way to apprehend Indian social reality as a whole. But to the extent that the texts which are actually studied or recommended to be studied are invariably Hindu texts[3] what we get, even if the argument is conceded, is in effect Hindu sociology which is not exactly Indian sociology. I am not suggesting that this is not a worthwhile exercise but only pointing to the implications involved.

Those who invoke Hindu religious texts to understand the values of Indian society, if not the facts, assume that Hinduism is the most ancient religion of India, an assumption not entirely uncontested. It is necessary to refer here to the religions in India[4] in terms of their *sources of presence*. They may be categorized as follows:

1. The primal vision of indigenous social categories such as the Adivasis and Dalits.[5]
2. The earliest migrant religion which got 'nativized' and emerged as the dominant religion: Hinduism.[6]
3. The religions which emerged as the result of protest against Hinduism: Jainism, Buddhism, and Sikhism.
4. The religions which are perceived to be the products of conquest or colonization: Islam and Christianity.[7]
5. The religious groups which came as migrants: Jews, Zoroastrians, and followers of Baha'i faith.

The first three categories of religions are usually reckoned as Indian religions not only in popular perception but also in terms of constitutional provisions—Hindu Code Bill and the application of Personal Laws. On the other hand, notwithstanding the fact that Christianity came to India in the first century AD and Islam has been in India for 13 centuries, they are taken to be 'alien' religions. Similarly while 80 per cent of the world's Zoroastrians lived in India in the mid-twentieth century and Buddhism is practically an expatriate religion from India, the former is perceived as an alien and the latter as an Indian religion. I submit that this is sociologically untenable for a variety of reasons but let me mention just two of them. First, when we refer to India as a geographical-political entity today, the reference is to an entity only 70 years old. Second, it is sociologically untenable to view millions of people who have been inhabiting the very same geographical area for centuries as 'aliens' for the simple reason that they profess religious faiths which originated elsewhere.

It is against this background that the implications of the attempt to reduce Indian values to those contained in Hindu texts will have to be seen. Therefore, the contention that ' … the very existence, and influence, of the traditional higher, Sanskritic civilization demonstrates without question the unity of India … it does not only demonstrate, but actually constitutes it' (Dumont 1957: 10) is undoubtedly unacceptable not only to Muslims, Christians, Baha'is, Jews, and Zoroastrians but also to the Dravidians,[8] Adivasis, and Dalits, who do not share this 'higher' Sanskritic civilization. Even the Buddhists and Sikhs, I am afraid, are not likely to be persuaded to accept the proposition insofar as Pali and Gurumukhi texts are ignored. In the final analysis, invoking the route of Hindu texts to arrive at Indian social reality would only give us an understanding of the values of the 'mainstream' people of present-day India: the twice-born Hindus inhabiting the Indo-Gangetic plain.

It is important to note, however, that we can speak of Hindu sociology in another sense, that is, in the sense in which we refer to Hindu Law. But Hindu Law is clearly distinct from say, Muslim Law, Christian Law, etc. And in India the modern state legal system co-exists with varieties of religious/folk legal systems, applicable to and actually applied in the case of different groups. Similarly, in medicine we have the western allopathic system co-existing with Ayurvedic (predominantly Hindu), Unani (mainly Muslim), and folk systems of medicine. In the case of academic disciplines, we do not have live competing systems of knowledge such as Hindu economics, sociology, and political science and the like, although we can speak of Hindu economic, social, and political thought. It may be legitimately argued that this situation of knowledge vacuum has inevitably led to the domination by western theory and methodology in social sciences once they were implanted in India.

But even in those areas where competing indigenous professions (for example, medicine and law) did exist, the western brands of them came to dominate the native ones gradually. I will revert to this point later.

There is yet another reason why sociology in India (for that matter anywhere) could not develop mainly based on analysis of texts, ancient or contemporary. Those who argue for the tapping of Sanskritic sources anchor their argument on the richness and variety of thought contained in Hindu texts. There are others who suggest that precisely because of this, one cannot easily endorse one or another normative pattern or value system as representing the Indian collective conscience. Although this argument can be countered by suggesting that plurality of thought is the very essence of the Hindu collective conscience (see Chandra 1977), the more serious objection that the texts are normative and prescriptive and do not reflect the behavioural realities cannot be easily met. In fact, excessive dependence on the book is a characteristic feature of those branches of knowledge, such as theology and law, which attempt norm-setting and value-giving. Therefore, those who are concerned with behaviour tend to argue that the book view does not reflect reality, and for that one should resort to the field to get at 'facts'. Then, the tension between those who focus on the text and the field is anchored to their differential emphasis on the ideal and the actual. Viewed thus, the controversy appears to be not only sterile but puerile, because one cannot understand the actual without reference to the ideal. Levy aptly remarks:

> The distinction between ideal and actual structures is one of the most vital and useful tools of analysis of any society, any time, anywhere. In one form or another, men have been aware of it since time began for them. It is, however, so obvious and such a humble distinction that many social scientists either neglect it or overlook its importance. (1966: 26)

The only sane solution, it seems to me, is to follow the dictum: render unto the text that which is the text's and render unto the field that which is the field's. The constructed estrangement between the text and the field, value and fact, does not exist; it is largely an artefact of scholastic craftiness, a manifestation of intellectual trade unionism.

To focus on the text necessarily entails a focus on the past and to concentrate on the field willy-nilly implies that the major chunk of attention will have to be on the present. But how much into the past should we travel in order to illumine our understanding of the present?[9] To the extent the sociologists' concern to understand the past is tempered by his/her interest to comprehend the present, there is a critical slice in history in which s/he ought to be interested, not more and not less. Admittedly this critical slice of relevant history would vary depending upon the problem under investigation; for example, the study of communalism in India on the one hand, or Hindu kinship on the other. That is, the options here are not between indology or sociology and history or sociology, as is usually made out to be, but *how much* indology or history, as the case may be, given the prime concern of the sociologists, namely understanding and explaining the present.

Having noted earlier that to invoke the study of Sanskritic texts as the route to understand Indian society in effect boils down to confining our attention to the value systems of twice-born Hindus, I should add here that such an enterprise is beset with another danger (although it does not follow logically), the tendency to ignore oral traditions.[10] And a substantial proportion of the Indian population such as the Adivasis, Dalits, and even peasantry have had only oral traditions. To the extent their oral traditions are ignored, we cannot speak of an authentic history of the people of India. Even if sincere efforts are made to reconstruct their past through oral history or 'texts' the time period that we can 'capture' through this would be rather limited. Here we note a basic problem, the discipline of history confronted, at least until recently. History that is available to us, in the final analysis, is recorded history. But the actual history is the totality of human activities and events and recorded history forms only an insignificant part of this total range of human events.

To complicate matters, what is recorded is often the activities of those who occupied exalted positions—political, economic, sociocultural—in varieties of situations; recorded history is *history from above*. While this is valuable in itself, this history is partial and hence gives only a distorted picture of the past. What we need and what is so miserably missing is *history from below*, the history of the oppressed, the wretched of the earth (see Chapter 5). While the new-found enthusiasm to study people's struggles, popular movements, and revolutions partly correct this distortion, this has not been entirely successful in correcting our abysmal ignorance in this regard. Even here the focus of attention and analysis has been invariably on those who led the struggles, the movement elite.

The sociologist with his capital concern for the present has a tremendous advantage in this context. He can observe and record present-day events as they unfold with the focus on the people: the sociologist should view the *present as history*. But regrettably, even this is not done. If we miss the opportunity *now* the future generations will continue to experience all the disadvantages that we are experiencing presently, to understand our past in an authentic manner. That is, the sociologist should not only be concerned with the past to understand the present, but s/he should be involved in the study of the present precisely to aid the future generations to understand their past.

First, the domination of western knowledge system over the indigenous one is usually explained in terms of the western colonial intervention. Apparently, this explanation is appealing, nationalistic, even patriotic, but actually it does not measure up to rational considerations or logical arguments. Conquest and colonialism were not unknown in India. The Muslim intrusion in India is 12 centuries old and yet Muslim thought and knowledge did not pose any significant challenge to the Hindu systems of thought and knowledge; no displacement of the latter occurred. In fact, the interaction between

Hindu and Muslim systems of thought gave rise to some creative syntheses. The fact that the Muslim conquerors were not 'imperialists' as they settled down and made India their 'home' should hardly be any solace to those who argue that Sanskritic civilization provided the basic grid for Indian society. Even the by-products which grew out of the combined Hindu–Muslim thought systems could not successfully resist the intellectual conquest of India by the West.

Western colonialism in India is only a few centuries old and yet its impact is staggering. Then, notwithstanding the uniqueness of Hindu and Muslim systems of thought and knowledge and their creative combinations, there is something compelling in the western system of knowledge and its application. Its acceptance seems to be necessary for India's very survival in the modern world. It is this which explains the persistence of western knowledge and proliferation of professions which emerged in the West, although they came through the route of colonialism.

Second, if that which was initially imposed by the colonial ruler was not basically acceptable and useful and viewed as a yoke and a burden, when the ruler withdrew, the imposed elements would have been rejected. There is no evidence even after several decades of political independence that this is beginning to happen in India; the fact is quite the contrary. To argue that it is impossible to emancipate ourselves from the cultural claptrap of colonialism is to accept that humans are mere receivers and creatures of history. But this is only a half-truth; we are as much creators of history.

Third, it would be helpful to undertake a mental experiment in this context. If we would not have had the western colonial intervention, could it be that our knowledge systems would have remained essentially indigenous, uncontaminated by alien influences? The answer to this question would be in the affirmative if only we visualize insulated social systems. But contemporary societies with their frayed edges, loose textures, and thin boundaries are constantly exposed to alien influences and are bound to acculturate and assimilate values and institutions irrespective of the spatial locus of their origin. Of course, there is a qualitative difference between such voluntary adaptation and the coercive imposition that colonialism implies (see Chapter 9). Be that as it may, we cannot wish away the facts of history and all that we can do is to reject the undesirable and assimilate the desirable elements from among those which were initially imposed on us. This is more a question of our civilizational and rational potentials and not so much of colonialism (see Oommen 1983a).

Instead of perceiving the problem thus, the effort often is to 'protect' Indian sociology from external intrusions. This concern is often expressed through the phrase 'academic colonialism'.[11] The argument that Indian sociologists (as indeed other academics) are mere captives of an international reference model accords monopoly to the knowledge industry located in the West. However, it can be argued with equal force that the knowledge industry can operate in a free market situation although this is not so in reality (see Chapter 7). The academic entrepreneur of the West, as his counterpart in industry, would want to sell his products wherever he can. But the transaction can take place only if there are willing buyers. Therefore, the argument that Indian sociologists are mere captives of an international reference model denies them autonomy. And, the implied assumption that humans are mere victims of their circumstances is only partially correct; they are as much designers of their situations.

The point is, academic colonialism is possible not simply because there exists enterprising knowledge producers and hidden persuaders in the West but also because there are willing buyers in the East. At any rate, the answer lies neither in a total rejection of western knowledge without knowing what it is, nor imposing restrictions on the knowledge flow, but in developing a critical capacity to discern what is good and relevant for us (see Chapter 8).

I must make it clear here that the rejection of an international model in the case of knowledge implies academic 'nationalism' and even academic 'communalism', both of which are not without their share of dangers. Academic nationalism, that is viewing all issues exclusively from the perspective of the interests of a nation-state, is not likely to be in the long-term interests of man and society for several reasons. First, formation and dissolution of nation-states do take place within a short span of history and these are not always likely to be in the best interests of the people involved in the process. In the last 60 years we have witnessed this in ample measure in the Indian subcontinent itself. Second, to be 'nationalistic' invariably means supporting the state and the government, that is, the party in power. This, under the conditions prevailing in many nation-states, would mean supporting the structures which perpetuate structural, physical, and symbolic violence.

Third, given the near absence of support from corporations and foundations for research in many nation-states, the state has near monopoly in defining priorities of research which are ultimately geared to tension management mechanisms to perpetuate the party in power. Admittedly, only the officially preferred brand of social research would usually get encouragement and recognition, which is detrimental to 'creativity'. Fourth, as social science research has ideological underpinnings, unless diverse orientations are encouraged to creatively confront one another, the distortions and ambiguities created by the state-sponsored perspective cannot be corrected. Finally, to investigate and analyse sociological issues to suit 'national' needs is both a challenge and a danger. It constitutes a danger to the scientific enterprise in that one can easily get into 'patriotic' slants pandering to popular emotions.[12] It is a challenge in that social research is rendered relevant to social needs.

It has been frequently pointed out that the handful of sociologists who practised the discipline during the colonial period were nationalistic and that they focused on Indian problems (see Joshi 1975; Mukherjee 1979). But it is often forgotten that after independence the national goals got diffused as there has been a sea change in the *historicity of context*. The sociologist, as everybody else, during the colonial regime was a subject and there existed a commonly perceived enemy, namely colonialism, both of which together invested tremendous legitimacy to a conjoint concern, namely political freedom. But once political freedom arrived not only did the national goal change to nation-building, but genuine differences of opinion were crystallized as to the paths to be pursued to achieve the goal and also the perception regarding the obstacles to nation-building.

Second, what has been hitherto perceived as national interests took different manifestations in the forms of 'communal', regional, class, or linguistic interests. These differing conceptions and consequent conceptualizations of national interests are reflected in the pursuit of sociology. Therefore, what is reflected in sociology in independent India is not an erosion of national concern but a reconceptualization of national interests; a redefinition of sociologists' constituency. This may not always be clearly articulated but it is easily evident to the discerning eye.

The change in the constituency of sociologists is a welcome one to the extent s/he enthusiastically highlights the issues of the collectivities to which s/he belongs, but it also contains a danger, that of 'academic communalism', which I have referred to earlier. Academic communalism implies that social researchers select specific constituencies based on primordial identities and they tend to study only these and emerge as the spokespersons of their constituencies. Thus, the tendency today is that the women are studied by women, the Dalits by Dalits, the Muslims by Muslims, the Punjabis by Punjabis, etc.[13] Indeed, the advantage of building instantaneous rapport and empathy with the people among whom one works is an argument in favour of such a trend. But the advantage of studying social segments to which one does not belong is equally clear and important.

First, if the advantages of studying 'other cultures' are recognized and established (see Chapter 2), the advantages of investigating the social categories to which one does not belong are self-evident. Second, the pay-offs that a researcher accrues from his being a 'stranger' to one's research constituency cannot be altogether denied (see Simmel 1950).[14]

Apart from these advantages, there are other reasons why one should not confine social research to the social categories one belongs to because there are segments of population which cannot throw up their own sociologists—the mentally challenged, the 'deviant', and the like. Further, this would mean that the study of marginalized categories—Dalits, Adivasis, unemployed, minorities, and the poor—will get neglected. To a certain extent this has already happened in Indian sociology and academic communalism is often a response to this neglect. On the other hand, the personal background of a sociologist may often be a liability to study certain categories or issues. For instance, the possibility of a Brahmin sociologist undertaking a study of Dalits through participant observation, or a Hindu sociologist investigating the issues of communalism amidst Muslims or vice versa, a male sociologist understanding the 'problems' of women, etc., is limited. That is to say, we face a genuine dilemma here: the acute fragmentation and extreme segmental insularity of Indian society renders the entry of sociologists into several areas of enquiry extremely difficult. On the other hand, if each social category 'produces' its own sociologists it will lead to academic communalism which is likely to reinforce the prevalent primordial collectivism. Clearly, we need to strike a balance by encouraging studies of different communities and groups both by 'insiders' and 'outsiders'.

This brings me to the last point that I would like to make in this context, namely academic feudalism and scholastic parochialism that reign in Indian sociology (as indeed in the 'republic' of the Indian academy). It is not so much the professional hierarchy or gradations which debilitate the profession but the patron–client and network ties. This is evident in the recruitment of academics, distribution of 'rewards', be it membership in committees or referring to the works of fellow sociologists. Let me illustrate this point with reference to the last of these, which is perhaps the least visible and most intractable.

If one were to look at the footnotes and references by Indian sociologists, what I am trying to convey will be clear. Depending upon one's positioning in the profession one refers to the works of (and this is invariably reckoned as one's obligation to, reward for, deference to, expression of friendship with, rather than the relevance of) one's patrons/bosses, one's clients/students, and those who are involved in one's own network: 'ethnic', national, and ideological. This creates a situation of internal academic colonialism, which to my mind is much more detrimental than international academic colonialism. And, paradoxically enough, those who beat their breasts about academic colonialism are the easiest prey to this internal colonialism.

While one can be indifferent to or even reject the international reference model, one cannot do so with regard to the internal, that is, the national reference model. This is because what sustains one professionally is the recognition one gets from fellow professionals from the same country. It seems to me that it is the frustration generated by the behaviour of professional peers that often drives out at least some of the capable ones to seek asylum either in the international network or in cognate disciplines. What is denied at 'home' is sought after elsewhere.

The argument I put forward is that academic nationalism is not the answer to academic colonialism and the former contains within it seeds of academic communalism and academic feudalism. The way out is to develop an authentic concern for man and society, a concern informed of humanism and not simply a concern for fellow citizens, co-religionists, co-nationals, or academic network.

While considering the issue of commitment to broad human concerns, the problem of motivation for entry into the profession becomes important. We many think of at least three broad types of motivations in this context: instrumental, professional, and existential.

To the vast majority of sociologists entry into the profession is a matter of bread and butter; it is a career and not a calling. This is not something to be deprecated or denigrated; in all probability they may develop an appropriate orientation through occupational socialization. Two sources have gradually enlarged the career opportunities of Indian sociologists: (1) introduction of sociology as an undergraduate teaching subject and (2) recruitment by the state, as collection and analysis of data for policy formulation by the planner and administrator became a prerequisite in the 'socialist'/'welfare' state. In the case of most college teachers, they look upon themselves mainly as communicators of available knowledge to the students and not as producers of knowledge.

Those who work with the government are expected to collect and analyse data through quick surveys as is evident in the numerous studies of community development, Panchayati Raj, land reforms, urban problems, studies on Scheduled Castes and Tribes, and the like. These sociologists are not involved in, perhaps not even expected to formulate concepts or build theories and there is no point in decrying their work as is done by some (see, for example, Srinivas and Panini 1973: 198–9). It is not even correct to characterize them as power hungry sociologists in search of lucrative positions in the establishment as Dhanagare (1980: 24) does. If a sociologist can be and should be a social critic, s/he can also be involved in social policy formulation and planned development: sociology can be and should be social criticism *and* a policy science at once. All that one can insist on is that the sociologist should consciously choose his/her role and what role s/he chooses at a given point in time depends on his/her evaluation of the 'establishment', the party in power.

Even most of those who project themselves as sociologists dedicated to the cause of developing the discipline of sociology—the teachers and researchers of university departments and research institutes—look upon their profession as a platform to demonstrate their intellectual ability to fellow sociologists within India and perhaps more importantly to those abroad, an international community of scholars from whom they seek professional recognition, rather than creatively attending to the problems of their immediate social milieu. To secure the eagerly sought after recognition from this international community, they have to demonstrate their ability in terms of what is valued by that community, which alone can bring in pay-offs: fellowships, visiting assignments, invitation to seminars and conferences, and the like. Understandably India has its share of Durkheimians, Weberians, and Marxists involved in the international professional network. (But alas! we do not have, say, Gandhians and if anybody dares to do sociology with reference to Gandhi, he is treated with contempt.) In this process we got alienated from the issues and problems which confront us here and now. It is my contention that our concern with issues of our immediate social milieu in the broader perspective of humanism will render us relevant not only nationally but globally.

Perhaps what I have in mind can be illustrated by referring to the works of Latin American social scientists. The notions of centre and periphery, metropolitan and satellite countries, pedagogy of the oppressed, conscientization, deschooling—the 'radical' ideas eagerly devoured in the contemporary West and metropolitan centres of the East—have been developed through an in-depth examination and critical understanding of the Latin American empirical situation and yet they seem to be relevant far beyond the boundaries of Latin America. It is not my intention to suggest that these notions and conceptualizations are necessarily foolproof; but I do want to affirm that these conceptualizations illustrate the potentiality of theory building even as one concentrates on one's own specific empirical situation.

The third possible motivation I have listed for pursuing sociology as a profession is rooted in one's biography, one's existential conditions, and life experiences. While I do not have any data to support this argument, it is my suspicion that most sociologists in India do not enter the profession to fulfil a 'mission'—be it to bring about social transformation, to revive the past glory of India, to perpetuate the present system, or to launch revolution. This is perhaps because most of them are middle-class climbers whose sense of success and achievements is rooted in upward mobility in material terms. If the recruitment base were predominantly upper class for whom one's profession is not the route to achieve material success, or of lower class/caste origin which prompts one to identify with the miseries of one's fellow citizens, or persecuted/marginalized minorities, perhaps the experiential base would have provided a compelling mission to fulfil. (Perhaps it is not mere accident that the Jews, the perennial minority of the world, have produced many outstanding intellectuals, including of course sociologists.) It seems to me that the majority of sociologists in India are without a goal which transcends the immediate mundane needs and aspirations; they are steeped in pragmatism. And this, I submit, at least partially explains why the sociologists of independent India do not respond to the critical human issues of their time and environment.

Having suggested that the Indian sociologist is impervious to the critical issues of his time and social milieu, it is necessary to pursue the argument so as to demonstrate its validity. This is perhaps best done by citing a few examples. Let me begin with the issues thrown up by the very birth of independent India: the partition and the 'refugee' problem. Between 1946 and 1951, nearly nine million Hindus and Sikhs came to India from the present territory of Pakistan and six million Muslims left India. By any account the holocaust was one of the biggest human uprooting in history. And yet hardly any serious sociological study was attempted on a scale and nature warranted by the event.[15] And the reverberations of partition are still with us: Hindu–Muslims conflicts, Akali and Northeast mobilizations, etc., none of which also is being studied adequately by Indian sociologists.

Second, the practice of untouchability has been decried almost universally: social reformers fought against the practice, social legislations are passed to ban it. And yet, the practice continues. In spite of this we do not have even a reliable and accurate sociography of untouchability of the various regions in India.[16] That more than one-third of India's population is below the poverty line is well known. Typically, and certainly fallaciously, the problem of poverty is assumed to be an economic and at best a political (in that the poor are also voiceless) one and rarely a sociological issue. Consequently, Indian sociologists hardly paid any attention to the study of poverty. The issue of nationalities in India is admittedly crucial in the ongoing process of 'nation-building'. Notwithstanding the expression of occasional anxiety regarding 'national integration' by both politicians and social scientists, we do not have a single comprehensive study on this problem by a sociologist of Indian origin.

I can go on adding to the above list but that will only increase the length of this chapter. But I hope the message is communicated. And, what is more, Indian sociologists seem to define the boundary of their substantive concerns rather rigidly and they tend to maintain the same very zealously. If anybody takes the risk of crossing the boundary what awaits him are ridicule and indifference.[17] This attitude of professional peers and elders is highly debilitating for the less distinguished and the new entrants and consequently for the profession, as it is constituted mainly by them.

—◆—

A recurring theme of debate in Indian sociology has been the unit of analysis. This is postulated in terms of micro versus macrostudies, a misconstrued juxtaposition (see Oommen 1972a). True, India is a national state (which is different from nation-state) or if you prefer, a civilization. But it is not one society or culture; we have a multiplicity of cultures and societies co-existing under one political roof. Therefore, investigations of 'regional' variations, that is, variation based on culture zones, are crucial in Indian social enquiry. It should be made clear that what I have in mind is not only states (administrative units) such as Madhya Pradesh or Bihar, but also folk regions such as Bhojpur, Chhattisgarh, Mithila, and the like.

What we have in India as of now is either study of institutions as they operate at the local levels (as if they are not linked with a wider universe) or studies which deal with the country as a whole. While there is no denying the fact that there is a set of all-India structures (for example, upper echelon of bureaucracy, a few political parties and professions), two points are to be noted. First, the processes involved in the functioning of these all-India structures may vary from region to region.

Second, there are institutions which vary both in terms of structures and processes in different regions: family, caste, agrarian system to list just three. The specificities of these institutions can be understood only through studies specifically designed for the purpose. Therefore, we should not juxtapose microstudies with macrostudies; the postulated polarity between them does not always exist. It seems to me that we need to concentrate our attention at three levels simultaneously. First, studies of villages as they operate at the grass roots level but trying to understand their linkages with the wider universe; second, studies of 'regions' which are more or less culturally homogeneous or politically bound; third, studies which consider the country as a whole as the unit of analysis. What is important to be kept in mind is that it is the nature of the enquiry and the substantive theme which would determine the unit of study.

The unit of analysis along with the substantive concerns of a study determines the appropriateness of techniques of data collection to be employed. The inadequate appreciation of this consideration results in arguments for or against a particular technique of data collection. As I have dealt with this issue in Chapter 2, I do not intend to elaborate on it here. But I do want to affirm that no technique of data collection is eternally valid or appropriate and therefore, there is no point in making a fetish of one or another technique. The question is not one of accepting or rejecting the 'western' empirical methods in sociological analyses of India but choosing the appropriate ones, amending the existing ones, or innovating and devising new ones depending upon the purpose of study and nature of the theme (see Chapter 4).

A serious objection that is advanced in this context is that some of the techniques, such as survey research, assume the autonomy of individuals and the Indian individual does not have any autonomy in decision making. Once again, this is only a half-truth and we get at this conclusion precisely because we assume that the traditional values are completely accepted and internalized even today. It could be argued on the other hand that democratic values are increasingly being accepted and internalized by Indians, which in turn means that the Indian individual is assuming autonomy in varying degrees in different contexts. But both these remain largely plausible hypotheses as of now in the absence of relevant studies.

The debate on units of analysis entails another issue, the kind of concepts to be employed. Generally speaking, those who undertake microstudies tend to argue for native concepts and categories. On the other hand, those who grapple with macroanalyses prefer concepts which are abstract in nature, usually concepts originally developed based on western empirical experience. I submit that it is the context of study which determines the suitability of 'native' or 'western' concepts. Thus, if one is studying a culturally homogeneous unit, native concepts can be profitably employed. But if the study envelops a variety of culturally heterogeneous units, the use of native categories is likely to be more confusing than enlightening. The way out seems to be in distinguishing between the form and substance of concepts. While the terms used by the people of one cultural region may vary from that of another region, these terms usually connote more or less the same meaning across the regions. Admittedly, one can think of a set of abstract concepts which are applicable to a variety of cultural regions although these may not be used by the people as such. Therefore, the advocacy of native concepts is logically linked with the study of culturally homogeneous units and that of abstract concepts go with the analysis of culturally heterogeneous situations.

I must enter a caveat here. Even as we employ concepts of western origin (which I do not think can or need be avoided altogether but need to be redefined to suit our purpose) we must guard ourselves from a possible danger, the tendency to postulate conceptual dichotomies or oppositions, such as caste versus class, joint family versus nuclear family, rural versus urban, tradition versus modern, and the like, which persist in sociological writings on India. This assumes a *displacement syndrome* fixated on the western epistemological dualism which does not fit our situation. This has been one of the greatest liabilities in our understanding the nature of social change in India.

＊

To conclude, let me reflect on the reasons for lack of innovativeness and the consequent crisis of relevance in Indian sociology. It has been suggested that social science developments in the West occurred in response to the transformative challenges in western society (Singh 1973). Responding to religious thought, western secular thought effectively challenged religious values and institutions. This is evident in the emergence of Darwinism, Positivism, and Marxism to mention just three. Similar secular trends originated in ancient India, as illustrated by *Lokayat*s and *Caravak*s which denied the existence of soul or the *Samkhya* school of thought which was initially atheistic. But these strands of thinking remained intellectual museum pieces and scarcely became powerful ideologies or social forces with a large following.

It is useful here to look at the evolution of Indian consciousness in the recent past. By the latter part of the nineteenth and early twentieth centuries, the antiimperialist movement gained strength. And during this period we have *demonized* not only colonial politico-economic dominance but also the institutions and values of the domestic society of the colonizer; we have indulged in an indictment of western civilization. As a corollary to this, it was necessary to sacralize indigenous values and institutions as is evident from Gandhi's *Hind Swaraj*,[18] Bankim Chandra Chatterji's *Ananda Math*,[19] Maithili Saran Gupta's *Bharat Bharati*,[20] etc. Given the fact that the British rule was preceded by several centuries of rule by Muslims, who were also perceived as aliens, it was necessary to invoke the glory of the hoary past of Hinduism. The simultaneous demonization of the western and sacralization of the 'indigenous' values and institutions was only partially functional in that the sources of sacralization were Hindu texts, which did not appeal with equal force to the Adivasis and Dalits not to speak of Dravidians, Muslims, Christians, and Sikhs. This tendency had its predictable consequences in the alienation of these collectivities and the one with sufficient political clout, namely Muslims, managed to get a separate sovereign state for itself.

The arrival of freedom heralded our rejection of western political dominance but at the same time we accepted western political institutions, economic values, and social goals. Our Constitution endorsed western values—socialism, secularism, democracy. The compelling need of independent India was to repeat the exercise we undertook during the colonial rule, but in the reverse order: selective *desacralization* of ancient Hindu institutions and values as well as *resacralization* of the constitutional values so as to bring about a judicious and creative reconciliation between the two. And there is no denying the fact that we have utterly failed in doing this and the crisis that we face in India today is the resultant of this failure. Admittedly, confusion pervades the whole of Indian society and sociology in India cannot be an exception to this. It is my contention that the failure of sociology in independent India is its inadequate anchorage in a set of relevant values.

Independent India has two sets of competing value packages: one, traditional values of hierarchy, holism, and pluralism and two, constitutional values of socialism, secularism, and democracy. There is no clear evidence that one set of these values is replacing the other; often one comes across reconciliation in some contexts but contradictions in regard to others. We cannot simply dismiss the friction thrown up by the confrontations of these value packages in contemporary Indian society as a mere transitional aberration which will disappear in course of time (see Oommen 1983a). This is because the displacement syndrome cannot operate effectively in the Indian context. We did not have in Indian thought the opposition and dualism between subject and object, matter and spirit, state and church, emperor and pope, and the like. Understandably, the process of change comes gradually through adaptation to and accretion of structures and values and not through sudden displacement. It is of vital importance that we recognize the pluralist paradigm in Indian thought and the reconciliatory ethos in Indian praxis (see Oommen 1983b).

In conclusion, if sociology is to be relevant for India as a discipline, it should endorse and its practitioners should internalize the value package contained in the Indian Constitution, the differing interpretations of these values notwithstanding. Although these values have not originated in India and we have borrowed them from the West, undoubtedly they are values widely endorsed in the contemporary world. But our social ethos does not permit total displacement of the old and internalization of the new, at any rate all of a sudden. Admittedly, the route to and style of implantation of these values will have to be our own. It is here that Indian sociology can and should play a critical role in the process of national reconstruction as a part of its commitment to broader human concerns. It is my submission that it is possible for sociology to play this vital role through a process of contextualization.

The process of contextualization of sociology in India involves the following dimensions. First, recognition of the fact that tradition/past contains both assets and liabilities viewed in terms of the present needs and aspirations. The ingenuity of a people lies in rejecting the liabilities without apology and accepting the assets unequivocally. Second, we should not be shy of adopting appropriate values and institutions from other societies and cultures and should judiciously graft them on to our own society. Third, in doing this we should take into account the central tendency in Indian society, which seems to be one of gradual adaptation and reconciliation. At the same time, we should recognize that such a societal ethos is capable of bringing about social transformation only at a slow pace. Therefore, it is necessary to mobilize people to protest against exploitation, injustice, and oppression. But the strategy of mobilization and the style of protest will have to be specifically Indian. Fourth, the social engineering involved here—the selective retention of our tradition, informed borrowing from other civilizations and the judicious mutation of the two—will have to be a process peculiar to India. The primary task of Indian sociologists today is to understand, analyse, and facilitate this process.

NOTES

1. For the present purpose I am ignoring the distinction between sociology and social anthropology.

2. The earliest of these was Mukherjee and Majumdar (1952). In 1957, Dumont and Pocock started *Contributions to Indian Sociology*. This was followed by a large number of publications, notably: Saran (1958, 1962); Saksena (1961, 1965); Bottomore (1962); Clinard and Elder (1965); Unnithan et al. (1967). By the 1970s we come across almost an uninterrupted discussion on the 'sociology of Indian sociology'. The most comprehensive of these to date is Mukherjee (1979) and Singh (1986).

3. This is recognized latterly. See for instance, Saberwal (1981). But even here the lacuna is seen mainly in terms of the neglect of Muslim texts. One wonders why Jain, Buddhist, Sikh, Zoroastrian, or Christian texts are not relevant!

4. This categorization draws from but modifies the one made by Schermerhorn (1978) in regard to 'ethnic' collectivities in India.

5. Adivasis literally means the earliest inhabitants. They have been referred to as Girijans (inhabitants of hilly tracts and mountains) in popular writings and as Scheduled Tribes (STs) in the official parlance. However, they prefer to be designated as Adivasis. There are 461 different communities of STs in India and according to the 2001 Census there are 88.8 million of them constituting 8 per cent of the total population. Dalits literarily means the oppressed, a term coined by them, although M.K. Gandhi preferred to call them Harijans, the children of god. In official parlance, they are designated as Scheduled Castes (SCs); there are about 1,000 different castes of this category, together numbering 80 million according to the 1971 Census of India constituting 14 per cent of the total population, the latest figure being 160 million making for 16 per cent. Today, most Adivasis and Dalits are reckoned as belonging to one of the 'world' religions: Hinduism, Buddhism, Sikhism, Christianity, or Islam. However, from 1871 to 1931 we come across a religious category designated as 'primitive' or 'tribal' in Indian census data. But some sociologists, notably Ghurye (1963 [1943]) consider that Adivasis are but backward Hindus, indeed a sociologically untenable proposition. As for Dalits, notwithstanding the current tendency to include them under the fold of Hinduism,

the *Purusha Sukta* in the *Rig Veda*, which refers to the theory of the origin of man, only mentions the Brahmin, the Kshatriya, the Vaishya, and the Shudra. The Dalits reckoned as 'untouchables' traditionally were not accounted in the *chatur* (four) varna scheme of Hinduism. In all probability they were the indigenous people who resisted the invading Aryans, the latter day caste Hindus.

6. According to some historians, Hinduism is the religion of Aryan migrants, however ancient might have been their arrival in India.

7. Christianity came to India in the first century AD and Arab Muslims' migration to the Malabar coast started from the seventh century AD. Pre-colonial Christianity and pre-conquest Islam existed in India and yet, in popular perception, these religions are products of conquest and colonization. But as the Thomas theorem goes: 'If men define situations as real, they are real in their consequences,' and this is sociologically significant.

8. Dravidians are those whose mother tongue belongs to the Dravidian family of languages. There are three main branches of Dravidian languages distributed into four main languages and several dialects, together constituting about 25 per cent of the total Indian population. The Dravidian language came into India centuries before the Indo-Aryan languages, the latter consisting of languages such as Hindi, Punjabi, Gujarati, Marathi, Assamese, Bengali, Oriya, etc. The most numerous and 'developed' Dravidian languages are Telugu (with 66 million), Tamil (with 53 million), Kannada (with 32.7 million), and Malayalam (with 30.3 million) speakers as per the 1991 Census of India.

9. It is conjectured that *homo sapiens* emerged some three million years ago. It is neither possible nor relevant to pitch our attention at history so far back and hence the need to identify the time period appropriate for particular analysis.

10. Admittedly, I am using the term 'text' in its usual limited sense of written text. While it may be legitimately argued that one can speak of oral texts, the difference between the two is clear.

11. This was articulated in a major way for the first time through a public debate (see *Seminar* 112, 1968). Later Saberwal (1982: 36–49) designated anthropology and sociology as 'uncertain transplants' in India.

12. This is already evident in many contexts. For example, almost all social researchers in India attest the proposition that Hindu–Muslim conflict in India is the handiwork of the British. If an Indian were to argue that there is a basic cleavage between Hindu and Muslim societies and that the intrigues of colonial policy could not have created it as Dumont (1964) did, he would be accused of creating obstacles to 'national integration'. Or if one were to argue that the multiplicity of 'nationalities' within the Indian national state would call for a highly decentralized political system, it is likely to be viewed

as creating obstacles in the nation-building process and is likely to be dubbed as a regional or linguistic chauvinist.

13. There is enormous scope for misinterpreting my position in this context. I am not suggesting for a moment that sociologists should not pursue the studies of the social categories to which they belong, but am only indicating that such studies need to be supplemented by studies undertaken by 'outsiders' to get at a rounded picture as it were. At the same time, aroused political consciousness renders studies by 'outsiders' increasingly difficult, if not impossible.

14. Simmel writes: '... he [stranger] often receives the most surprising openness—confidences which have the character sometimes of a confessional and which would be carefully withdrawn from a more closely related person' (1950: 404).

15. I could locate only two books by Indian social scientists apart from a few government reports. For details, see Oommen (1982).

16. An exception to this is Desai (1976) who gives a graphic account with regard to Gujarat.

17. Let me illustrate the consequences of deviating from 'mainstream' research by drawing from my own occupational biography. In 1962, I started studying the Bhoodan-Gramdan movement, which was widely acclaimed as a unique and novel method to tackle the agrarian problem, an approach hitherto unknown in history. And in 1963, an eminent Indian sociologist asked me: 'Is it a subject for sociological research?' obviously with ample sarcasm. Of course those were the days one studied religion, caste, village, family, or kinship. Anybody who attempted to cross this 'sacred boundary' was a butt of ridicule. But even by the 1970s the situation does not seem to have changed much. Thus, another eminent sociologist who undertook an extensive survey of sociology in India in the mid-1970s did not even mention the study although it was published by then (see Oommen 1972b) and his bibliography had over 700 items! If the references cited in the survey were selected on the basis of their 'quality' perhaps my study would not have qualified for inclusion. But the survey did deal with the emerging trends in Indian sociology including the new areas of investigation. And my book happens to be the first monograph on a social movement in India by an Indian 'sociologist'!

18. *Hind Swaraj* was first published in 1938. It was not only an analysis of why the British enslaved India but was an indictment of western civilization and a plea for restructuring Indian society based on its ancient wisdom as contained in Hindu texts.

19. *Ananda Math* was first published in 1882 in Bengali. Several of its Hindi translations appeared subsequently. The first English translation appeared in 1904. The central characters in the novel are Hindus who constitute into bandit gangs and plunder for an altruistic purpose, the

'national' cause. It was essentially an invocation to the Hindu psyche to restore the ancient glory of India which was essentially Hindu in character.

20. *Bharat Bharati* published in 1912 was instrumental for the mobilization of peasantry against the British. While the 'national' sentiment invoked by it appealed to all sections of the peasantry in parts of north India, the book was essentially couched in imageries and idioms glorifying the Hindu past.

2

Data Collection Techniques
The Sterile Controversy

Basically there are only three techniques of data collection: (1) eliciting verbal responses from respondents by asking questions either through an interview schedule, or interviewing informants, in an informal way, with or without the aid of an interview guide; (2) observing behaviour, either as a participant observer or as a non-participant onlooker; (3) analysing documents, which may be public (for example, a census report) or private (for example, a personal letter).

It is necessary at this point to bear in mind the distinction between the techniques of data collection and the methods of arrangements and analysis of data for one frequently comes across this confusion. For instance, while discussing the techniques of data collection, scaling techniques are occasionally mentioned. Scaling technique is a method of arranging data collected through verbal responses. Similarly, content analysis is not a technique of data collection; it is but an analysis of the raw data available in a document. Thematic Apperception Tests (TATs) of various kinds are devices to elicit either verbal responses from the respondent or mechanisms which lead to the production of a document, if the respondent is asked to record his feelings. Biograms are also to be regarded as documents, since the respondent is asked to write about his opinion or feelings about a given theme or incident.

It is commonplace to recall here that the relevance of a particular technique of data collection is dependent upon the type of data sought to be collected. Yet, for a variety of reasons, not always rational, each discipline has employed one or another of these techniques. Thus, economists usually collect their data through verbal responses using questionnaires and interview schedules or from public documents. The psychologists, by and large, collect their data by asking questions or observing human behaviour under controlled laboratory conditions. The social anthropologists have invariably preferred participant observation or unstructured interviews of selected informants. Sociologists are probably more eclectic in this context and employ almost any of the techniques depending upon the nature of the study at hand.

The advantage or disadvantage of a particular technique of data collection cannot be understood unless it is examined against the purpose of the study for which it is employed. Yet, one frequently comes across arguments for or against a given technique; the demonstration of the superiority of one technique and/or the debunking of another technique. To my mind, such exercises stem from an abysmal ignorance of the fundamental relationship between the nature of the data collected and the purpose for which it is collected. In this chapter, I propose to demonstrate that the substantive concerns of a particular discipline and the nature of the society that it investigates are important determinants of the techniques it employs for data collection. Since my familiarity, though inadequate, is largely confined to sociology and social anthropology, I will develop my discussion with special reference to these cognate disciplines.

To start with, one may ask, are sociology and social anthropology separate disciplines at all? We frequently come across suggestions to 'combine' departments of sociology and social anthropology and to 'integrate' these disciplines (Srinivas et al. 1961). It is implied in such suggestions that these disciplines differ, at least in some respects. However, there are a few sociologists and social anthropologists who consider that these disciplines are basically the same. In fact, I know of only three writers who have made bold and categorical statements in this connection. Eisenstadt, while evaluating the contribution of social anthropologists to the study of complex societies, wrote: 'It should be emphasized from the beginning that in my view there is no theoretical distinction between sociology and social anthropology' (1965: 69). Fallding, while discussing the subject matter of sociology, opines: ' ... cultural and social anthropology comprise neither more nor less than the sociology of simpler peoples. So I think one is entitled to claim all of it for sociology' (1968: 71). Srinivas, talking about the problems in the study of one's own society laments: ' ... the traditional but irrational distinction between sociology and social anthropology is so disastrous. A true science of society must include the study of all societies in space as well as time—primitive, modern, and historical' (1966: 164).

We should not make the mistake of dismissing a viewpoint as insignificant because it is upheld only by a small number of persons, especially since the majority of sociologists and social anthropologists are trained only in their respective disciplines. The large majority of social anthropologists emphasize the distinctiveness of their discipline; I will refer only to a few here. Lévi-Strauss (1966) considers social anthropology as a discipline devoted to the study of simple (primitive) societies and John Beattie (1964) regards it as a discipline mainly discussing 'other cultures'. Not only is the distinctiveness of social anthropology emphasized, but its superiority over sociology is insisted upon. Thus Dumont asserts: ' ... sociological understanding is more advanced by the social anthropologists looking upon a foreign society than by the sociologist looking at his own' (1966: 23); and Barnes is convinced of the superiority of the slow and indirect field techniques specific to social anthropology. He writes, while reviewing Frankenberg's *Village on the Border*, 'The ethnographer, with his traditional distrust of direct questions and questionnaires, and his desire to do more than test a bald hypothesis or establish a correlation, is particularly well qualified to observe these lengthy and devious sequences of social action and to analyse them in sociological terms' (1959: 15). It is therefore obvious that at least to some social anthropologists, not only is their discipline distinctively different from sociology, but it is also 'superior'. It is against this background that the discussion which follows is to be viewed.

Traditionally, social anthropologists concerned themselves with relatively simple societies ('primitive' or 'tribal' societies) and sociologists usually studied complex societies; this was one of the distinctions employed to denote the differences between these disciplines. The differences in the nature of societies investigated were an important determinant of the techniques employed for data collection. Thus, social anthropologists collected their data mainly through participant observation and informal interviews of a handful of informants. On the other hand, sociologists employed mailed questionnaires and interview schedules along with observation (not necessarily and always participant) and combed documents of various sorts to collect data.

For a variety of reasons, which are not my concern for the moment, social anthropologists extended their interests to folk/peasant and urban societies.[1] Thus, we have today anthropology of peasantry, urban anthropology, anthropology of industrialization, etc. While minor concessions are occasionally shown in regard to the techniques of data collection, by and large, the majority of social anthropologists cling to observation, particularly participant observation, to collect their data. That is to say, while there is a marked shift in the substantive interest of social anthropology, from simple to complex societies, there is no concomitant shift in the techniques employed for data collection. This seems to be an anomalous position; there is a lack of fit between the nature of the society investigated/subject matter studied and the techniques of data collection.

The assumption in the above statement is this: *the nature of the social system from which we collect data is an important determinant of the data collection.* In a simple society, which is relatively more integrated and homogeneous, the interdependence of the structural components will be more intimate. Unless we look at the system as a whole, we are likely to miss the meaning of several aspects of behaviour which we need to know. Second, these systems[2] have greater internal autonomy for they are small-scale societies. The dependence of a simple society on the outside world is relatively less and this too facilitates a clearer understanding of the society as a whole through observation. Third, simple societies usually are small-sized societies where it is physically possible for an investigator to observe most of the situations over a period of time.

Fourth, the events and activities in a simple society are relatively less as compared with complex societies. For instance, the absence of a multiplicity of secondary groups or the near absence of political recruitment through periodic elections all confine the activities of people to a few situations. All these factors which favoured the employment of participant observation and are eminently suited to study a simple society may be disadvantageous if employed to study a complex society.

In a large-scale society with considerable structural differentiation, it will not be possible for a researcher to observe even most of the situations, not to speak of all situations, for a variety of reasons. I will list a few here. (1) If s/he 'participates' and observes one of the segments of the population s/he may become unacceptable to other segments. Therefore, in order to be a participant observer in one of the segments s/he should alienate himself/herself from one or more of the other segments. This is particularly true of a hierarchical society like the Indian society[3] (see Chapter 5). (2) In a highly differentiated society, there are a variety of situations and all these cannot be faithfully observed, within the time usually available or expended by the researcher for his fieldwork. This is true also of specific communities in a complex society. Thus, it is far easier to study a village through participant observation as compared with a city. (3) Since the autonomy of complex societies is very limited, it is virtually impossible to draw their boundaries, except in geographical and/or political terms. At any rate, complex societies with frayed edges and loose texture are constantly exposed to alien influences and this makes them less amenable to tidy observation.

The above reasons make it clear that it is virtually impossible to undertake participant observation of complex societies as a whole. All that one can do is to observe a particular subsystem and/or confine the observations to specific situations or institutions. This means, the holistic orientation of social anthropology to the study of societies will necessarily change. We can, however, retain the holistic orientation while studying 'total institutions' in a complex society (Goffman 1961). The point I want to make is this: if social anthropologists opted for participant observation as the technique of data collection while studying simple societies, there were sound reasons for that. But to employ the same technique while analysing a society/situation which is far more complex and hence different, will not be very rewarding, to say the least.

There is yet another reason why participant observation became the favourite technique of data collection for social anthropologists. Conventionally, they have studied 'other' cultures and every anthropologist attempted to study a new culture or society. This means that the researcher was innocent of all aspects of the system he studied. Therefore, it was necessary to study the system in toto and there was a strong case for pursuing the holistic approach. This called for ravenous collection of data, to observe and record whatever one comes across, without always knowing the full meaning of these events and occurrences and their interrelationships while they were observed or studied. On the contrary, if one studies one's own society, one starts with some understanding of the system under observation. Insofar as one knows the values and ideologies underlying actions in a society, observation need only be undertaken to locate gaps between the ideal and the actual,[4] that is, to understand behaviour in specific contexts. There is no need or virtue in observing all people in all situations under such circumstances. Available documents can be analysed or questions can be asked in order to ascertain what proportion of the population subscribes to the prevalent value system or ideology.

One serious limitation of participant observation as a technique of data collection stems from the context of participation itself. The investigator can 'participate' in community or institution only through certain roles. For instance, it may not be possible for him to play the role of a priest (as the community may not accept him in such a role) but he may enter the community as a shopkeeper. This may mean that the researcher cannot 'participate' in most of the 'core roles' in the system. Even when he participates in 'peripheral roles' it can be only in relation to specific activities and events in the system. In any event, it will be very difficult to decide when the community has actually accepted him as 'one among them'. This is to say that the dividing line between non-participant and participant observation is not at all clear. The question to be asked, therefore, is when can we say that a researcher is accepted as an insider, as a participant in the system? Several Indian social anthropologists, when they recall their field experiences, claim that they were inducted into the communities they investigated by ascribing a specific 'kinship status' or they were recognized as 'insiders' by being called upon to act as conciliators in quarrels or as medicine men, etc. These overt manifestations of 'acceptance' are more apparent then real. At any rate, if I undertake to do participant observation in a particular urban settlement, I do not know how a specific kinship status will be accorded to me. Again, if I undertake an investigation of a hospital, I do not know how I will be inducted into the status-system of the hospital. Of course, one can resort to disguised participation and refuse to disclose one's identity. This, in turn, creates a number of ethical and moral problems.[5]

Though the need to study behaviour and hence the merit of participant observation as a technique of data collection is universally acclaimed by social anthropologists, much of the anthropological data is based not on observation but on verbal responses. The difference between the anthropologist and the sociologist in employing the questionnaire as a technique of data collection stems from the fact that, while the former selects a few respondents as key informants and interviews them in an informal way without the aid of an interview schedule, the latter usually interviews a larger number of respondents selected in a systematic way through a certain statistical procedure and invariably employs a structured schedule. These differences notwithstanding, it is safe to say that much of the data is collected by sociologists and social anthropologists by asking questions and eliciting verbal responses. Yet, it is true that social anthropologists usually look at the data collected in a sociological study through questionnaires and interview schedules with distrust. This distrust and probably distaste, I feel, is a carry forward of the obsession of social anthropologists with their earlier universe of study—the tribal society. With the level of formal education being low in tribal and even peasant societies, the use of mailed questionnaires is ruled out. Even asking structured questions for definite answers regarding complicated issues will not always be a rewarding exercise when the respondent is illiterate. The researcher working with simple societies will find it more rewarding to frame his/her questions to suit the intellectual and educational level of the particular respondent s/he interviews and, since interviewing is usually confined to a handful of key informants, the processing and arrangement of data do not pose a problem.

A special problem emanates from the collection of information by social anthropologists from a small number of informants. Only infrequently, social anthropologists make the 'status' of their informants known to their readers. There is good reason to believe that most of these informants are either those who occupy exalted positions—priests, kings, chiefs of castes, community leaders, and the like—in the society,[6] or the aberrant, maladjusted, and atypical individuals in the community. The very fact that they agree to be informants renders them atypical. The important personalities would consider it as their 'duty' and the deviant individuals may regard it as a welcome opportunity to air their dissatisfactions. If the informants are well integrated members of the community, their views represent the ideal rather than the actual position. On the contrary, if the researcher selects the low status or marginal individuals who are less integrated into the system as informants, there is good reason to believe that s/he will get a different account of the situations and events in the society studied.

What I am hinting at is that just as there is observer or interviewer bias, there can also be an informant bias. In order to counter this problem, we need to select a representative sample of informants or respondents from different strata or segments of society and try to understand their articulations. To achieve this we have to employ certain systematic procedures to select the sample of informants. These call for the use of statistical techniques which would, in turn, help in quantification of data. I am not suggesting that quantification is a virtue in itself, but if we stand to benefit by quantifying the relevant data we must do so. To recall the pertinent words of Homans, 'Let us make the important quantitative, and not the quantitative important' (1951: 22).

One merit of data collected through participant observation and from a small number of key informants is that it is qualitative data. Indeed it offers important insights towards an understanding of the society under investigation. However, since the data are not collected from a representative population, their amenability to generalization is considerably reduced. While the social anthropologist usually asserts the 'uniqueness' of the situation s/he studies by saying, 'this is not so in my village', even this is an erroneous generalization, for s/he does not know the viewpoint of the community as a whole, or a representative sample in the community, but only that of a few individuals who are his/her informants.[7] This is a case of mistaking the part for the whole.

I have suggested at the very outset of this chapter that the nature of the data collected is dependent upon the purpose for which it is collected and this, in turn, influences the techniques employed. The main concern of social anthropologists, as pointed out earlier, was to understand other cultures, the way in which people live and behave. Therefore, most of the social anthropological studies do not have a hypothesis. This 'diffuse orientation' and lack of initial 'focus' also permits the collection of qualitative data through participant observation. In contradistinction to this, since sociologists study their own societies they are already participants to a certain extent and hence participant observation is a contradiction in terms in such a situation. Second, since it is virtually impossible to participate in all situations in a complex society, sociologists confine their interest to and focus their attention on one of the aspects of the system. This being so, to achieve their object sociologists should start with certain assumptions and hypotheses and look for certain correlations and causal links. In so doing, their studies become 'explanatory' in character. Preoccupied with this end, the sociologist is compelled to collect data through sources other than observation. Insofar as this is undertaken systematically, the data yield themselves to quantification.

First, the sociological concern for explanation calls for an understanding of the causes of social pathology. In attempting to explain the causes of various 'social problems', the sociologist cannot depend upon the technique of observation. It will not do if s/he observes a few selected situations and gathers interesting information. He should also know the magnitude of the problem. Moreover, it is not always possible for him/her to 'participate' in the event or the sub-system concerned. To illustrate, if a sociologist is to study prostitution, he may not be in a position to collect the data through participant observation. At any rate, in order to locate the various causes of prostitution s/he should know the details regarding a large number of cases and for this s/he should undertake a social survey of prostitutes. If our concern is to understand the magnitude of a social problem, we cannot secure the result by knowing how a few individuals affected by the problem live and behave but we should also know how many such persons exist. Second, if the data is to be useful for the social planner or social reformer, it is insufficient to have a description of the pattern of life of the persons concerned. We need specific data in a quantitative form regarding the relevant aspects which will aid the contemplated rehabilitation. All this calls for the employment of questionnaires and interview schedules as tools of data collection.

It may be noted here that my purpose is not to argue for or against a particular technique of data collection. Rather the contrary, I would emphasize that all techniques of data collection are important and useful. More specifically, the relevance of a particular technique is to be viewed contextually. I believe there is no merit or defect in a particular technique of data collection. However, if the technique is employed in the wrong context it becomes a liability instead of an asset. I have argued that the reasons for the emphasis on participant observation as a technique of data collection by social anthropologists is to be located in the nature of societies that they have investigated, the purpose of their investigation, and the type of data they have collected. That is to say, it is not because of the inherent strength of the technique that social anthropologists have adopted participant observation as their method, but because of the nature of the society they studied and substantive content of their studies. Similarly, if questionnaire, interview schedule, and the like are more popular techniques of data collection among sociologists, it is not because sociologists are always eager to quantify their data and ignore the importance of qualitative data, but because their subject matter and areas of concern facilitate the employment of those techniques.

—◆—

Is there any perceptible change in the data collection techniques in Indian sociology? To answer this question one needs to understand the recent trends. While the first three sections of this chapter were written in 1969, an attempt was made after 20 years (see Oommen 1988a) to revisit the issue.

One possible route to understand the recent trends in the change of data collection techniques in sociology is to identify the substantive areas in which research is done (assuming that certain areas are more amenable to qualitative data generation) and to take note of the techniques of research employed by researchers. The ICSSR had commissioned two surveys in research in sociology and social anthropology (ICSSR 1974a, 1974b, 1974c, 1985a, 1985b, and 1986). The first survey reviewed researches in 18 and the second in 16 specializations in sociology.

Ten areas were common to both the surveys: social demography, tribal studies, rural studies, urban studies, industrial sociology, social stratification, sociology of religion, education, law, and political sociology. These may be viewed as conventional areas of sociological research in India in which there is continuing interest. Eight themes surveyed in the first review were dropped from the second survey. These may be grouped into two categories. Those areas in which substantial amount of work was done in the past but have witnessed a perceptible decline of interest at present—caste, SCs, community development and democratic decentralization, kinship—and those themes on which enough work does not exist so as to warrant a review—social change, historical sociology, sociology of economic development, sociology of medicine—as the time span covered by the second survey was only a decade (1970–80). The five new areas added in the second survey were social movements, sociology of science, professions, communication, and deviant behaviour. This indicates the direction in which sociology is moving in India.

In the first survey, in addition to the 18 substantive themes covered, there was a survey on research methodology and a social anthropologist was commissioned to undertake the same. After analysing 50 monographs and books and 532 articles published in seven journals of sociology and social anthropology during 1950–70, it was concluded that, ' ... in an overwhelmingly large proportion of the cases examined, data have been drawn from secondary sources or collected through observation and interviews' (Madan 1974: 301). This conclusion is largely valid even today although more than a quarter of a century has elapsed since it was arrived at. In any case, in the second survey there was no review of research methodology and hence one is not in a position to make a more definitive statement on the trend in this regard.

If one relates the theme of investigation with the type of research techniques used for data collection, the following broad picture emerges. Of the 23 substantive areas of research covered in the two surveys, quantitative data are generated and/or analysed in four areas—social demography, urban studies, industrial sociology, and education—though not to the exclusion of qualitative data, and in five areas—economic development, communication, science, professions, and deviant behaviour—the generation of quantitative data is at its incipient stage. The data generated and analysed in the remaining 14 areas are completely or predominantly qualitative in nature. Therefore, it would not be wrong to conclude that much of the data generated and analysed by Indian sociologists are qualitative in nature.

As I have argued in this chapter, while the age-old controversy between quantitative versus qualitative data still persists in India, as perhaps elsewhere, there has been an increasing awareness that the appropriateness of the tools and techniques of data collection is inextricably intertwined with the purpose for which data are generated and the nature of society or social situation from which it is collected.

NOTES

1. In my view, we can distinguish between three basic types of societies: tribal, folk, and urban. For a detailed statement and clarification, see Oommen (1967a).

2. Howley (1950: 223–32) distinguishes between 'independent communities' and 'dependent communities' based on their ecological patterns. The tribal societies with their virtually self-sufficient residential aggregation and social integration are independent communities. As compared to this, the peasant and urban societies are dependent communities. This dependence in turn means that the destiny of the dependent community is not entirely endogenously controlled.

3. For a pointed discussion of the problems that a fieldworker faces in a caste-ridden society, see Béteille (1966: 9–12). While describing the dilemma he faced, Béteille writes: 'Had I lived with the Adi-Dravidas, the agraharam would have been inaccessible.' He continues: 'I have tried in some measure to understand social life from within, in terms of the values and meanings attributed to it by the people themselves.' I fail to understand how this is possible in the light of the first statement quoted above. Discussing the advantages in living with the Brahmins and studying Sripuram, the Tanjore village, Béteille notes: 'Had I lived with the Adi-Dravidas this study would perhaps have had a different focus. A somewhat different picture of Sripuram ... would perhaps be the outcome.' And this is the basic weakness of the technique employed.

4. To concentrate on this dimension of the problem is a challenging task. As Levy observes: 'The distinction between ideal and actual structures is one of the most vital and useful tools of analysis of any society, any time any where. In one form or another men have been aware of it, since time began for them' (1966: 26).

5. I will not go into this problem here. Other students of methodology have discussed this issue at length. See especially, Edward Shils (1959) and Erikson (1967).

6. See for instance the heavy reliance of Firth (1967) on the Tikopia Chief. In studying the family and kinship among the Pandits of Kashmir, Madan (1965: 243–6) relied heavily on five informants. His description of the five informants shows that they are all educated and land-owning individuals.

7. At any rate there is no virtue in ceaselessly emphasizing the uniqueness of one's universe; this is an activity no better than a butterfly collection as Leach (1961: 1–10) would put it. The point is that the emphasis on the unique circumscribes the possibility of any valid generalization which is the aim of scientific endeavour.

3

Theory, Concepts, and Empirical Research
An Analysis in Reciprocity

The problems of social research are basically two, 'epistemological' and 'technological'. The epistemology of research relates to issues such as choosing a theme for research, the evolution of one's conceptual–theoretical framework, the interaction between empirical research, concept formation, and theory construction, all of which have a dominating influence on the nature of knowledge and its production. To be precise, I pose three questions in this chapter: Why did I study social movements? How did I arrive at the frameworks of these studies? What bearing did my empirical research have on concept formation and theory construction?

In my academic career spanning four decades, one of the thrust areas of my research has been social movements centring on two major field studies. The first of these, an analysis of the Bhoodan-Gramdan movement (*bhoodan* means land-gift and *gramdan*, village-in-gift) with special reference to Rajasthan, began in 1962 as my PhD research project and its findings were published in the early 1970s (Oommen 1972b). The second study, an analysis of the agrarian movement in twentieth-century Kerala, was initiated in the late 1960s and was published by the middle of the 1980s (Oommen 1985).

The Bhoodan-Gramdan movement, the theme of my first study, began in 1951, a year before the launching of the Community Development Programme (CDP) by the Government of India. These were then viewed by many as alternative approaches to the socio-economic reconstruction of rural India. By the time I began my research in 1962, several social scientists had written extensively on CDP and most of these studies had been sponsored and financed by different agencies of the government. But even a decade after its inception, hardly any researcher had made a serious attempt to evaluate the impact of the Bhoodan-Gramdan movement although it was (and still is) the only agrarian movement in independent India with an all-India spread. However, this movement did generate some interest, as it was an attempt to reconstruct Indian rural society relying on voluntary action and on faith in the goodness of human nature. It attracted the attention of a few foreign writers, none of whom was a social scientist, who characterized it in an idyllic fashion; the movement to them was a 'miracle' and a 'superhuman' achievement which could happen only in Gandhi's India (see Hoffman 1961; Lanze 1956; Tennyson 1955). Two social scientists, a foreigner (Yinger 1957) and an Indian (Sekhar 1968) attempted a macrolevel evaluation of the movement, based on secondary data. No investigation of the impact of the movement at the grass roots, its real target, had been undertaken by any researcher, foreign or Indian. Therefore, I thought of studying the 'Sociology of Gramdan Villages'.

When I started my research in 1962 the air was thick with the purported 'success' of the movement; the national press and All India Radio regularly reported its progress and the Planning Commission, in its evaluation of land reforms in India, published statistics relating to the collection and distribution of land through the movement. Official patronage was readily extended to the movement and was very visible. Even the United Nations' documents on land reforms made references to the success of the movement.

At that time two sets of questions played on my mind. The first set included the following: Why was it that no sociologist had ventured to make a thorough analysis of the movement thereby either vindicating or contradicting the prevalent popular and official opinions and claims about the movement? Such a study had great potentialities for building a theory of rural social transformation not only for India, but perhaps for other developing countries as well. Further, such a study could have helped in examining the efficacy or inadequacy of several social policy measures initiated by the governments in developing countries to bring about rural social change. Why was it that such an opportunity was missed?

I do not intend to catalogue all possible reasons for this serious omission but let me list a few. First was the intellectual claustrophobia created by the professional conservatism of Indian sociologists. During the 1950s and the 1960s, Indian sociologists studied religion, caste, family, village, and urban communities. Any deviation from these 'sacred themes' was not only discouraged but was even ridiculed. Second, as the movement drew its inspiration from the Sarvodaya (literally, upliftment of all) ideology propounded by Mohandas Karamchand Gandhi and as it was initiated by Acharya Vinoba Bhave, his foremost disciple, social scientists dismissed the movement as 'conservative' and hence not worth studying. Third, given the state patronage extended to and accepted by the movement, it came to be identified with the government and the party in power. Admittedly, the movement did not operate as a countervailing power to the state and therefore it did not attract much attention. Fourth, the movement was avowedly non-violent and hence non-controversial, had no nuisance value, and hence did not attract the attention of the law and order agencies. Finally, hardly any material incentive in the form of financial assistance or a possible career advantage was available to those who could have undertaken the study.

The second set of questions which occurred to me were comparative in nature: If the movement was successful in certain regions or villages in tackling the basic agrarian problem of India, namely, redistribution of land in favour of the tiller, what conditions favoured it? Were these conditions replicable elsewhere? And, if these conditions were recreated in areas where the movement was absent or unsuccessful, would it then spread to the entire countryside, thereby solving one of India's crucial problems, namely concentration of land in the hands of a small proportion of absentee and non-cultivating landlords? I do not think that it is a *post-factum* rationalization to state that while my enquiry was primarily motivated by intellectual curiosity, it also had an indirect practical concern, namely the improvement of the lot of the rural poor, the landless agricultural labourers. This in turn moulded the content of my study.

Since I set out to study the impact of Bhoodan-Gramdan movement at the grass roots, it was necessary to investigate whether its ideology had been adequately disseminated among Gramdan villagers, the strength of their motivation to donate villages-in-gift, the economic and political changes in these villages following Gramdan, the role of the local leadership in effecting these changes (if changes did occur), and the value orientations of the villagers.

As I proceeded with the investigation of Gramdan villages, I discovered that a meaningful analysis of the movement was possible only by a conscious effort to view the village situation against the backdrop of the functioning of the movement at the macrolevel. Understandably, my initial theme 'Sociology of Gramdan Villages' changed to 'Ideology and Social Change'. Broadly speaking, the movement had three layers: the micro- (village and district), the macro- (all-India), and the meso- (provincial state) levels. The macrolevel supplied the ideology, the broad organizational pattern and the top leadership; the mesolevel subjected the first two dimensions to a filtration process and moulded them to suit local conditions. For example, in states having a sizeable tribal population, Gramdan rather than Bhoodan was accorded greater importance, considering the traditional tribal pattern of communal land ownership. At the microlevel the ideology was translated into actual programmes through organizations inducted into the system for the purpose. This realization led to further shift in the emphasis of my study. While retaining the focus of investigation on Gramdan villages, I started concentrating on the role of ideology in bringing about change which necessitated a macrolevel analysis of the movement as well.

As I became familiar with the available writings on the emergence of the movement, I found that its origin and spread could not be attributed solely to its ideology. During the pre-independence days, Gandhi's Sarvodaya ideology had been overshadowed by the nationalist preoccupation with the goal of Swaraj (independence). Its tenets had scarcely been translated into concrete action, particularly in dealing with the inequality in land distribution. Further, the movement needed a style of functioning, different from that of the anti-colonial struggle and yet, acceptable and appealing to the people. This was precisely what Vinoba Bhave attempted and he functioned as a charismatic leader (Rambhai 1954, 1958). Taking a cue from this, I finally reformulated the theme of my study as 'Charismatic Movements and Social Change'. At that point I had simply assumed, following Max Weber, that charisma was a system changing force in society. But by the time I concluded my study I was convinced that charisma could as well be a system stabilizing force and hence the title of the book: *Charisma, Stability and Change*. In the book, I first attempted a general analysis of the movement in India based on its origin, ideology, organization, and macroleadership pattern before presenting details of its functioning at the grass roots level in the Gramdan villages of Rajasthan.

Based on this experience, I suggest that analysis of social movements should comprise of two aspects, the macro and the micro. By the macrodimension of a movement, I mean its ideology contained in the documented and undocumented pronouncements by its leaders; organization, the machinery through which the ideology is sought to be propagated and communicated; strategy and tactics, the specific programmes, organizational devices, and procedures adopted to put its ideology into practice. The microdimension refers to movement's actual operation and its consequences at the grass roots level, wherein we observe the filtration or accretion process to which the ideology and organization are subjected to, in order to meet the demands of specific local conditions and the mechanisms through which the movement ideology is put into practice. Thus an analysis of the macrodimension of a movement informs us of its ideology and organization, a study of the microdimension acquaints us with its actual functioning on the ground; the former offers us a perspective from above and the latter a view from below. In order to arrive at a meaningful understanding of a movement, then, we should view it from both these angles. And this is precisely what I attempted to do in the case of the Bhoodan-Gramdan movement, although my initial intention was to analyse the movement only from a microperspective.

My analysis of the macrodimension of the movement added new aspects to the study. In the case of the Bhoodan-Gramdan movement, most of its basic tenets were contained in Gandhi's Sarvodaya philosophy. In analysing the ideology of the movement I drew upon the writings of its chief architects—Gandhi, Vinoba Bhave, and Jayaprakash Narayan. Similarly, I found that its organizational core had pre-dated the emergence of the movement in its present form, the Akhil Bharat Sarva Seva Sangh (All India Social Service Society). When the movement started functioning as a concrete programme for the collection and distribution of land, the need for a specific new organization was keenly felt. In fact, soon after the first land donation in 1951, in Pachampalli village in Andhra Pradesh, Bhave constituted a 'trust'—a tripartite committee consisting of the donor, village influentials, and Sarvodaya workers—to administer land distribution. As the number of donations multiplied, the need for co-ordinating organizational tasks arose. Thus village, district, state, and national level organizations developed gradually. Generally speaking, except at the village level, co-ordination of the movement activities had been taken over by the existing Sarvodaya organizations. Therefore, it was necessary to analyse the organizational innovations of the movement at the village level in order to understand the problems of translating the movement ideology into practice.

Another 'feedback' from the field provided the rationale for the shift in the focus of the study. My analysis of the communication pattern revealed that most of the villagers viewed Vinoba Bhave, the initiator of the movement, as a saint-on-march; they were gifting away their lands to a saint! Further, while analysing the local leadership pattern of the movement, I observed a process of vertical transmission of charisma; local charismatic heroes donned the mantle of charisma and adopted a style of life akin to that of the national leaders and maintained their appeal through contact-charisma. This led me to conclude that the change propelling force in the movement was not so much its ideology as it was the charismatic appeal of the national and local leaders. Thus I became convinced of the tremendous importance of the charismatic resource to mobilize people into collective action. It was this realization which emboldened me to stick to the new focus of the study, 'Charismatic Movements and Social Change'. The point I want to emphasize is this: even as a researcher starts with a specific plan of study, the focus of his investigation is likely to change as he interacts with the field. What is important is his flexibility and ability to respond to the demands of the field situation.

An indirect pay-off due to successive shifts in the focus of study needs to be noted here. As I indicated above the analysis of the movement at the macrolevel showed the existence of an ideology and an organizational core prior to the emergence and spread of the movement in its present form. The critical factor facilitating the movement's spread was charismatic leadership. This led me to conclude that we could identify three distinct aspects of any movement for purposes of analysis: ideology, organization, and leadership. Any of these dimensions may emerge first and some aspects of a movement may have primacy over the other aspects at a specific point of time. If this is so, we can speak of three types of movements depending on which of these aspects emerges first in its life cycle: ideological, organizational, or charismatic, a typology I proposed in the study.

Reflecting back on the life cycle approach I proposed and the typology formulated based on that, I note two major omissions. First, I failed to account for the societal conditions which facilitated or thwarted the emergence of a particular type of movement. This lacuna emanated from the failure to link systematically the theory of social movements with a theory of social structure. A more fruitful analysis could have been attempted by focusing on the system conditions more systematically. The crucial question then to be posed in a study of movements is: What type of movement emerges in what kind of society and why?

Second, I had overlooked the importance of analysing the mobilizational activities of the movement. The main reason for this was the style of the movement itself. In the case of the Bhoodan-Gramdan movement, the most important mobilizational activity was *padayatra* (walking a long distance) by movement workers to propagate its ideology and to collect donations of land. Apart from this, the movement attempted very little mobilizational acitivity, partly because of the absence of any organized opposition to it. The cause the movement championed, land to the tiller, had been accepted by the government and most of the political parties. Further, the movement elicited support by adopting non-violent means. Hence, there were no major confrontations between the supporters of the movement and their opponents and therefore mobilization was not a particularly exciting area of analysis. However, analysis of mobilization is too important an area to be neglected in the study of social movements.

I did not begin my fieldwork with an 'open mind'. The very fact that I had decided on the broad area of my investigation beforehand made it incumbent on me to have an outline of what I was looking for in the field. The impression conveyed by some researchers which can be stated as: 'I went (to the field), I observed, and I analysed', is to my mind quite contrary to the 'natural' research process. On the other hand, the way in which one presents one's argument and data may impart the impression that the author started with a preconceived framework. For instance, readers of *Charisma, Stability and Change* may get the impression that I started with the argument stated in Chapter 1 and collected 'convenient data' to 'prove' my argument. This is quite contrary to my experience in evolving my strategy of research. I stated my argument at the very outset in order to inform the presentation of data with some consistency and order. In fact, the argument, although stated in the beginning of the book, was the end product of my research.

I started with the assumption, as noted earlier, that charisma is a change generating force in societies. Similarly, it was my hunch in the beginning that charismatic endowment existed only at the macrolevel, that it was a quality to be found only among the national level leaders of the movement. Although I started with these assumptions and hypotheses, it was possible to float counter-hypotheses, not always in a cut-and-dried fashion but as a sort of 'mental experiment'. Thus, in effect there was a constant interaction between the assumptions that I entertained, the concepts I employed, and the empirical evidence I gathered. It was through this process that I arrived at my argument whose guiding principle was neither deduction nor induction but retroduction. Let me elaborate.

I gained my initial insight in characterizing the movement as 'charismatic' from the descriptions of the conditions under which the first land-gift was obtained and Bhave's response to it (Rambhai 1954, 1958). However, as soon as I undertook my first field trip the empirical manifestation of charisma became clearer to me. The incidence of Gramdan villages was high along the route of Bhave's Padayatra; the people were gifting away their land to a peripatetic saint. But gradually I noticed that the charismatic quality was also attributed to, or found in the regional and village level leaders as well and hence I started working with the notion of local or 'little charismatic'. The local leaders of the movement were often looked upon as charismatic heroes by the people, linking them with national ones. For instance, I came across Bagad Gandhi (Bagad being a folk region constituted by Dungarpur and Banswara districts of Rajasthan) and little Bhaves and Gandhis even at the village level. In the light of this evidence I postulated that there were two types of local charismatic leaders: (1) those who came to don the mantle of charisma independently of the leaders of the wider system; this possibility obtained in systems in which leaders operated independently of the wider context, their independence being rooted in the cultural autonomy of their systems. (2) the mantle of charisma may be passed downward by the macrolevel leader by grooming regional or local leaders or the latter may establish sufficient communication with the former thereby assuming the role of his spokesmen at the local level. This vertical dispersion of charisma was designated contact charisma.

The notion of local charismatics also led to a reformulation of the attributes of charisma. While the local leaders emulated the lifestyle of macroleaders in their dress, dietary practices, and daily work schedule, they operated in a very limited locale. They were in constant interaction with the people and it was not possible to create a smokescreen and mystify relations between the leaders and the followers. Admittedly, we would search in vain for the charismatic qualities of a Gandhi or Bhave in a local charismatic leader. Therefore, I argued that charisma was an amorphous attribute qualitatively different at different levels and contexts. I then reformulated the notion of charisma as follows: 'The attributes of charisma are not given for ever, they are contextual; charisma is ultimately a product of social structure and it undergoes qualitative transformation concomitant to the changes in the nature of society' (Oommen 1972b: 6).

Another insight I gained from the application of the concept of charisma to a specific empirical context was the system stabilizing function of charisma. Analysis of charismatic authority was crucial to Weber's explanations of social change. Within the framework of German historicism, Weber sought to explain the problem of change at the macrolevel through the concept of charisma. The charismatic leaders were innovators and creators who brought about large-scale change, whom Weber distinguished from the maintainers of tradition. But I found that the unconventional means a leader employs to achieve his objective could render him a charismatic hero even if he proved to be an agent of system stability. Further, I observed that the leaders of the Bhoodan-Gramdan movement were instrumental for system conservation, at least in certain respects (Oommen 1967b: 88–9). Bhave wanted to establish a society from which exploitation was rooted out through peaceful means. Partly because of his approach to change, the movement could not effectively confront vested interests and unwittingly even reinforced them. Thus, in spite of its charismatic force, the movement often led to the perpetuation of the system.

Yet another instance of the bearing of empirical research on concept formation may be noted here. The prevalent tendency in community power structure analysis was to emphasize a given approach—positional, reputational, or decisional—in locating influentials which often led to the failure to net all the leaders in an analytical framework (Oommen 1970b: 226–39). I employed all the approaches to locate the leaders in the villages studied. In Gramdan villages there were two important formal bodies, the executive committee of Gram Sabha (village assembly), making routine decisions and the Sabha itself constituted by all adults in the village, those who were above 18 years, in which the ultimate authority for local affairs was vested. The usual practice in the executive committee was to get the decisions endorsed by all its members who appended their signatures or thumb impressions. But the Gram Sabha meetings were too unwieldy to collect signatures of all present and, therefore, they were collected only from a limited number of persons. The significant point to observe was, who were the persons from whom signatures were collected in Gram Sabha meetings and what were the bases on which they were qualified to sign? In one of the Gram Sabha meetings at which I was present, the secretary of the executive committee was collecting signatures from a few additional individuals *other than* the executive committee members. On enquiry I was told that these were *khas admis* (men who matter) in the context of village affairs. Such observations led me to a fuller understanding of the nature of the power structure in villages on the basis of which I made the following formulations:

1. All those who wield real power, *power-reservoirs*, in a village community may not be on the formal decision-making bodies.
2. The power *exercisers* who constitute the formal decision-making structures have legal or formal power but they may not wield actual power.
3. The *power pool* in a community is constituted by power reservoirs and exercisers.
4. The power exerciser may be able to use his position to become a power reservoir but one can be a member of the power reservoir without being a power exerciser. That is, membership in formal bodies is a resource for acquiring actual power, but actual power can be acquired independent of formal structures.
5. If the power reservoirs are not power exercisers or if the power exercisers are not falling in line with the power reservoirs, political instability is likely.
6. Political stability is assured when power reservoirs are also power exercisers or power exercisers are willing to be controlled by power reservoirs.

Thus, an empirical observation in the field yielded fresh insights about the nature of the power structure and political instability.

The point I want to make is this: even as a researcher starts with a conceptual framework, it undergoes constant revision as s/he confronts empirical reality. The field situation offers him/her opportunities to reformulate existing concepts and invest them with new meanings, if s/he has the required flexibility and openness. Additionally, the field situation also continuously provides the researcher the context for enunciating new concepts.

The three very well-known approaches in history to tackle agrarian problems are: violent uprising by deprived peasantry, legislative intervention by the state, and non-violent mobilization. A large number of studies on the impact of land reforms initiated by the government were completed in India by the 1960s, particularly by economists. Having analysed the Bhoodan-Gramdan movement in India, the best known non-violent effort in history to tackle agrarian problems, I came to the conclusion that in terms of its announced aim of establishing communitarian villages based on collective landownership, the movement was an abortive experiment. Ever since, I had wanted to study an agrarian movement with a different orientation in rural India. An opportunity to start studying such a movement emerged in the early 1970s.

With the ushering in of the 'green revolution' in India, the role of economic development in accentuating income disparities became a favourite theme of social science research. The widespread agrarian unrest in India's countryside culminating in the emergence of the violent Naxalbari revolt in West Bengal in 1967, released shock waves throughout India. Unlike the non-violent Sarvodaya movement, the Naxalbari uprising was widely discussed, debated, and analysed. Everybody seemed to attest to the presumed linkage between the green revolution and rural unrest. Even the then home minister Y.B. Chavan articulated the popular stereotype when he declared in Parliament that the green revolution would turn into a red one if the strategy of rural change was not immediately reoriented.

Having followed this debate carefully for some time I made an initial effort to contest the widely heralded hypothesis, based on the data available in the home ministry report (Oommen 1971a). I suggested that the presumed causal linkage between the green revolution and agrarian unrest was naïve, simplistic, and was not sustainable. But it was necessary to explicate my position with hard and detailed empirical data. My native district in Kerala, Alleppey, provided an excellent empirical context to pursue the analysis. Although an Intensive Agricultural Development Project (IADP) district, Alleppey scarcely experienced the green revolution. On the other hand, Alleppey had a long tradition of agrarian unrest, very high agricultural wage rate, and low productivity. My detailed and intensive study of the district conclusively proved that the presumed causal sequential explanation—development–›disparity–›discontent–›conflict—was facile and misleading. I found that mobilization of the peasantry and agrarian proletariat by a multiplicity of political parties competing for clients substantially contributed to agrarian conflicts (Oommen 1971b). This was my first study of Kerala.

Given my interest in rural social transformation and familiarity with rural India, I favourably responded to a request from the Food and Agriculture Organization (FAO) of the United Nations in 1972 to undertake a study of agrarian organizations in one of the districts, as a part of a wider study covering 20 districts from all over India. Without hesitation I selected Alleppey district. The purpose of the FAO study was to collect and analyse data on agrarian organizations keeping in mind what factors facilitate or obstruct the building of organizations for the welfare of the rural poor.

I came across a large number and a wide variety of agrarian organizations in Alleppey. From the perspective of building organizations for the welfare of the rural poor they could be classified into two: those sponsored by the government and those initiated by political parties. The archetype of the first being Harijan co-operatives and of the second being peasant and agricultural labour unions. In terms of their aims, while the co-operatives were dismal failures, the unions were a thumping success. One of the main reasons, which accounted for this differential performance, was the nature of leadership in these organizations. I therefore argued that if co-operatives were entrusted to the leaders who organized labour unions they may perform better (Oommen 1976).

The FAO study clearly revealed the importance of agrarian unions in bringing about substantial change in rural Kerala. For a fuller understanding it was necessary to analyse their style of operation.

This called for a new study. If the FAO study concentrated on the organizational dimension, the focus of the new investigation had to be mobilization. I then launched such a study with financial assistance from the Jawaharlal Nehru University (JNU) in 1974, where I was faculty since 1971.

As I have noted earlier in the Bhoodan movement study, the mobilizational dimension was neglected, partly because it was a non-violent movement. But in Kerala, what characterized the functioning of agricultural labour unions was their frequent confrontations with farmers' associations. Understandably, the focus in this study was on the varieties of mobilizations by a multiplicity of agrarian unions and associations.

Given the findings of my initial study of Alleppey district which dispelled the causal linkage between the green revolution and agrarian unrest, I was persuaded to enlarge the scope of my new study. The following questions became pertinent. Was there a tradition of peasant movement in Kerala? If yes, when did it emerge and crystallize? Were there basic differences in these traditions among the three regions—Travancore, Cochin, and Malabar—which came to consititute Kerala? If so, what were the bases of the differences? What was the relationship between peasant mobilization and anti-colonial struggle? What changes, if any, did the agrarian movement undergo after independence? Which parties and organizations took the lead in mobilizing different agrarian classes? How did the collective actors define and perceive their identities and what were the consequences of this cognition? What was the impact of state policies in determining the course of agrarian movement?

I might not have satisfactorily answered all these questions in my book *From Mobilization to Institutionalization* (1985). But I am sure that these questions shaped my investigation and they occurred to me precisely because of my previous studies and familiarity with the studies of fellow students of agrarian movements. And yet I believe that this 'prior knowledge' did not constrict and choke me intellectually.

Having stumbled on the idea of career of a movement (the life-cycle approach) while studying the Bhoodan movement, I was inclined to pursue the same strand of analysis in the case of the Kerala agrarian movement too. While the Bhoodan movement had a rather short and prosaic career, that of the agrarian movement in Kerala was long and eventful. Further, while the former was initiated by a charismatic personality at the national level and had subsequently

spread to distant parts of the country, the Kerala agrarian movement was autonomous to begin with but subsequently got linked
with all-India movements (for example, the anti-colonial movement)
and structures (for example, political parties). This facilitated the
following conceptualization:

... in the origin and spread of movements in India we can discern two
patterns: (1) Independent local origin (at the micro levels) either simultaneously or sequentially and then getting coordinated ... (2) Simultaneous
emergence in different regions through the inspiration of charismatic
heroes or sponsored by all India structures such as political parties.
(Oommen 1977: 34)

Given the fact that I was studying a movement which survived and
continued for nearly a century, a question arose as to whether
the nature of the movement remained the same throughout its
existence. This prompted me to examine closely the goal transformations, value orientations, the nature of enemies, and the styles
of mobilization in the different phases of the movement. Based on
this analysis, the movement was divided into four major historical
phases: the pre-political, the anti-colonial, the anti-Congress, and
the pro-government phases. It is necessary to briefly explain the
rationale behind this classification.

The pre-political peasant revolts and rebellions usually had independent local origins and were rarely co-ordinated at the regional
level. Notwithstanding their economic goals, these revolts were characterized by primordial collectivism. Their ideology, organizational
weaponry, and leadership were closely linked to and utilized the
symbols of caste and religious collectivities. They were rarely exclusively agrarian in content and most of these movements were also
cultural revolts. That is, an undifferentiated social structure gives
birth to an amorphous 'agrarian' movement with multiple goals.

The anti-colonial phase was distinct in several specific ways: co-
ordination of the movement on a wider, almost on an all-India basis;
confrontation with a clearly identified and hierarchically ordered
set of enemies namely, the British, the 'fedual'/absentee landlord,
the moneylender, and the big landlord; emergence of political
parties with distinct pro-landlord anti-peasant and anti-landlord
pro-peasant orientations.

In the first decade of independent India, the peasant movement
of Kerala was explicity anti-government for the following reasons.
First, the mobilization of peasantry and agrarian proletariat was

undertaken mainly by the Communist Party of India (CPI), which was in the opposition. Second, the Congress party, having acquired power, took or appeared to be taking a pro-landlord posture.

In the fourth phase, beginning with 1957, the Kerala agrarian movement took a different turn as the party or parties which were the chief mobilizers of the peasantry and agrarian proletariat either formed the government (intermittently) or remained as substantial opposition parties with sufficient political clout to challenge the parties in power. This rendered the possibility of the agrarian movement operating as an agent of the establishment and/or an extension of the party in power.

Based on this empirical evidence I argued that any effort to generalize about the role of particular peasant classes irrespective of the contextual variations would be misleading. I have suggested that (1) the notion of the vanguard should be viewed in the spatio-temporal context and (2) the same agrarian class may play diametrically opposite roles in different historical phases. Much of the prevalent confusion relating to the analysis of the role of agrarian classes in revolution is the result of ignoring the *historicity of context.*

The conceptual distinction between party, voluntary association, and movement is well documented and widely accepted in sociology. This conceptualization is based on the empirical experiences of western liberal democracies. But these distinctions are scarcely applicable to one-party systems and even to the Indian situation. For example, what is labelled as a peasant or agrarian 'movement' in India is invariably the mobilizational activities of agrarian unions, that is, voluntary associations which are front organizations of political parties. Viewed thus, if one makes a comprehensive study of the activities of political parties that would encapsulate movement activities too.

In Kerala there are several agrarian front organizations based on parties and classes. Thus, a particular political party may sponsor two or more such organizations (and in fact some of them do)—a peasant association and an agricultural labour union—while others may sponsor only one such association or union. The usual tendency among movement analysts is to concentrate on the activities of one set of these associations or unions—farmer's associations, peasant unions, and agricultural labour unions—ignoring others, thereby mistaking the part for the whole. In reality, the agrarian movement is constituted by the co-operative and conflicting interactions between and among these unions and associations. Keeping these considerations in mind, I defined a movement as a stream of associations in interaction. Such a definition helps to distinguish movements from parties and associations and to concentrate on the specific activity of movements as distinct from that of particular associations or parties.

Discussions on the role of the peasantry in the freedom movement in India are viewed from two perspectives, macroholism and microindividualism (Oommen 1985: 2–3). The first overemphasizes the political content and motivation and the second highlights only the economic grievances and interests of the peasantry. While emphasizing the specific attributes and motives of the peasantry, both these perspectives ignore the properties of the situation in which mobilizations take place. In reality, peasant collective action particularly under colonial conditions is largely prompted by political considerations, the aspirations they share with others to move from subjecthood to citizenship. But the concretization of this aspiration as far as the peasantry is concerned is to be found in the redressal of its economic hardships. Even as the holistic perspective informs peasant collective action, the individualistic (class-categorical) interests and needs cannot be overlooked. That is, neither macroholism nor microindividualism can fully explain peasant involvement in anti-colonial struggles. Therefore I suggested *situational interactionism* as an appropriate and adequate perspective which recognizes: (1) the *reciprocity* between local mobilization and national movement and (2) the importance of the properties of the situation (ibid.: 3).

There is yet another reason behind the linkage between the macro- and microevents and situations in the context of movements as I have recognized.

Movement ideology is usually formulated by the leadership and often in abstract terms but is a necessary input which provides the requisite passion to the rank and file to plunge into collective actions. But this ideological vision of the leadership needs to be translated into problem-oriented and issue-centred programmes taking into account the existential conditions of the specific social category which is sought to be mobilized into collective actions. (Oommen 1977: 32)

The tendency to juxtapose collective protest actions with state actions and hence movements and legislations is widespread in contemporary social science writings of the western liberal democracies.

But this conceptualization does not adequately portray the empirical realities of either the socialist countries or of the developing counties. The state in these countries not only initiates a series of legislative measures to bring about 'radical' transformation, but even sponsors collective actions either to legitimize its measures and/or to accelerate the process of social transformation. Further, legislation itself can be an initiator or indicator of change depending upon the role the state assumes. Keeping these considerations in mind, I tried to highlight the *complementarity* between legislation and movements. That is, legislation plays a pivotal role in order to institutionalize the changes initiated by social movements. Conversely, even when change is initiated through the instrument of law, collective actions become important to legitimize and complete the process of change. One cannot understand and appreciate these observations unless one conceptualizes state's actions and collective actions as complementary, a pay-off obtained by recognizing the difference between India's empirical situation and that of western capitalist democracies.

It is widely recognized that the mould for the emergence of movements is provided by relative deprivation, its perception and articulation by the concerned collectivity. In contrast, very little theroretical work exists in regard to the termination of movements. However, it has been proposed that the specific processes which lead to the termination of a movement are: repression, discreditation, co-optation, and institutionalization (Rush and Denisoff 1971: 367).

My analysis clearly showed that no effort was spared in the pre-independence phase and even in the first decade of free India by the then establishments to repress the agrarian movements in Kerala. In spite of this virulent repression the movement gained in strength, notwithstanding temporary setbacks. Therefore, the critical variable is not repression *per se* but the collective conscience which bestows legitimacy on the agent of repression and attributes *illegitimacy* to movement participants. That is, insofar as the state is perceived by the collectivity as a 'legitimate authority' which should repress the 'illegitimate movement', which offends the collective conscience, repression will be an effective instrument for terminating a movement. On the other hand, if the state is perceived as an illegitimate intruder and/or supporting the vested interests in society and movement participants are viewed as martyrs to a cause in the wider interests of the collectivity, then repression will not weaken but strengthen the movement. Thus my analysis unfolds as to how ignoring the 'properties of the situation' leads to the formulation of erroneous theoretical propositions.

With the arrival of freedom and transfer of political power from the British to a national government, a critical proportion of people invested the Congress government with legitimacy. That is why the repression of agrarian movements by the Congress government was not viewed with the same disdain by people at large. Conversely the Congress tried its best to *discredit* the then CPI thanks to the latter's refusal to 'co-operate' with the Congress. But after the split of CPI into CPI (Right) and CPI (Marxist), CPI (R) opted for a policy of peaceful transition to socialism and entered into an alliance with 'progressive' bourgeoisie, that is, the Congress party which was in power. This in turn led to partial co-optation of several movement leaders directly or indirectly into the establishment. But thanks to the CPI (M)'s refusal 'to co-operate' with the Congress, the possibility of co-opting leaders associated with CPI (M) diminished. CPI (M) front organizations continued to be the most persisting factor in keeping the vitality of the agrarian movement in Kerala and hence the strategy of co-optation did not produce the desired effect, namely the demise of the movement. That is, in order that discreditation and co-optation be effective means of terminating movements, a series of prerequisites should exist.

As noted earlier, I began the study of agrarian movement in Kerala within the framework of the natural history or lifecycle approach according to which institutionalization is an inevitable tendency leading to the termination of a movement. Simply put, the argument runs as follows: the development of an organization, however rudimentary, is inevitable for the realization of movement goals. But the emergence of such organization inevitably sets in motion forces which defeat the very purpose which necessitated it. The instrument—the movement organization—becomes instrumental in frustrating the initial objective for which it emerged.

Contrary to this conventional theorization I found enough support in the empirical evidence available to me that there is no inherent tendency towards institutionalization. Further, even when it occurs, institutionalization does not necessarily stop or always decelerate the process of mobilization which is so fundamental and primary to the continuance of a movement. In fact, mobilization and institutionalization co-exist and the latter may provide new possibilities for mobilization. Therefore I concluded: ' ... mobilization

is not displaced by institutionalisation *but both go hand in hand ...* '
(Oommen 1985: 254).

The recounting of my experiences in undertaking studies of two
social movements reveals that a multiplicity of considerations goes
into the selection of research themes. The researcher may not be
conscious of all these factors particularly in the beginning. But it
is rewarding to bring the unconscious elements into the realm of
consciousness because that would at least partly reveal the value
biases and preferences the researcher has. To be aware and conscious of one's value preferences is the first step in the journey
towards objectivity.

There is an inevitable risk in choosing research themes which
foment contemporary political and academic controversies. The
possibility of getting grafted into one or another camp is fairly
high. To take a position independent of the prevalent popular sentiments and opinions calls for tremendous courage and fortitude.
And yet, one has to do precisely that if one is to deserve the label
of an impartial analyst.

Those who have a definite issue to investigate and questions
to answer would invariably begin their empirical studies armed
with a conceptual-theoretical framework. But this need not be an
intellectual liability if one is sufficiently open, flexible, and creative
to reformulate one's framework in the light of one's exposure
to empirical evidence. That is, while it is not possible to begin
research with an 'open mind', one should constantly keep open
one's partly-filled mind to provide scope for creative confrontations between concepts, theories, and data. The captive mind is
not simply a product of western academic colonialism but also of
the inability to transcend 'trained incapacity' and inappropriate
indigenous work habits.

4

On the Craft of Studying
Social Movements

❖

This chapter addresses the issues relating to what I have designated as 'technology of research' in Chapter 3. More specifically, I propose to deal with problems I encountered in the selection of units of study, in choosing appropriate tools and techniques of data collection, and in defining my identity as a researcher in the field.

There are two volumes (Béteille and Madan 1975; Srinivas et al. 1979) dealing with these issues. Although there are 29 contributions by 28 sociologists and social anthropologists in these two volumes, covering a wide variety of themes and situations, none deals with the investigation of a social movement. While the issues discussed in this chapter are certainly not entirely specific to the study of social movements, they do highlight certain issues exclusive to its analysis.

I shall discuss my experiences in undertaking studies of social movements in two different field settings. The first of these, an analysis of Bhoodan-Gramdan movement with special reference to Rajasthan was undertaken to write a PhD dissertation. The second study attempts an analysis of agrarian movement in twentieth-century Kerala. I shall discuss my experiences in relation to these in succession.

As a young student initiated into the world of social research my first problem was the focus of study. Although my field investigation was to be done in gramdan (village-in-gift) villages, my aim was *not* to analyse the social structure of these villages or even to understand the style of life of the villagers. My purpose was to evaluate the role of the Bhoodan movement to bring about social change and to observe the manifestations of this in gramdan villages. Therefore, the questions that arose in my mind were: One, how can one establish that changes, if any, taking place in gramdan villages are exclusively or at least predominantly due to the movement? Two, assuming that there are multiple causes of change, how can we isolate the specific contribution made by the movement in effecting changes in gramdan villages?

The fact that I started my investigation with a definite purpose called for the invoking of an 'experimental' research design. It is widely recognized that a study of change is methodologically sound only if it is attempted either in a time-perspective or in a space-perspective. While in the former case the same working universe is subjected to analysis through time, the latter calls for a comparative study of at least two spatial units with the provision that the variable assumed to be causing the change is absent from one of the units. Since the Bhoodan-Gramdan movement was in existence barely for a decade when I started studying it in 1962 and further that the villages actually selected for the study were gramdan villages only for about five years, it was felt to be unrewarding to attempt an analysis of these villages in a time-perspective. Therefore, I decided to study two sets of villages, gramdan (experimental) and non-gramdan (control),[1] in order to understand the changes in the former set of villages which may be attributed to the movement.

Since the movement operated in the whole of India and over 5,000 villages were donated in gift (gramdan) by 1961, it was necessary to decide upon a specific locale from which the villages were to be selected. I cannot offer any compelling rationale in selecting the state of Rajasthan as the locale of my study, except that it was convenient for me as I was attached to one of the universities in that state at that time. However, discussions with movement leaders revealed that Rajasthan was one of the states wherein the movement was active and 'successful'. In 1961 there were 234 gramdan villages in Rajasthan and I had to select a few villages for intensive observation. Although a complete list of these villages was obtained from the co-ordinating agency of the movement in the state, the Rajasthan Sarva Seva Sangh, most of them could not be located or if located the requisite data to facilitate the selection of villages were not available. Therefore, I decided to select a few villages from among the 65 gramdan villages brought under the purview of legislation, the Rajasthan Gramdan Act, 1960,[2] since some preliminary information was available about these villages. Thus the factor which influenced the selection of villages was limited resources—time and money—available to the researcher.

These 'social' factors apart, a few research issues conditioned the selection of specific villages. An examination of the details relating to the 65 gramdan villages brought under the Act revealed that these villages were generally speaking atypical when regarded in terms of their population and/or number of households, the area of land held by the villagers, and social complexity, viewed in terms of the number of social categories, castes, and tribes, found in these villages as compared with non-gramdan villages. There was yet another factor which contributed to the atypicality of gramdan villages. In the process of becoming gramdan villages, they had undergone a process of bifurcation usually in terms of the village 'core' and the hamlets.[3] Thus if a 'revenue' village had three hamlets, apart from the village core, as a result of gramdan four 'villages' emerged out of it. The search for gramdan villages similar in size and social structural complexity as compared with non-gramdan villages prompted me to select as far as possible unbifurcated villages. If I were to select typical gramdan villages they would have been atypical villages of Rajasthan. Thus, the gramdan villages selected were more or less typical of the villages of the region but were atypical gramdan villages.

The villages selected were atypical from another angle too. I wanted to examine the conditions which led to the successful operation of gramdan villages as communitarian enterprises, because the assumption was that the replication of these conditions in other villages would facilitate their being brought under gramdan. Therefore, it was necessary to select 'successful cases' and this was precisely what I did. In consultation with the movement leaders at the local level, I made a list of successful gramdan villages from the pool of 'typical' villages for closer analysis. Thus, both theoretical purpose and practical concerns of my study dictated the selection of gramdan villages.

A final consideration which conditioned the selection of gramdan villages was their spatial spread. On examination of the relevant data I found that, out of the 65 gramdan villages brought under the purview of legislation, 62 were located in five of the 26 districts of Rajasthan. I decided to confine the selection of villages to these five gramdan 'clusters'. In turn, these five districts belonged to three major regions of the state—the eastern plain, the dry (arid) zone, and the southern highland. Two of the gramdan clusters each belonged to the dry and highland areas and one to the plain area.

I decided to select one village each from three regions. In the case of the plain area, since there was only one gramdan cluster, I faced no problem of selection. But there were two clusters each in the case of the dry and highland regions and I settled on one or another of the clusters depending on certain practical considerations, such as relatively easy accessibility to the village and amenability of the movement leaders at the district level.

However, the problem I had to tackle in the selection of villages was not yet over as 12 per cent of gramdan villages brought under the Act were new colonies, villages established on land donated by local landlords or on government land. Since these colonies were established *de novo*, I anticipated their functioning to be on a different footing, as traditional animosities based on neighbourhood and factions may not be present in these villages. In order to give representation to this category, I selected a fourth village (a new colony) from the highland region in which the incidence of new colonies was the highest. Thus, I selected four 'successful' gramdan villages, which were also unbifurcated typical revenue villages, from four out of the five districts to which most of these villages belonged, the districts being drawn from the three major regions of the state. It may also be noted here that the selection of villages from the three regions also facilitated the inclusion of villages with different sizes, quality of land, and varying social composition (castes and tribes) in the study.

While four gramdan villages were selected, only three non-gramdan villages needed to be selected because the category of new colonies was non-existent in the case of non-gramdan (control) villages. The three control villages were selected from the same districts, talukas, and panchayats as that of the experimental cases, the distance between them ranging between five to ten miles in all the cases. The selection of both the experimental and control cases from the same administrative units was intended to neutralize the impact of state initiated programmes like community development and Panchayati Raj. The use of an experimental design thus affected the choice of control villages because of the need to select two sets of villages, the control set being comparable to the experimental set except in regard to the additional factor, namely gramdan. Although sufficient care was taken to ensure similarity between experimental and control cases in regard to landholding pattern, size of population, and social structural features, there were some differences between them. This is an inherent limitation in applying the experimental design to a natural setting. Thus the control villages had more households, their complexity greater in terms of the number of social categories, and the inequality of landholdings more telling as compared with their gramdan counterparts. However, these differences, I was convinced, were not so crucial as to abandon the design itself. At any rate, instead of adopting a 'methodologically naked' design, I thought it was necessary to attempt a rigorous comparison since my purpose was to understand the rate and directionality of change.

The choice of tools of data collection is to be made based on several considerations such as the nature of the social system in which the study is launched, the subject matter, the purpose of the study, the kind of research design, etc. (see Chapter 2). However, it is not always possible to fathom all the problems in this context at the initial stage. Right from the beginning I thought of employing several techniques of data collection: structured interviews, observation, and documentary analysis. Most of the data, I thought, could be collected through an elaborate interview schedule to be administered to all heads of households in the selected villages. But it took only a little time for me to realize that interviews by themselves could not yield adequate and reliable data and the respondents from whom I sought to collect data (heads of households) were not always the most suitable. Admittedly, I had to improvise in the field. While I continued to use the interview schedule, I stopped administering certain parts of it, for example, those relating to intergroup relations, factions, and landholdings. I found that the data collected on these aspects were unreliable for different reasons. Let me illustrate.

Collectivization of land being an important objective of gramdan, I wanted to know whether disparities in landholdings existed between different households in gramdan villages. But most respondents did not have any clear idea of the size of land held by them. This lack of clarity was partly related to the structure of households, most of which were consumption units but not independent production units. While two or three brothers may commonly cultivate the undivided ancestral land and divide the produce, they had separate kitchens, that is, households consisting of their wives, children, and other dependants. Even when the ancestral land was partitioned, the procedure of land transfer was such that it did not enable the landholders to have a clear idea of their size of holdings. Often the *kathedar* (the legal owner) continued to be one of the great grandfathers and the land was apportioned between the legal heirs for the purpose of cultivation, but legal ownership was not transferred. Therefore, in order to know the amount of land cultivated by each household, I had to undertake an analysis of kin relations (as division of property is invariably based on inheritance rights) and investigate the land transfers (selling, donations, etc.). While this procedure was cumbersome and time consuming, I found it highly satisfactory to get at reliable data in this context.

As for the data on intergroup relations or details on factions which I needed to understand, the political dynamics of gramdan villages, several heads of households were either not sufficiently communicative, or inadequately informed, or simply indifferent. Further, I realized that a summation of these responses would only provide me with an understanding of the opinions, attitudes, and value orientations of respondents. My interest was to collect factual information about the dynamics of factions and intergroup relations. In order to collect data on these aspects I resorted to informal interviews and observations. In the case of informal interviews I discovered that a given set of informants did not suit my purpose in all contexts. Therefore, I had to identify different sets of key informants with whom I could enter into prolonged conversation. A key informant is a person who can supply vital information regarding a particular aspect of the problem under investigation. Admittedly, it was necessary to interview different sets of key informants to secure information regarding different dimensions. For instance, in order to understand the historical background—animosities and alliances—of village factions, the elders were found to be more useful, whereas the youth were found to be more communicative in reporting current factional alliances. Here again, I had my share of difficulties.

I came across a variety of informants. Apart from the *routine* type of informants who constituted the majority, there were the *eulogisers* who were highly integrated with the system and invariably gave a positive picture of everything in the village; the *marginals,* drawn from the stock of 'unimportant' social categories; the *unintegrated* (in the system) who always criticized everything that happened in the village; and the *enthusiasts* who had a tendency to over-report about men and events. To construct a consolidated and balanced picture, I had to sift the information received from each of these categories of informants. As for observation, I could participate only in a limited range of activities partly because my stay in each village was short (usually about eight weeks) and partly because all contexts and occasions were not equally open to me for observation. Generally speaking, I confined my systematic observation to the meetings of formal and informal bodies such as the gram sabhas, co-operative societies, neighbourhood groups, caste panchayats, smoking groups, workgroups, and the like, since routine rituals of various kinds were not my immediate concern.

The autonomy of the individual in formulating and articulating his opinions, it is argued, is a prerequisite for the meaningful application of 'survey research'. Since the Indian individual is not autonomous, it is unrewarding to employ survey techniques to collect data (Rudolph and Rudolph 1958), particularly from rural India. On the other hand, there are authors who have demonstrated that reliable data can be collected through survey research in rural India (Elder 1960). It is not my intention here to revive this controversy but to suggest that the problem is wrongly posed.

The real problem I experienced was not so much the incapacity of Indian villagers to articulate their points of view at least in regard to certain aspects, but the difficulty in locating my respondents individually. I found them invariably in small groups of kin, friends, and workmates and to disengage them from these groups for purposes of interviewing was almost impossible. The way out was to interview them while they were in groups. This proved to be advantageous in several ways. First, if my 'respondent' did not remember a particular fact or wilfully distorted it, others operated as a check and corrective either by directly correcting him or by reminding him that what he reported was not altogether right. Second, some of the attitudes and values which he held in a nebulous fashion could be articulated clearly with the help of his companions so that I got a clear picture of these. Third, if the formal head of the household was docile the 'operational head of the household' answered the question, thereby partly reducing the problem I faced in locating the effective respondent.

However, this procedure of interviewing brought to light new difficulties. For instance, if my respondent was a person of inferior status (lower caste, young, agricultural worker, woman) and if a person of superior status was present, the former either became non-communicative or tried to respond in a way which would not invite the latter's anger or disapproval. Occasionally, there would be no response until the persons of superior status indicated the direction in which the answer should be furnished. Conversely, the presence of persons with inferior status restrained the response of respondents with superior status, particularly in freely expressing their contemptuous or hostile attitude to the former. Having faced such situations on a few occasions, I changed my 'strategy' of inter-viewing. I decided to interview individuals only when they were in 'homogeneous groups' and these for my purpose were constituted of persons belonging to more or less the same hierarchial level, composed of kin or workgroups. Thus a workgroup of carpenters, a group of jats sharing a *hookah*, or a group of agricultural labour-ers belonging to a low caste living in a village *mohalla* (street) were homogeneous groups for my purpose. Once I devised this proce-dure of 'interviewing-in-group', I found the reliability of my data increased, the issue of the autonomy of respondents relegated to the background, and the efficiency and speed of my work enhanced. An unanticipated but rewarding pay-off of this mode of data col-lection was that I could occasionally resort to group interviewing wherein a set of informants conjointly responded to my questions, provided such a procedure was amenable for the purpose at hand.

The relationship between data collection techniques and the nature of the data sought to be collected is well recognized in social research (Zelditch Jr 1962). I had to collect data of a wide range—facts about material conditions, attitudes and value orientations, the dynamics of human behaviour manifested in events and incidents. This called for the employment of multiple techniques, relying on different tools of data collection for different dimensions. The tech-niques I employed included structured interviews for enumeration and frequency data, unstructured informal interviews to understand institutionalized norms, observation to describe specific incidents and events, and analysis of relevant documents and informal interviews to understand historical background. It is of great significance to note here that insofar as an analyst of movement has to deal with both micro- and macrodimensions, s/he cannot but combine a multiplicity of tools of data collection. By the time I finished the fieldwork I became a sceptic about the infallibility or superiority of any particular technique of data collection. Further, I became convinced that the substantive content and purpose of study and the nature of social system one analyses influence the techniques one employs to collect data (see Chapter 2).

Of the problems I faced in the course of my fieldwork, those related to my identity as a person was the most difficult. While doing fieldwork in Rajasthan villages, I tried to proximate my lifestyle to that of the villagers in terms of dress and dietary practices. Yet the differences between me and the villagers could not have been wished away by 'acting Rajasthani' and in fact my clear impression is that they wanted me to maintain my distinctiveness. The differences between me and them were mainly two: cultural and social. I was a 'Madrasi'[4] and they were Rajasthanis; I was an educated middle-class person and they were illiterate peasants. The fact that I was a 'stranger' often facilitated the flow of information from them; they did not suspect that I had any axe to grind in collecting the information or that I would malign them by circulating the information to 'significant others', as I did not have any kinship ties or territorial affinities in the region. They did not accept me as one of them and this I think was helpful to secure zealously guarded secrets. However, this is not to deny that they might have concealed some other vital information from me, precisely because I was a stranger.[5] The point I want to make is this: the fact that the researcher is an outsider to the society in which she/he does fieldwork facilitates accessibility to certain types of critical information, although this may also handicap him/her in getting certain other types of information.

Being a 'Madrasi' they could not automatically assume my religious identity. I was mistaken by some as a Muslim, thanks to my name and the beard I used to grow those days.[6] Because of the concealed estrangement, if not open hostility, that existed towards Muslims in rural Rajasthan, I knew that it could have been a great disadvantage to be identified as a Muslim, particularly in having close social intercourse. Therefore, I was keen to establish my identity as non-Muslim. If I were not a Muslim, the villagers thought I could only be a caste-Hindu and a Brahmin at that. I did all that I could to reinforce this impression about me among the villagers and this for several reasons. First, Brahmin as a 'caste' was the most universal in India and no other caste of Kerala (my home state) was comparable with the non-Brahmin clean castes of Rajasthan, either in nomenclature or in status. This prompted me to accept the label of Brahmin which the villagers put on me.

Second, I did not consider it prudent to tell them that I was a Christian by birth. The Indian Christians that they knew were either low-caste converts or Anglo-Indians and both these categories did not rank high in their estimation or in the local status hierarchy. My anxiety was not to be accepted as a person of high status but to escape stigmatization so as to avoid difficulties in social intercourse between them and me. Further, in the tribal belt, there was widespread belief that Christians went to villages to convert people. They have heard of priests and nuns doing so and this stereotype about Christians would have been a great disadvantage if I were identified as a Christian. On all these counts, I thought it was pragmatic to accept the status of Brahmin bestowed on me by the villagers and behaved as one. For instance, throughout my stay in Rajasthan villages, I remained a vegetarian and told the inquisitive among my informants that I was one. As a Brahmin I was expected to be present at the time of religious rites and community celebrations. And I conformed to this.

The fact that I was regarded as a Brahmin by the villagers created some difficulties. Perhaps an illustration is helpful. I preferred to live in village schools or in office buildings of co-operative societies, where ever they were available, while doing fieldwork. In those villages where such facilities were not available, I hired an independent building to live in. But in all cases I lived in the areas inhabited by clean castes. During one of my visits to the Chamar mohalla of one of the villages, I accepted the tea offered to me. The news spread within a couple of days in the village and I was unaware of this. I noticed that the usual visitors to my room started being absent or avoiding me and even those who came refused to accept the usual cup of coffee I used to offer them. Soon I discovered that their response was based on my being a 'guest' in the Chamar mohalla. I told them that I did not subscribe to the norms of the caste system, and hence it should not matter to them if I established commensal relations with 'untouchables'. Their point of view was different: if I wanted them (clean castes) to interact with me or if I were to be entertained by them in their households, I should not have commensal relations with 'untouchables'. They were not bothered about my belief or ideology; they were not willing to accept me as a 'social equal' insofar as I had commensal relations with 'untouchables'. I gave them the understanding that I would behave appropriately in the future and avoid such instances and the matter was settled.

I could not have gained equal acceptance from both the groups, the clean castes and the untouchables. It is clear that the researcher cannot put into practice his values during fieldwork without risking the loss of valuable field data. One must try to operate within the limits of institutionalized norms of the system in order to collect data; one cannot be social reformer and researcher in the same context. Of course, one can take a contrary position and collect data from that perspective: live with 'untouchables' and prepare to be boycotted by caste-Hindus. But then, the project one undertakes should be such that to identify with 'untouchables' has a higher pay-off and acceptance by clean castes not crucial.

The other context of identity related to my marital status. I was a bachelor in my mid-twenties during the days of my fieldwork in Rajasthan's villages. It was unusual in those villages for a person of my age to remain unmarried and among the enquiries about me as a person in the first few days figured my marital status. As I knew the norm in rural Rajasthan (marrying at a relatively low age), it was somewhat risky to reveal my marital status; every movement of mine could have been a matter of close scrutiny and inspection. Therefore, I pretended to be a married person. Occasionally some villagers expressed the desire to see my wife. Since in no case did I live in a village for more than two months, I could always postpone bringing her under some excuse. My non-existent wife was ill, pregnant, or just gave birth to a child, all of which rendered it difficult for her to come to one or another village from faraway Kerala.

Admittedly, in posing as a Brahmin and as a married person I had run the risk of disclosure. I am not quite sure whether this constituted an unethical act, but I am convinced that these construed identities improved susbstantially my chance of being accepted as a person by the villagers which in turn facilitated my establishing quick rapport with them. The point I want to make is this: the researcher faces certain dilemmas while doing fieldwork, some of which emanate from one's personal identity. Whether or not s/he should reveal all aspects of his/her personal identity is to be dictated by his/her own background, the kind of field situation in which one operates, and the pay-offs or the obstacles one expects from such disclosures.

In the late 1960s when I began my study of agrarian unrest in Kerala, the most widely studied territorial/spatial unit in Indian sociology and social anthropology was the village. But my effort to understand the Bhoodan movement through an investigation of gramdan villages unfolded that if I were to link the microdimensions with those of the macro—ideology, organizational pattern, leadership—I needed to go 'beyond the village' as my unit of study. This experience prompted me to consider the viability of a unit of analysis bigger than the village but manageable for doing fieldwork.

In arriving at the appropriate unit of analysis for a study, several considerations are relevant. The most important of these are: the theme of the study, the spatial coverage of the phenomenon, and its historicity. Generally speaking, a phenomenon such as social movement is rarely confined to a territorial entity such as a village and it may have existed for a long span of time. The Kerala agrarian movement, notwithstanding its independent and autonomous origin in the three regions which came to constitute Kerala—Malabar, Cochin, and Travancore—got co-ordinated during the freedom struggle and subsequently came to constitute and operate as a single stream with the emergence of Kerala as a state. Further, insofar as agrarian mobilizations in India are essentially activities of front organizations of political parties, the macrodimensions of agrarian movements are linked to a spatial unit bigger than the particular state in which they function. Thus the agrarian mobilizations in Kerala initiated by parties such as the CPI (M), CPI, Congress (I) are tempered by the ideology and styles of functioning of these 'all-India' parties.

The above considerations make it clear that I could not have selected a 'fixed' unit of analysis while studying the Kerala agrarian movement. Rather, it was necessary to constantly shift the unit of analysis as a frame of reference depending upon the specific dimension under investigation. Thus, while examining the pre-independence phase of the movement, the analysis of the event-structure had to be kept separate for the three regions of Kerala even as these mobilizations were informed of the same spirit and ideology, namely anti-authoritarianism, be it against the British or the monarchy, and pro-peasant.

Once Kerala emerged as a separate state it was possible to attempt the analysis on an all-Kerala basis. But whether or not this could actually be done would depend upon the nature of data available and needed to be generated. Insofar as one is drawing from various types of records and documents, it is possible to construct a picture of mobilizational activities of a given region or state, say of

Malabar or Kerala. But in those contexts and/or periods for which the documents were not available and the researcher generates data through field studies, s/he must have to confine to a much limited spatial unit. Thus, historical analysis usually undertaken on the basis of documents relate to a wider spatial unit as compared with field investigations done by the researcher. And this shift in the unit of analysis was inevitable. While analysing the current phase of the movement about which I had to collect field data, my unit of analysis was one district, namely, Alleppey. But wherein I developed my analysis based on documents, the units were either a region (for example, Malabar) or the state, that is, Kerala as a whole.

Why is it that I selected Alleppey district as the unit of my field investigation? The fact that it is my native district and that I had already undertaken some fieldwork there were important but not clinching factors which influenced my decision in favour of Alleppey. The central focus of my field investigation was the nature and magnitude of mobilization of different agrarian classes and Alleppey was an excellent case befitting the purpose.

First, Alleppey had a long tradition of agrarian protest, the famous Punnapra-Vayalar revolt of 1946 occurred in two talukas of the district, Ambalapuzha and Shertala. Second, while the agrarian mobilization in the Malabar region was largely confined to peasantry, that of Travancore enveloped both peasantry and agrarian proletariat. And Alleppey was the epicentre of the agrarian movement in Travancore. Third, with the implementation of land ceiling legislations and abolition of intermediaries, the erstwhile feudal landlords had disappeared as a class in Kerala. The emergence of the former tenants as owner-cultivators and the ushering in of the green revolution coincided and these two in conjunction led to the growth of a prosperous class of capitalist farmers. The latest phase of the agrarian movement in Kerala was characterized by organized and continuous confrontations between farmers and agricultural labour. In 1971, 23 per cent of farmers in Alleppey district were members of one or another farmer's association, sponsored by different political parties, probably the highest figure for the whole of India. Although only 12 per cent of the agricultural labour force of Alleppey district were union members in 1971, this was the highest figure for Kerala, followed by Trichur and Palghat districts with barely 5 per cent unionized agricultural labour force. All these convinced me that Alleppey was an ideal unit for my field investigation.

From what I have said above it is clear that in analysing social movements one cannot confine either to the micro- or to the macro-situation; one has to draw from both. This in turn means that one cannot rely entirely on field data or documentary analysis; it is imperative to combine both if one were to study an ongoing movement, with a long career. As the Kerala agrarian movement fits this description I resorted to collecting data from a multiplicity of sources employing a variety of techniques. However, even here the kind of perspective one adopts becomes crucial in determining the nature of data one collects. Let me illustrate.

Those who attempt to reconstruct the history of social movements usually rely on two major sources: archival records and the 'official texts' of the movement, both of which may provide a view from above. Archival records mainly relate to the correspondence between and among the administrative and movement elite. The official texts of a movement usually discuss its ideology, organizational pattern, strategy, and tactics as conceived by the top movement leadership. Consequently, an effort to reconstruct movement history from these sources misses the view from below, the views and articulations of the ordinary participants. It was possible for me to capture a bottom-up view of the contemporary phase of the movement through the field data I collected. To match this data I had to tap appropriate sources relating to the historical phase of the movement. The most authentic and useful data I could find was the writing by and on grass roots movement activists—biographies, memoirs, 'historical accounts', literary writings (novels, short stories, and dramas)—and informant interviewing, that is, 'oral history'.

An important source of information widely tapped by most researchers is reports by journalists. I have also used these sources. But usually journalists report only when the incidents are violent or when political heavy weights are present on specific occasions. Thus the routine activities particularly at the grass roots go unreported. An invaluable source to get at these activities is the police records, which are usually not accessible to researchers. Fortunately, I was permitted to go through the police records and this helped me to get a picture of the activities of different agrarian associations on a continuous basis. Once I knew that a particular incident had taken place, it was possible for me to pursue its investigation by collecting data through other sources. However, there is one disadvantage if one relies exclusively on police accounts of such incidents and activities.

The unusual tendency (and this seems to be based on an official brief) is to concentrate on the activities of those associations and leaders affiliated to the political parties in opposition. But given the political situation prevalent in Kerala, the associations affiliated to all parties got their 'attention' in turn as they circulated in and out of power. At any rate, the mobilizational activities were usually kept high by a party when it was in the opposition and therefore it was also natural for the police to concentrate on them.

I have defined the event structure of the movement as the interactions between the different unions and associations. The record of activities kept by them was another important source of data for me. As is well known, the local (village) units of these organizations rarely keep comprehensive accounts of their activities. Even the decisions were taken in informal meetings. Therefore, the data about local units were invariably collected through informant interviewing, the informants constituting a pool of persons drawn from all the organizations.

Yet another source of data was the records of government departments of revenue, welfare, labour, and newly created organizations such as the Industrial Relations Committee (a tripartite committee to process disputes which arose among and between farmers and workers) or Land Tribunals (to settle the disputes between landowners and their tenants).

The foregoing account clearly unfolds that the major chunk of data for the study was drawn from records of various types and informant interviewing (with the help of interview guides devised for different categories of informants). In addition to this, I had the opportunity to observe specific incidents of mobilizations and meetings of agrarian organizations for nearly a decade, although intermittently, beginning in the early 1970s, during my several visits to Kerala, ranging from two to eight weeks.

Although I was not a typical anthropological 'fieldworker' observing a specific universe (village, factory, co-operative, etc.) for a prolonged period, during the course of this study I collected considerable amount of field data. I visited numerous offices, met and talked to scores of persons, and my social identity was, I am afraid, both an asset and a liability. If in Rajasthan villages I was a 'stranger' anxious to be accepted, in Alleppey district I was a 'native' who needed to distance myself from my informants. Having lived the first 20 years of my life in Kerala, I had no difficulty in taking to the local dress, food, language, and lifestyle in general. On the other hand, it was easy for the people to place me socially. And the source of the problem was precisely this easy social identification.

I belong to that small 'ethnic' group called Syrian Christians who claim that they were upper castes who converted to Christianity in the first century AD. In the area where I conducted my fieldwork they are a dominant group viewed numerically, economically, and politically. An economically enterprising group, they have experienced rapid upward social mobility. In the wake of land reforms, a substantial proportion of erstwhile tenants who became prosperous owner-cultivators were Syrian Christians. Understandably they took a leading role in meeting the challenge posed to them by the agricultural labour unions usually sponsored by the Communist parties. Inevitably, they aligned with those political parties which opposed the 'onslaught' from Communists. In fact, the social origins of the Kerala Congress in which the Syrian Christians dominate can be traced to this situation of social unrest which prevailed in several pockets of Kerala, particularly in Alleppey district.

Given this background the Syrian Christians were perceived as a pro-capitalist, pro-Congress, and anti-leftist community. (I must add here that this stereotype cannot be sustained if one looks at facts.) To be identified with such a collectivity is of no comfort when one has to collect a large part of one's data from agricultural labour unions and peasant associations affiliated to leftist parties. This was evident from the initial response I received from several movement activists of the leftist agrarian unions and associations. In order to establish my credentials as a 'progressive' Syrian Christian, if not a 'radical', (and such persons are quite a number) I had to obtain the necessary certifications and appropriate introductions preferably from Syrian Christians belonging to leftist parties. Further, I had to conduct myself in such a manner that should contradict the pro-capitalist and pro-Congress image initially attributed to me.

If I were to project the image of a progressive with the leftist unions, I had to establish my non-leftist, if not anti-leftist, inclination with farmers associations affiliated to the Congress parties. This was relatively easy partly because I was accepted as 'one of them' at least to begin with and partly because I could invoke appropriate kinship links to establish my 'credentials'. And yet, I had to 'distance' myself sufficiently from both the groups to secure adequate and relevant information so as to construct a rounded picture of the situation I was investigating. To identify exclusively with either would have been disastrous.

The point I want to make is the following. To be an outsider or insider to the field is a mixed blessing. Further, what aspect of one's identity becomes a 'liability' or 'asset' would vary from situation to situation. In Rajasthan villages, my cultural identity and marital status assumed saliency, but in Kerala it was my attributed political affiliation, thanks to my community membership, which became salient.

NOTES

1. The reader may note that the concept of property-space is implicit in my discussion of research design of the study at several points: gramdan (experimental) versus non-gramdan (control) villages, revenue villages versus hamlets of villages, old villages versus new colonies. For a short discussion on the concept of property-space, see Barton (1955).

2. Two legislations passed by the state assembly, the Rajasthan Bhoodan Yajna Act, 1954 and the Rajasthan Gramdan Act, 1960, were used as reinforcement mechanisms for the successful operation of the movement. The legal requirements for a village to be called gramdan, according to the Act, are (1) that not less than 51 per cent of the total extent of land under private ownership in that village should be donated; (2) that the donors should constitute at least 80 per cent of the total number of persons owning land and residing in the village; and (3) that not less than 75 per cent of adult persons residing in the village should have declared, in the prescribed form and manner, their desire to participate in gramdan community life.

3. Generally speaking, a typical Rajasthan village has a number of parts attached to the village core or central village. The definition of the village for purposes of the Rajasthan Gramdan Act, 1960 was the same as given in the Rajasthan Land Revenue Act, 1956. According to this, parts of villages whether called *thok, patti, dhani, pura, fala, wada,* or otherwise are included in the village and are not considered as separate units. However, as many as 14.5 per cent of gramdan villages were former hamlets and this was the main reason for their atypicality.

4. 'Madrasi' is a pejorative term employed in north India to refer to south Indians in general.

5. After the completion of my fieldwork, I came across Simmel's seminal essay on 'the stranger' which reinforces the point made here. Simmel writes: ' ... he [stranger] often receives the most surprising openness—confidences which have the character sometimes of a confessional and which would be carefully withdrawn from a more closely related person' (1950: 404).

6. In one of the villages I was to be the guest of a Rajput family on the day of my arrival, according to the understanding I had with the Sarvodaya worker who gave me a letter of introduction. But having seen me (I used to keep a beard those days) and learnt my name upon arrival, my host suggested that I move to the school building immediately. I was dead tired having walked about six kilometres to reach the village and it was already 8 p.m. His behaviour was incomprehensible to me and I was very upset. Later my host confessed that he mistook me to be a Muslim and profusely apologized for the mistake and compensated by inviting me several times over to his household for meals.

5

Apprehending Social Reality in a Hierarchical Society
The Rationale for a Perspective from Below

❧

Indian society is a product of a long and complex historical process. The seven major events which contributed to the formation of this process are the Aryan 'advent'; the emergence of Indian Protestant religions—Jainism, Buddhism, and Sikhism; the entry of non-Indic religions into the subcontinent as immigrant religions; the Muslim 'conquests'; western colonialism; anti-colonial freedom struggle; and the partition of the Indian subcontinent in 1947 on the eve of the British exit (Oommen 1998). The product of this long process is a four-in-one society.

Like all societies, Indian society's stratification is based on age, gender, rural–urban differences, and class. But unlike many others, Indian society is marked by considerable cultural heterogeneity too, particularly because of a large number of speech communities counting more than 1,500 including 460 tribal communities. India's religious plurality complicated by the uneasy co-existence of religions of Indic and non-Indic origin is a rare phenomenon in most contemporary societies. However, what is unique to India is the all pervasive caste hierarchy legitimized through the Hindu doctrine of karma and reincarnation. It is my contention that apprehending social reality of a hierarchical society poses certain methodological issues specific to that society.

As one observes the complex entity called Indian society by the end of the twentieth century, four major trends of social transformation are in evidence (Oommen 1998). First, a transitional trend from cumulative to dispersed dominance. If status, wealth, and power were earlier concentrated in the hands of the twice-born caste Hindus—Brahmin, Kshatriya, and Vaishya—accounting for a mere 15 to 20 per cent of the population, now there is an incipient trend towards dispersal of political power to the Other Backward Classes (OBCs), SCs, and STs together constituting the vast majority of Indian population. This is the resultant of universal adult franchise introduced in India with the arrival of independence and the reservation of seats in legislatures proportionate to their population.

In addition to the acquisition of political power, a small middle class is emerging among the above categories. But the reasons for the emergence of the middle class vary across them. The policy of protective discrimination reserving seats in educational institutions and government service are primarily responsible for the emergence of a bourgeoisie among the SCs and STs. The Kulaks among the OBCs are a product of agrarian reforms which transferred land from absentee landlords to the tenants and share croppers drawn from among OBCs, and the green revolution which provided subsidized inputs and assured minimum prices for agricultural products to owner cultivators.

The changes in power and wealth are not matched by change in status, that is, weakening of the importance of the ritual dimension. Interdining, intermarriage, and social interaction between the twice-born and SCs are still rare particularly in rural areas due to the practice of untouchability. This result in status incongruence, that is, their upward social mobility in wealth and power is not matched by mobility in the ritual context. In the case of the OBCs, status incongruence results from their low representations in the high echelons of bureaucracy and professions even as they became politically powerful.

The second major trend in social transformation manifests in the gradual movement from hierarchy to equality resulting in the decline of traditional collectivism and emergence of individualism. With the emergence of individualism, the salience of traditional collectivism manifested through the joint family, jati, village, etc., are being gradually relegated to the background. While there is no neat and tidy displacement of collectivism by individualism, the birth of the Indian individual is clearly evident. I am stressing this point because autonomy of the individual was non-existent in the traditional social order unless one became an ascetic (Dumont 1970). This is not true any more. And yet, the central feature of Indian society, namely, hierarchy still persists.

The third important trend in social transformation in India is the simultaneous demands for individual equality and the assertion of collective identity. The Indian constitution unambiguously assured equality and concomitantly social justice to all individuals irrespective of gender, caste, creed, or class. Initially, most of the traditionally disadvantaged groups believed that the implementation of the constitutional promise would automatically follow and the maintenance of their group identity was irrelevant. But the persistence of the stigma associated with their identity prompted them to abandon it and plumb for assimilation, as the process of Sanskritization implied. But gradually it dawned on them that their efforts to sanskritize were not accepted by the higher castes and individual equality *per se* would not emancipate them. Consequently they became aware of the need to reinvent dignity in their collective identity; expressions such as 'Dalits' and 'Adivasis' clearly point to this trend.

While the constitution does not clearly recognize identities based on religion, caste, language, and tribe, it does not completely overlook these identities either, if these are disadvantageous to the collectivities concerned. This ambiguity is evident both from constitutional provisions and administrative measures as exemplified in special rights conceded to religious minorities (for example, upholding their civil codes), the policy of reservation in the case of SCs and STs, the recent steps taken to provide representation to OBCs and women in selected contexts, the special treatment extended to tribal communities, and the linguistic reorganization of Indian states as administrative units. All these steps have inevitably given fillip to the relevant collectivities to assert their identity when it pays off.

The fourth transition that I am referring to is the movement from plural society to pluralism (Oommen 1997a). Plural society as initially conceptualized by J.S. Furnivall (1948) alludes to an arrangement in which different social and cultural segments uneasily co-exist, interacting in the economic context but prohibiting legitimate transfusion of blood (intermarriages) or transmission of culture. This arrangement prevailed within the Hindu society through the operation of the *jajmani* system for centuries. Latterly, the twice-born castes interact with the OBCs and SCs both in the political and economic contexts but have very limited interaction in sociocultural contexts and no interaction in the ritual context. This description also fits in the mode of interaction which prevails between Hindus, particularly the upper castes, and those who profess the non-Indic religions, particularly in the rural areas.

I suggest that the four trends of change listed, namely, the movement from cumulative to dispersed dominance; from hierarchy to equality and the consequent birth of individualism; the simultaneous demand for equality and identity; and the gradual transition from plural society to pluralism (the dignified co-existence of different sociocultural segments as equals in the polity) have tremendous methodological implications for the study of Indian society. However, I do not propose to discuss all the dimensions but shall confine my attention to those which are relevant for the present theme, namely the perspective from below.

⇥◆⇤

The 'view from below' is an old and persisting issue in social science, particularly, in sociology and social anthropology. But concomitant to the emergence of the traditionally oppressed and stigmatized collectivities as partially emancipated and empowered ones, their conventional silence is being replaced by audible new voices. In turn, the need for their representation in the process of knowledge production is grudgingly being recognized. That is, the very framing of the issues and terms of discourse have changed over time. The demand for a perspective from below is an indication of this massive change in society. If earlier those who occupied the bottom of society were invisible due to the cognitive blackout perpetuated by the upper caste, middle class, urban, male researcher, today they are in full view and demand their legitimate share of representation in the production and representation of knowledge.

All societies have their bottoms; in those which are homogeneous and merely stratified this space is occupied by women, youth, and the proletariat. These categories have questioned the knowledge produced by their counterparts—men, adults, and bourgeoisie. Over a period of time, the specific role of each of these disadvantaged categories in the production of knowledge has come to be recognized.

In the case of culturally heterogeneous societies, if the constituted segments are unequal either because they are numerically
small or economically weak or culturally 'backward' or all of
these, the tendency is to ignore them in the representations of
reality. There are numerous instances when those ignored or
marginalized communities demand to be represented in the
process of knowledge production. A familiar example in India is
the neglect of the numerous, numerically small, less developed
linguistic communities. Their emerging identity assertions are also
indicative of their clamour for representation in the context of
knowledge production.

In plural societies, the unrepresented bottom categories are
invariably viewed as outsiders to the society, as in the case of followers of non-Indic religious categories in India. Voices of protests
from them have gradually led to the provisioning of space to their
experience in the context of knowledge production. For example,
the distinctiveness of religious minorities is increasingly recognized
in studies of sociology and social anthropology in India.

The bottom layer in hierarchical societies is constituted by the
cumulatively deprived section of society. Unlike women, youth, proletariat, culturally backward or 'alien' segments, which are deprived
in one of the contexts, the cumulatively deprived are subjected to
multiple deprivations. They are found only in hierarchical societies. The ex-untouchables of India afford an ideal type example of
this category.

For the reasons listed above, I shall confine my attention to the
most 'oppressed bottom' found in hierarchical societies. It is also
necessary to indicate here what the perspective from below is not.
First, the view from below should not be confused for the study
of other cultures, the conventional avocation of anthropologists
(Beattie 1964). Anthropologists did not consider other cultures,
at least by definition, as inferior but only as different (cf. Chapter 9). It is another matter, however, that the colonial context in
which anthropology was practised did create an inferior–superior
dichotomy between native tribes and western anthropologists.
However, once the native anthropologists started investigating their
co-citizens who were tribals, this dichotomy became irrelevant. At
any rate, the rise of anthropologists from the tribal communities
rendered redundant the original distinctiveness of anthropology
as the discipline which studied other cultures.

The specificity of the anthropological 'method' is the distinction between etic and emic approaches, both of which employed the technique of participant observation which is often mystified (see Chapter 2). But the demystification of participant observation was bound to happen when anthropologists started investigating their own societies. The point of interest for the present is that in hierarchical societies the anthropologists/sociologists drawn from upper castes were invariably reluctant to interact with the bottom rung of the society, given the norms and values associated with the practice of untouchability. Should an effort to participate in the life world of the 'untouchables' be made by a *savarna* social researcher, it would be disapproved not only by his own jati peers but also by the untouchables themselves, given the grip of the doctrine of karma and reincarnation on them.

Even the distinction between etic and emic approaches remained problematic. The etic approach identified and studied social reality independent of the natives' cultural judgements. The emic view, in contrast, is an insider's view. However, there can also be different emic views insofar as different cultural segments within a society have their own constructions of social reality and value orientations about them. The researcher should not appropriate the monopoly of defining the people, nor can s/he uncritically endorse the self-definitions advanced by the people. Having said this, I should insist that self-conceptualizations such as Dalits are emancipatory as contrasted with terms such as exterior castes, panchamas, Harijans, SCs, and others. What is required is resorting to double hermeneutics to incorporate both the emic and the etic perspectives.

The different cultural segments in heterogeneous societies may have differing insiders' views. Further, the lack of co-terminality between political boundaries and cultural boundaries creates problems. This is exemplified in the difference between an Indian Bengali anthropologist studying the Bengali society spread across India and Bangladesh, and his investigating Tamil society, divided between India and Sri Lanka. While in West Bengal he is both a political and cultural insider (that is, a citizen and a national), in Bangladesh he is a cultural insider (national) but a political outsider (non-citizen). In Tamil Nadu, he is a political insider (citizen) but a cultural outsider (non-national) and in Sri Lanka he is both a political and a cultural outsider (non-citizen and non-national). (For an exemplification of these concepts see Oommen [1997b].) It is difficult to believe that these differing identities of the investigator will not affect the process of investigation. But yet it is important to note that the etic–emic distinction is an insider–outsider distinction and not an inferior–superior distinction.

Second, the perspective from below should not be confused for the much heralded subalternist perspective. Subalternists focused their attention on elite politics and have emphasized the insurrectionary activities and potential of the 'subaltern classes' (artisans, poor peasants, and landless labourers which are essentially economic categories) who, according to them, possessed self-conscious and coherent conceptions of resistance that were directed against rich peasants, urban traders/merchants, or the colonial revenue administrators. Subalternists claim to have unfolded the incapacity of nationalist historiography to incorporate the voices of the weak into the project of history writing (see Guha and Spivak 1988).

The setting for 'subaltern history' was provided by colonial India and the freedom struggle. If nationalist historians were macroholists who ignored the 'voices from below', subalternists are microindividualists who missed the view from above (Oommen 1985). But both confined their attention to different dimensions of and actors involved in the freedom struggle. The perspective from below goes much beyond this. It focuses on the implications of the nature of social structure and the location of the researcher in the process of knowledge production. Hierarchy as a feature of Indian society existed much before colonialism arrived and the freedom struggle started.

Third, the view from below is different from the proletarian, feminist, or generational perspective. Class in the sense of social gradations exists in all societies and there are no immutable boundaries between classes. Both embourgeoisement and proletarianization are perennial possibilities. Indeed, declassing has been advocated and successfully attempted by many investigators. There was a time, say in the 1960s, when the widespread belief prevailed that the youth alone had the capacity to cognize truth; those above 30 were adjudged to be incapable of perceiving truth (Feuer 1969).

The extremists among feminists seem to take the view that only women can understand and analyse issues concerning women. The corollary of this is that only men can understand their problems. Even as one concedes the existence of differences between men and women, those who belong to the same class within a society and share the same culture have many things in common irrespective of gender differences. But as I have noted above differences based on class, age groups, and gender exist in all societies, including homogeneous societies. And, both age groups and sex groups are distributed across classes. To a large extent, method verstehen advocated by Max Weber will help one to cope with the problem.

Fourth, in plural societies the segments even when they are equal remain cultural strangers. That is, even as they interact in the economic and political contexts which results in interdependence, culturally they are insulated. To the extent sociocultural insulation persists, hostility could develop between them. But they could be equals; what strangers suffer from is externalization. Following Simmel's notion one can even accept the advantages of doing research among strangers (1950). The point I want to make for the present is that the perspective from below is the specific need of hierarchical societies, such as that of India, wherein the society is so tightly compartmentalized that one segment cannot penetrate into the other.

Having said the above I need to add a caveat here. If one were to take a position that there is no possibility of an outsider ever investigating a segment of society to which she does not belong, then each segment will have to produce its own set of researchers. This will leave some segments uninvestigated forever. For example, who will study children, invalids, imbeciles, or insane people? At any rate, there is an advantage for those segments which can be studied by its own representatives and by outsiders also. None of these preclude the need to have a perspective from below.

—◦—

The need for a perspective from below is inextricably interlinked with the hierarchical nature of societies such as those of India. All the available evidence suggests that Indian sociologists and social anthropologists, predominantly drawn from the twice-born caste Hindus, at least until recently, have largely neglected the social realities of the lowly placed and oppressed, the OBCs and particularly the SCs. This is not simply a matter of praxiological aberration but also that of theoretical neglect; a product of *cognitive blackout*.

I propose to pursue this argument invoking the first presidential address to the Indian Sociological Conference held in 1955 delivered by D.P. Mukherji. There are several reasons why this address is used as a case in point. First, of all, it was the first presidential address. Second, D.P. Mukherji was not aligned with or sympathetic to the Hindutva ideology. Third, many thought that he was a Marxist, although he preferred to call himself a 'Marxiologist'. Fourth, there was no doubt that he was a 'modernist' and a 'progressive'.

In this address, which was pregnant with fertile ideas, Mukherji insisted that it was not enough that an Indian sociologist be a sociologist but should be an Indian first. And how does a sociologist acquire Indianity; by situating himself in Indian lore, both high and low, according to Mukherji. But, 'unless sociological training in India is grounded on Sanskrit, or any such language in which the traditions have been embodied as symbols, social research in India will be a pale imitation of what others are doing' (Mukherji 1961: 23). Although Mukherji wanted sociologists to be familiar with Indian lores both high and low, he thinks that our traditions are embodied in Sanskrit. There are several problems with this advocacy.

First, only the twice-born caste Hindus were allowed any access to Sanskrit, the texts in which traditional knowledge was embodied. By insisting that Sanskrit is the route through which Indian sociologists can cultivate originality, Mukherji is narrowing the recruitment base of Indian sociologists. Second, by the time education became a constitutional possibility to the vast majority of Indians, Sanskrit ceased to be a live language. That is to say, if one is not traditionally privileged to learn Sanskrit one can scarcely have the opportunity to learn it. Third, the reference to 'such other languages' may be an allusion to Pali and Tamil, but it should include Persian too. If indeed all the four languages—Sanskrit, Pali, Tamil, and Persian—are under reference, one cannot talk of tradition in the singular; indeed there is a multiplicity of traditions in India.

Fourth, even if one takes such an accommodative view, still all the traditions under reference are Great Traditions. And the traditions of the vast majority of the peoples of India are Little Traditions confined to folk regions. No sociologist can afford to neglect this rich variety of traditions and remain authentic. In fact, there is greater possibility of cultivating sociological originality by familiarizing oneself with these grass-root and ground realities. Fifth, it is difficult to comprehend why training in sociology grounded on Sanskrit and/or other such languages can inform sociology of originality.

By Mukherji's prescription, an overwhelming majority of Indian sociologists are pale imitators. On the other hand, that handful of Sanskrit-knowing sociologists hardly demonstrated any originality; they invariably indulged in exegetical analyses. In turn, this would blur the distinction between indology and sociology.

Mukherji in his presidential address entitled 'Indian Sociology and Tradition' made another curious observation pertinent to the present discussion. He said: 'All our Shastras are sociological' (Mukherji 1961: 21). There is an interesting link between the need to anchor sociologists' training with knowledge of Sanskrit and the observation that the Shastras are sociological because the latter are in Sanskrit. But a few uncomfortable facts may be noted here.

First, *Our* in the quotation presumably stands for Hindus, but Indian sociology cannot be equated with Hindu sociology for the simple reason that one out of every eight Indians is a non-Hindu. Second, Hindu sociology necessarily implies Muslim sociology, Buddhist sociology, and the like, the very antithesis of sociology as a humanistic and encapsulating enterprise.

Third, *Our* does not stand even for all Hindus; the majority of the Hindu population (the OBCs and SCs) have no role in the making of these Shastras and they are treated as congenital inferiors by twice-born Hindus. In fact, the *panchamas*, those of the Fifth Order (the 'untouchables') are not even accounted for in the *Chaturvarna* theory which deals with the Hindu doctrine of creation. Not only that, the Shastras also assign a marginal position to women of even the twice-born varnas. To put it pithily, the Shastras privilege upper caste males and treat the vast majority of Hindus as inferiors. Can they be sociological? Sociology cannot ignore the experiences of any segment in society, much less treat them as inferior. The mission of sociology is all embracing and ought to be humanistic.

While some shastras are sociological (for example, *Arthashastra*) some other shastras are theological (for example, *Dharamashastra*). At any rate Shastras deal with the issues of Ought. The concern of sociology is primarily with Is. That is, Shastras are prescriptive and normative. True, sociology cannot ignore the normative and it should take into account the Ought, but its primary concern is with reality as it exists and operates in society. To anchor Indian sociology to Hindu Shastras is to undermine sociology's secular and humane foundations. Finally, I may recall here that B.R. Ambedkar in his debates with M.K. Gandhi in the 1930s insisted that only if the Puranas, Shastras, and all scriptures that supported caste (that is, inequality and injustice) were disowned could he call himself a Hindu. As is well known, the challenge was not admissible to caste Hindus and Ambedkar embraced Buddhism in 1956.

Indeed the 'book view' of sociology in India was/is excessively in favour of projecting the view from above. To counter this, the field view would have been greatly helpful if executed with care. But that was not to be. Almost all field studies in sociology and social anthropology until recently were undertaken from the perspective of twice-born middle-class Hindus. For example, there is hardly any study of village, a much celebrated theme in Indian sociology, which views the village reality from the perspective of the Cheri, Maharwada, or Chamar mohallas. In field studies as in texts those below the pollution line are designated as Chandals, Mlecchas, exterior castes, untouchables, etc., if they are referred to at all. Even the designations such as SCs proffered by the state and Harijan coined by Narasinh Mehta and propagated by M.K. Gandhi are not acceptable to Dalits. That is, the very labelling of these categories has been debilitating and stigmatizing. The compelling need for a view from below will have to be situated in this context.

But let it be noted here that the bottom layer of Indian society itself is no more uniform and homogeneous. The upwardly mobile, urban educated Dalit elite are qualitatively different from the cumulatively dominated rural, illiterate, economically stagnant Dalits. While it is the rise of the former which eventuated in the plea for giving proper space to the voice of the latter, embourgeoisement of the urban Dalit elite should not be allowed to endanger the cause and interests of the cumulatively oppressed rural Dalits. That is, the perspective from below is the epistemological privilege of the cumulatively oppressed. Those who are incorporated into the establishment often get distanced from their roots.

It is time I indicated the theroretical foundation of the approach designated as the 'perspective from below'. If experience and knowledge are inextricably interlinked in social science, then the location of the knowledge producer, the researcher, in social structure is crucial from the perspective of production of knowledge. That is, the perspective from below is necessitated due to the politics of location. The process of production of knowledge and the advantages and disadvantages emanating out of one's location in social structure are inevitably linked. One can dismiss this formulation as excessively ideological, indeed political, and hence harmful to the generation of 'objective' knowledge only at the cost of ignoring the quality of knowledge produced. And the proof of the quality of knowledge is in its content and orientation.

There has been a cognitive blackout in Indian social science, at least until recently, as far as knowledge regarding the life world experiences of Dalitbahujans. The fact that the lifestyles of upper castes and Dalitbahujans vary dramatically in terms of food habits, worship patterns, or gender relations is tacitly acknowledged. But instead of squarely recognizing these variations and explaining why they exist, the dominant tendency in Indian sociology, at least until recently, has been to suggest that the Dalitbahujans are abandoning their way of life in favour of the lifestyle of caste Hindus. This is what sanskritization is all about. In this perspective, not only are the norms and values of caste Hindus privileged, but the Brahmins are also christened as norm setters and value givers for the society as a whole. Conversely, the norms and values of Dalitbahujans are knocked out, ignored, stigmatized, and delegitimized. Indeed, the field view has made Indian sociology more authentic compared with the book view, but its authenticity has been largely partial. To correct this imbalance we need the perspective from below.

If the white anthropologist indulges in the 'invention of primitive society', to invoke the felicitous phrase of Adam Kuper (1988), the twice-born sociologist of India projected an idealized picture of Hindu society mainly based on classical texts. Even the field view has not interrogated this deficit successfully. That is the reason why we need a counter view even if it is an idealized version of Dalitbahujans. I shall attempt to present such a view based on the analysis by Dalitbahujan intellectuals (see, for an example, Ilaiah 1996). What is important about this perspective is not its present performance but its future promise. Such a view was non-existent and considered to be inadmissible in the lexicon of savarna social scientists of India.

First, the Dalitbahujans do not subscribe to the notion of all-India or pan-Indian Hindusim, not even regional Hindusim, ideas widely accepted in Indian sociology (see Srinivas 1952). In fact, the Dalitbahujan identity is essentially a localized caste identity and a series of mini-traditions, not even a Little Tradition. Their religion does not admit patriarchal Hindu gods and the absence of professional priesthood is a pronounced feature. In the Hindu pantheon, as and when they are acknowledged, the Dalitbahujan gods are assigned a low status matching the status of their worshippers in the social structure.

Second, the Dalitbahujan women enjoy considerable economic independence and sexual equality. Absence of a sharp sexual division of labour is a prominent feature of their society. These traditional values of Dalitbahujans are actually much acclaimed values of modernity and even post-modernity. But they tend to lose these values as and when they get sanskritized.

Third, in the Dalitbahujan society, gender relations are largely open and egalitarian; parent–child interactions, including father–child interactions, are intimate; widows are respected and not stigmatized; widow remarriages are practised. The incorporation of patriarchal values into their society is changing these norms and values.

Fourth, while there is an over-evaluation of occupations of caste Hindus (priesthood, administration, trading), there is a studied lack of respect for the occupations of Dalitbahujans such as agriculture, arts, and crafts. In turn, knowledge associated with production of wealth is undervalued. Generally speaking, only knowledge relating to the occupations of caste Hindus is given importance. There is a conspiracy of silence regarding the knowledge associated with Dalitbahujan occupations.

Fifth, the language used by Dalitbahujans in their everyday life is different from that used by caste Hindus. Their language is not only non-sanskritic but not even standard vernacular languages such as Hindi, Tamil, or Bengali. Not only is their language not recognized by the state, it is stigmatized by the caste Hindu society both of which undermines Dalitbahujan identity. The Dalitbahujan names are quite different from those of caste Hindus but as they are disparaged they are inclined to shift either to sanskritized or anglicized names.

Sixth, the ideas generated by the organic intellectuals of Dalitbahujans are hardly recognized let alone communicated to the new generations. Even when Dalitbahujan intellectuals are recognized reluctantly (for example, B.R. Ambedkar), the politics of knowledge transmission invariably renders their contribution insignificant. Given the localization of Dalitbahujan castes to their respective linguistic regions, their leaders rarely become all-India figures even when they have made signal contributions as illustrated by the cases of Mahatma Phule in Maharashtra, Basava in Karnataka, Narayana Guru in Kerala, or Narla in Andhra Pradesh. Consequently, the basic cleavages and differences between caste Hindus and Dalitbahujans remain unnoticed.

Seventh, generally speaking the exclusive political voice of Dalitbahujans remains muted and submerged due to the absence of political parties which champion their cause. As and when such parties emerge and operate, their influence is confined to certain pockets. For example, the Republican Party of India founded by B.R. Ambedkar is virtually confined to Maharashtra. And the recently established Bahujan Samaj Party's influence is confined largely to Uttar Pradesh and a few pockets in north India. Consequently, the political voices of Dalitbahujans are being articulated through mainstream parties wherein they remain subordinated.

Eighth, given the numerical importance of Dalitbahujans, universal adult franchise did make them politically salient. But this is not adequately matched by their upward economic mobility in spite of numerous development programmes initiated by the government to improve their economic condition. The change in the ritual context is the least and it continues to bestow on them low social prestige. Consequently, the existential condition of Dalitbahujans is characterized by status incongruence. Their efforts to interrogate the entrenched castes often result in atrocities against them.

Ninth, although rebels challenged the Hindu caste system periodically in the last 25 centuries and tried to establish separate religions or sects, they did not succeed; they were silenced by incorporation into the Hindu system and usually assigned a low status. Gautama Buddha was a Kshatriya who revolted against the Brahminic order. But he was gradually incorporated into the Hindu pantheon as an avatar of Vishnu and rendered powerless as a reformer. This has happened to the rebels of the Bhakti movements too which crystallized between the eighth and eighteenth centuries in different parts of the Indian subcontinent. This clearly points to the near impossibility of reforming the Hindu caste system as to provide a respectable position to the Dalitbahujans. That is, insofar as caste hierarchy exists, the perspective from below would remain relevant.

Finally, it is necessary to recognize that knowledge has two uses: oppression and perpetuation of hegemony and institutionalization of equality and justice. The view from above sometimes directly and almost always indirectly aided and abetted oppression and hegemonization. The view from below can and should provide the much needed antidote to this by facilitating the institutionalization of equality and social justice. This is the rationale and justification for the perspective from below.

PART II

6

Internationalization of Sociology
A South Asian Perspective

The issue of internationalization of sociology has different dimensions: production of that corpus of knowledge referred to as sociology; the rationale behind the acceptance of that knowledge by those who do not or cannot produce it; the obstacles in the spread of that knowledge; and the assumptions behind the flow of knowledge. It is widely acknowledged that the conditions conducive to the flowering of sociology vary vastly across societies/nations/states. Admittedly, the quantity and quality of sociology produced in different societies differ considerably. Those societies with favourable conditions for producing sociology are likely to have an abundant supply of it and those with constricting conditions would have only a skeletal sociology or no sociology at all.

The imbalance in the production of knowledge across societies affects the trajectory of the flow; an inevitable division of labour between the producers of sociology and its mere consumers ensues. But the flow itself may not be allowed and/or restricted, which in turn renders the spread uneven. Even if the flow is unhampered, the potential consumers may not always welcome it and may even reject the product. The flow may be disallowed or restricted by governments in spite of the consumers' preference for the product. The consumers may reject it even as the flow is facilitated because they may perceive it to be unsuited to their situation or may conceive it to be an instrument intimidating their creativity and productivity.

However, if the flow is unhampered and the consumers welcome it, the unstated assumption would be that sociology produced in society A is good enough for society B. This in turn entails the assumptions that all societies are essentially the same and that sociology is a 'universal' discipline. However, if sociology produced in society A is rejected by society B, the assumption implied is that societies differ vastly and hence sociology is a society-specific discipline. The problematic of internationalization of sociology is essentially one of sorting out these issues. But to do that, one should have some clarity about the very notion of nation/society. Therefore, even though I know that I am 'carrying coal to Newcastle', I am constrained to begin by providing that clarity.

⟡

In its original classical Latin sense, *nasci* meant a tribal-ethnic group, a people born in the same place or territory wherein the political dimension was not a necessary element. Nation as a community of citizens, that is, a political entity, is the creation of the French Revolution. However, in Europe, a nation is perceived both as 'a people, a folk, held together by some or all of such more or less immutable characteristics as common descent, territory, history, language, religion, way of life, or other attributes that members of a group have from birth onward' (Peterson 1975: 181) and 'as a community of sentiment which would adequately manifest itself in a state of its own; hence a nation is a community which normally tends to produce a state of its own' (Gerth and Mills 1948: 176). Thus it came to be believed that it is not only natural for a nation to have a state, but also necessary for a nation to have its own state so that its cultural identity is maintained and protected.

It is untenable to follow the Latin sense of the term 'nation', which refers to a tribal-ethnic group, in the contemporary world. Before the French Revolution the polities were either small (tribes, peasant villages, caste councils, city states) or large (empires, federations, universal churches). But today the tendency is to establish viable polities. In fact, there are not more than 220 or 230 states in the contemporary world. In Africa alone there are about 6,000 tribes and in South Asia over 600 of them. Not only are a large number of tribes too small in size to constitute viable nations, they may not always have any cultural distinctiveness. Further, if the political dimension is taken into account, many of them were either stateless societies and/or are incorporated into larger polities.

If in Europe, nations are essentially cultural entities, in the colonized parts of the world and in ex-colonial countries, nations are viewed as political units. Further, most of the 'new nations' are also culturally diverse. Thus, African nations emerged through the incorporation of many tribes which spoke different languages/ dialects and followed different religious faiths. While race is the most salient common feature, even this criterion is not universal as exemplified in the case of South Africa, which is a multiracial state. In Asia, almost all nations are multireligious and multilingual. In the case of Latin America, the populations of particular nations are multiracial, multilingual, multireligious, or all of these. In North America and Australia, national populations are constituted predominantly by migrants from Europe who spoke different languages and belonged to different religious denominations. Understandably, the connotation of the term 'nation' and the background of the national population vary across the continents. In the case of western Europe, the nation-states are intented to be culturally (that is, linguistically and even in religious terms) homogeneous, but in most other cases they are culturally heterogeneous.

The point to be noted is that it is the historicity of context which invests meanings on concepts. The 'people' of the United States of America did not have a pre-existent 'nation' (in the European sense) to latch on their nationalism and yet American nationalism led to the formation of a state. On the other hand, 'nations' may not always clamour for their sovereign states, as borne out by the experience of India and the former Soviet Union. (In fact, available evidence suggests that it is usually the smaller nations located on interstate borders or those nations which are vivisected across boundaries which exhibit secessionist tendencies.)

Ideally, the nation-state fuses three dimensions: territory, culture, and citizenship. That a whole nation can be uprooted from its territory and rendered into an ethnie (a people sharing a common culture, particularly religion and language but without a common territory and citizenship) only points to the historical process and possibility of one category being transformed into another.

The attributes of homeland and territory are crucial in the case of a nation. Even if all other attributes are present together, a nation does not come into being unless it establishes legitimate moral claim over a territory, which in turn provides it with the potential for state formation. The ethnification of a nation takes place precisely when it does not have the resources for state formation, namely a homeland and legitimate political authority over it. Therefore, ethnie, nation, and state should be viewed in a processual relationship. When an ethnie acquires legitimate moral claim over a territory it becomes a nation, and when a nation secures political jurisdiction it becomes a state. Consequently, to be an ethnic group is to operate within a nation-state or to be dispersed into several of them. By the same token, to be an ethnie is to be on the periphery and to be a nation is to be in the centre of the polity. If a state has different nations within its territory, that state will and should have multiple cultural centres (see Oommen 1986a). It may be noted here that cultural pluralism, that is, the dignified co-existence of a plurality of cultural groups within national states, needs to be accepted as axiomatic. It follows that such an entity, a multinational state, can and should have several national traditions in sociology. Internationalization of sociology in such a context means something quite different as compared to what is usually meant to be understood by the term.

To complicate matters, nation-states are universally referred to as societies in sociology. As Bauman observes, 'with hardly any exception, all the concepts and analytical tools currently employed by social scientists are geared to a view of the human world in which the most voluminous totality is a "society", a notion equivalent for all practical purposes, to the concept of the "nation state"' (1973: 78). Not only that. To quote Bauman again:

Sociology, as it came of age in the bosom of western civilization and as we know it today is endemically national-biased. It does not recognize a totality broader than a politically organized nation, the term 'society', as used by well-nigh all sociologists regardless of their school loyalties, is, for all practical purpose, a name for an entity identical in size and composition with nation state. (Ibid.: 42–3)

It is neither necessary nor possible to trace the course of events which resulted in this situation. I shall confine myself to listing a few plausible factors which seem to have contributed in assuming isomorphism between society and nation-state. First, the rise of sociology as an academic discipline is only a little over 150 years old; sociology was born into nation-states. Predictably, the discipline got conditioned by the womb from which it emerged. Second, society and polity were conterminous in those nation-states in which sociology emerged and thrived initially (for example, France, Germany, Italy), or the distinction between the nation (England, Scotland, Ireland,

Wales) and the state (the United Kingdom) was not always clearly maintained for purpose of analysis, perhaps for political reasons. Third, in North America (the USA and Canada), the polities in which sociology as an academic enterprise thrives, particularly after World War II, are polyethnic states wherein the distinction between nation and state is irrelevant as their populations are constituted by immigrants drawn from a multiplicity of nations.

The point to be noted is that particular historical circumstances and political conditions have contributed to the obliteration of the conceptual distinction between the entities such as polity and society, and nation and state. Admittedly, internationalization has different connotations in different contexts. To ignore this in the context of the present discussion is to imperil a meaningful analysis.

In the case of a multinational state, internationalization is a phenomenon which can happen *within* the same sovereign state. Thus in the case of India and the former USSR, for example, one can speak of different national sociologies—Bengali, Tamil, and Kashmiri or Russian, Ukrainian, and Uzbek—co-existing and influencing one another. In other contexts, it may mean the impact and influences of the sociology of the original nations on the ethnies, the segments which are dispersed—that of French sociology on French–Canadian sociology, Spanish sociology on Mexican sociology, Portuguese sociology on Brazilian sociology, and the like. Finally, one can speak of internationalization as an ongoing process of modernization/westernization of sociology. Since most of the problems of internationalization of sociology stem from this process, I shall confine my attention to this theme. Further, I propose to highlight the problems with special reference to what are usually referred to as developing countries, with special reference to South Asia.

—◆—

Before we turn to this analysis, it is necessary, even if briefly, to indicate that colonialism is the critical variable in the context of the present analysis and why it is so. Sociology was born in Europe and flourished there; it was a product of a European renaissance which was essentially cultural in its content. Understandably, national traditions in sociology gradually emerged and crystallized in Europe. Further, the main carrier of sociology was a professional middle class, which gradually *evolved*. As Schumpeter (1951) noted,

the professionals of Europe were incumbents of certain newly created roles, carrying out new and expanding social functions. They
gradually displaced the erstwhile self-made entrepreneurs, who had
earlier replaced the nobleman landlord and the knight as the occupational ideal of western societies. Thus the western professionals,
sociologists included, are simply the last link in the continuously
evolving system of an occupational prestige chain.

In contrast, the rise of sociology in colonial countries followed
a different trajectory; it was a colonial transplant and a child of
imperialism. Moreover, colonialism threw up an artificial middle
class which was a victim to the modernization strategy of the colonial
agents. The colonial middle class was *artificial* because the social
process during the colonial period led to the arbitrary liquidation
of the older middle class and the creation of professional groups to
consolidate and subserve the alien rule. Consequently, the possibility
of societal stirring which is a prerequisite to produce an authentic
renaissance did not take place in the ex-colonial countries. The
immediate concern was political freedom and the efforts at cultural
efflorescence were subdued if not aborted. To recall the pregnant
words of an Indian sociologist, 'it is not possible for anybody belonging to a free country to know how that Great Denial [that is,
colonialism] has worked havoc with various attempts at renaissance'
(Mukherji 1958: 206).

As there are different varieties of colonialism, the attitude to
and the destiny of sociology and its nature also varied across these
colonial situations. I propose to distinguish between four *essential*
varieties of colonial situation for the present purpose.

First set are the colonies of the migrants constituting polyethnic
states. Although the migrants were structural marginals and the colonies were initially politically subservient, gradually they emerged as
dominant nations and leading producers of sociology in the world
(see Chapter 8). North America, consisting of the US and Canada, is
the archetype of this variety. But Australia, New Zealand, and other
polyethnic states together constitute the emergence of what may
be called the Euro-American society and may be treated under one
rubric. Thus one can speak of two centres from which mainstream
sociology is produced in the contemporary world—the traditional
old European centre and the newly emerged Euro-American one.
The latter is a case of a periphery (colony) becoming a centre.

Second, colonies which have become politically independent and continue to be economically dependent but are largely cultural extensions of Europe: the nation-states of Latin America. The fact that the majority of migrants to Latin America are drawn from the then European periphery—Spain and Portugal—is itself important in this context. It is a case of the periphery reproducing itself at a different and distant geographical space. However, the peripherality in this case is moderated by the cultural similarity which obtains between the centre and the periphery. Thus populations of most Latin American states are mainly Christian and the dominant languages are European, particularly Spanish and Portuguese. This commonality in religion and language provides substantial similarity in the cultural lifestyles of Europe and Latin America.

The distinctive deprivation of this type of periphery is economic. Therefore, it is understandable that the paradigm of centre–periphery, which focuses on unequal economic exchange, is the preoccupation of Latin American sociology. Scarcely, if ever, is the cultural dominance of the European and Euro-American centres accounted for in this paradigm.

Third, the colonized native population sticks to the language and religion of the colonizer even after the latter's physical withdrawal. The African situation largely fits this description. Of the 50 states in Africa, over 80 per cent have one of the European languages, mainly French and English, as their official and/or leading language. The leading religion of 50 per cent of the African states is Christianity, the other dominant religion being Islam. Thus, both the native languages and religions are relegated to the background, thanks to colonialism and conquest in Africa.

Even as the modernized, which in effect means westernized, elite persists with its received lifestyle, the storm troopers of nationalism, a counter elite, insist on the distinctive non-western cultural identity. To them, the production of nationally relevant and authentic sociology is an important item in the context of the search for this identity. Each 'nation' aspires to anchor its sociology to the specificity of its society and culture, pan-Africanism notwithstanding.

Fourth, the colonies stick to the pre-colonial culture patterns, particularly language and religion, after the political withdrawal of the colonizer. Even if the language of the colonizer is retained for its functional value, it is given little constitutional sanctity or official recognition. Those who embraced the religion of the colonizer may not be reconverted, need not even be persecuted, but are viewed with suspicion, if not disdain, and are invariably marginalized. The South Asian situation largely fits this description wherein the difference in cultural terms between the colonizer and the colonized is loud and clear.

Of the 40 states of Asia only one, the Philippines, is predominantly Christian and, except for Hong Kong, the city state, no other state has a European language as its official or leading language. Among the seven states of South Asia the percentage of the Christian population ranges between 8.3 per cent in Sri Lanka and 0.1 per cent or less for Nepal and Bhutan. None of the states has English as the official language, although South Asia was a British colony. Small wonder then that discussions on the cultural imperialism of the West abound in South Asian sociology.

It is my contention that the attitude to and acceptance of the sociology produced in the Euro-American centre would vary vastly among the four ex-colonial situations depending upon their present existential conditions. I have indicated above that the first, the Euro-American society, has become the new centre in the production of sociology. But the new centre is by and large the carrier of traditions initiated in the old centre. As for the second situation, the Latin American, the deprivation experienced is mainly economic. The excessive attention given to the ideas of centre–periphery, unequal exchange, etc., is reflective of this. The third and fourth situations share several attributes: racial (physical) distinctiveness, economic underdevelopment, and even political subservience. And yet, the third, the African situation differs from that of the South Asian in that in the former, dominant elements of European culture—language and religion— are retained and accepted. That is to say the South Asian situation is the farthest from the erstwhile colonial cultural milieu. Admittedly, the attitude to sociology, a cultural product of the West, would be most critical in South Asia.

For this reason alone it is legitimate to undertake an analysis of the implications of the internationalization of sociology with special reference to South Asia. But there is an additional reason—my familiarity with the other ex-colonial situations is limited. In pursuing this analysis, I shall keep mainly to South Asia, which was the biggest colony of the British empire. Although now split into several states, the region is a civilizational unit and colonial India more or less covered the whole of South Asia.

———

Earlier, I referred to colonialism as a 'great denial' which thwarted the natural development of sociology as a discipline in the colonies. There are several reasons why colonialism was a great denial. First, disengaged the past from the present. Colonialism did not promote a creative tension and innovative interaction between tradition and modernity in India. Quite the contrary; it created a deep and wide hiatus between tradition and modernity, a disengagement between the past and the present. (Consequently, Indian modernity is artificial and could be alienating.) Further, colonialism, did not even promise an authentic new beginning.

England has broken down the entire framework of Indian society without any symptoms of reconstruction yet appearing. This loss of his old world, with no gain of a new one, imparts a particular kind of melancholy to the present misery of the Hindu, and separates Hindustan ruled by Britain from all its past history. (Marx and Engels 1955: 332–3)

This total break from history is particularly agonizing for a society and civilization with a long and uninterrupted history and that is the second reason why colonialism was a great denial. The ideal was articulated by many but let me quote just one, namely, Bankim Chandra Chatterji, the great revolutionary who composed the Indian national song during the freedom struggle. He was a teacher before he plunged into revolutionary action and in his last lecture to his students, he said:

You are not a race of savages who have no past to remember, you cannot discover yourself in a day for the associations and influences of the past which extends over at least five hundred centuries; you cannot annihilate in a day a past natural existence which has survived the annihilation of hundreds of empires, of a hundred systems of religion and which has surveyed unscorned the downfall and ruin of many kindred civilizations. (quoted in Das 1984: 212)

The Indian civilization was perceived not simply as long and continuous but also as unique and creative. Understandably, colonialism which sought to displace such a civilization was indeed a great denial. In the eloquent words of the celebrated poet, Rabindranath Tagore:

For generations you have felt and thought and worked, have enjoyed and worshipped in your own special manner; and this cannot be cast off like the old clothes. It is in your blood, in the marrow of your bones, in the texture of your flesh, in the tissue of your brains, and it must modify everything you lay your hands upon, without your knowing, even against your wishes. Once you did solve the problems of man to your own satisfaction, you had your philosophy of life and evolved your own art of living. All this you must apply to the present situation and out of it will arise a new creation and not mere repetition, a creation which the soul of your people will own for itself and proudly offer to the world as its tribute to the welfare of man (1937: 57).

Colonialism was particularly incarcerating because it was not merely a political and economic subordination but also a moral and intellectual one; it was unabashedly flaunted as a civilizing mission; and it systematically undermined the national identity. All these deepened the intensity of the great denial. As the art historian Coomaraswamy noted: 'modern education that Englishmen are so proud of having given to India is based on the assumption—nearly universal in England—that India is a savage country, which is England's divine mission to *civilise*' (1981: 99). As against this, the assertion of Indian national identity was based on the axiom:

... that every nation has its own part to play in the long tale of human progress, and nations which are not free to develop their own individuality and own character, are also unable to make the contribution to the sum of human culture which the world has a right to expect of them (ibid.: 2).

The inability to develop one's national individuality would inevitably result in blind imitation and incongruous assimilation of the dominant, in the present case the colonial ruler's, culture. However, it is judicious to opt for a selective assimilation of the alien culture. In the wise words of Mohandas Karamchand Gandhi:

I am humble enough to admit that there is much that we can profitably assimilate from the West. Wisdom is no monopoly of one continent or one race. My resistance to western civilization is really a resistance to its indiscriminate and thoughtless imitation based on the assumption that Asiatics are fit only to copy everything that comes from the West (1948: 126).

To overcome the great denial there ought to have been, and there was, an Indian renaissance. But it was qualitatively different from the European renaissance. The Indian renaissance, incarnated in political nationalism questioning western hegemony and manifested in asserting her political autonomy and cultural specificity, entailed a rejection of western dominance, political, economic, and cultural.

The vital forces associated with national movement in India are not merely political, but moral, literary and artistic; and their significance lies in the fact that India henceforth will, in the main, judge all things by her own standards and from her own point of view. But the two sides of the national movement, the *material* and the *spiritual,* are inseparable and must attain success or fail together (Coomaraswamy 1981: iv).

The prognosis, however, has not come true. India achieved political autonomy and even economic independence to a large extent. But the envisioned spiritual resurgence and cultural renaissance did not automatically follow. There are two main reasons for this. First, India is constituted by several cultural entities, 'nations' in the European sense of the word. Therefore, Indian cultural renaissance will have to occur either at the civilizational level or at the level of each of these nations, not an easy process as the co-terminality between culture, civilization, and polity is disturbed. Second, renaissance necessarily implies both renewal and retention of the assets as well as cleansing and/or discarding of the liabilities in the system (see Oommen 1983a). For this to happen, revolutionary forces should emerge and crystallize, which is a long drawn-out process. Free India has existed for too short a time for this to happen. Therefore, it is not surprising that sociology in India is still searching for its identity.

Academic sociology in India is scarcely seven decades old and several social forces successively shaped it: first, the rich and varied Indian social thought which crystallized several centuries ago and continues to have a strong presence even to this day; second, the colonial connection which facilitated the study of Indian society by British scholar-administrators and European missionaries who laid the foundation for contemporary sociological scholarship in India; third, the anti-colonial struggle and social reform movements, which invested Indian sociology with a strong political content and orientation; fourth, the emergence of the Indian state wedded to parliamentary democracy, planned economic development, and secularism; fifth, the continuous exposure of Indian sociologists to the professional trends in sociology at the global level, particularly of West Europe and North America (cf. Chapter 1).

Indian sociology is thus a hybrid; a product of the creative confrontations and dialectical interactions between an intense desire to retain Indian tradition, a passionate quest for evolving and maintaining a distinct national identity, and an abiding interest to acquire a prominent place in the world community of academic sociologists. The odd combination of 'captive mind', the product of persisting academic colonialism and national consciousness, moulded in the crucible of the freedom movement and reinforced by the objectives of the national state, and the enthusiastic response to the process of globalization of sociology have predictably led to the crystallization of a series of apparently contradictory but actually creative tendencies in Indian sociology.

The capital concern of the *pioneers* of Indian sociology, who had started practising their profession by the early twentieth century, the heyday of the antiimperialist struggle, was to *Indianize* and not to *professionalize* sociology. As Singh concludes:

The sociologists of this generation were torn between issues of objectivity and reflexivity which are basic to a paradigm of sociology that has universal appeal and the issues of relevance which bound it deeply with the ideology of indigenous national liberation and cultural reform movements, an ideology anchored in the objectives of ushering in basic changes in the structure and tradition of Indian society (1986: 6).

Further, as Ramakrishna Mukherjee observes:

Most of the pioneers were ardent nationalists, but only a few of them were actively involved in politics. Also, even those who were engaged in active politics were not dogmatists or doctrinaires in so far as their academic life was concerned. Apart from their intrinsic quality as scholars, their politics was an indication of the social situation in which they functioned (1979: 229).

While for the majority of the pioneers, Indian nationalism was political in its orientation, for at least a few its content was religious, that is, cultural. Consequently, the *traditionists* upheld a Hindu view of life and advocated Hindu sociology (for example, Motwani 1946, 1958). And some of the traditionists of the later generation argued that sociological cognition is genuinely alien to Indian tradition and hence Indian sociology is destined to remain essentially parasitic and imitative (see, for example, Saran 1958). While this perception hardly gained any currency in India, latterly a neo-traditional orientation has resurrected (see, for example, Dumont 1957; Mukherji 1958). These perspectives, perhaps unwittingly, advocated sociology of the cultural mainstream and the majority religious collectivity (see Chapter 1 for an elaboration). Understandably, the neo-traditionists are often perceived as conservatives and revivalists by the modernizers.

The traditionist and neo-traditionist emphasis on the study of Indian tradition and Hindu texts seem to be a reaction (perhaps an over-reaction) to the enthusiastic 'modernization' of Indian sociology in the 1950s and 1960s by the new generation of cosmopolitans who were not intimidated by (at any rate entirely emancipated from) the debilitating conditions of colonialism and not inflamed by the zeal of nationalism. They believed that methods, concepts, and theories of sociology developed anywhere can be applied to the Indian situation, at any rate, with minor modifications (see, for example, Damle 1965). Thus they invoke Durkheimian, Marxian, and Weberian frameworks or one of their numerous recent incarnations. If in the 1950s the cosmopolitans drew their inspiration mainly from British social anthropology, in the 1960s the tilt towards American sociology was evident. If the first was an indication of the yet-to-be severed academic umbilical cord from the colonial world, the second was an indication of the emerging academic 'imperialism' of the New World.

The cosmopolitans belong to several ideological camps: first, those who imbibe one or another brand of 'western sociology', including its current fads—functionalism, structuralism, behaviouralism, phenomenology, ethnomethodology, semiotics; second, Marxist sociologists who reject western sociology, but whose staple is the Marxist sociology produced mainly in the western liberal democracies either because the sociology produced in East Europe is not available in English or because it is not adequately creative; third, those who reject not only the conservative western sociology but also the state-regulated sociology of the eastern European countries and opt for 'radical sociology' produced in the Third World, particularly in Latin America; and finally, those who attempt to fuse two or more perspectives into new hybrids (for example, Marxist phenomenology).

Notwithstanding the differing perspectives pursued by cosmopolitans, one thing is common to them: the sociology produced by them is not rooted in the history and traditions of India. Also, they are the main agents of the internationalization of 'Indian sociology' which chokes creativity and blocks the development of authentic national traditions in sociology. If the cosmopolitans ignored the deep and specific historicity of Indian society, thereby creating intellectual alienation, the traditionists with their overemphasis on the uniqueness of Indian civilization created intellectual claustrophobia.

The young national state of India pursuing the goals of democracy, secularism, and socialism not only provided a new milieu to practise sociology, but also made heavy demands on its practitioners. The need to apply sociological knowledge to bring about social transformation in a desired direction came to be acutely felt. The linkage between sociology and social policy was increasingly acknowledged; sociology was perceived as an instrument of national reconstruction. Those who took such a perspective, the nationalists, argued that although academic sociology was a colonial importation into India, during the freedom struggle, its value orientation was explicitly nationalistic (see, for example, Joshi 1975). Further, it is suggested that western sociology itself emerged as a response to nationalistic urges and aspirations, and to develop an authentic Indian sociology the same path should be traversed (Singh 1973).

I want to suggest that unqualified commitment to a 'nationalist' sociology in the prevailing conditions of South Asia has several unanticipated consequences. First, boundaries of states could be redrawn in the course of a relatively short time-span and sociologists cannot and should not constantly redefine their commitments to suit the political expediency of states. Second, commitment to a national state would often entail participation in the formulation and implementation of the state policy, which may be oppressive in certain contexts and to some sections of the population. Third, the change in the historicity of context, from colonial state to national states may lead to the redefinition of the constituency of sociologists, and in many cases it did, drawn from different primordial collectivities. The value orientation and commitment of those who champion the cause of cultural minorities or the socially marginalized may often be perceived as 'parochial' or 'subversive' by those who hail from the dominant political groups or the cultural mainstream. This necessitates the distinction between academic nationalism and academic parochialism, that is, commitment to the welfare of one's own specific constituencies, be it primordial or civic collectivities, as against the commitment to the wider collectivity. This leads to erosion in commitment to basic human values by sociologists.

Given these reservations regarding the nationalist perspective, it is but natural that the pluralist paradigm of Indian sociology is slowly but surely emerging as a conjoint response to the traditionist, cosmopolitan, and nationalist orientations (see Chapter 1). The domain assumptions of the pluralist paradigm are the following. First, sociology stands apart from all other disciplines in that its mission can be fulfilled only if it is all-inclusive and totalistic. Its practice presupposes the authentic appropriation of all varieties of human experience (Oommen 1988b). Second, the conventional dichotomization of social reality anchored to western epistemological dualism is incapable of comprehending social structure, process, and change (Oommen 1990a). Third, the process of social transformation is rarely, if ever, total and it does not occur through the displacement of the old by the new as implied in the tradition-modernity paradigm, but through a process of reconciliation and accretion (Oommen 1983a). Fourth, it does not advocate unqualified commitment to nationalism or nation-state but pleads for selective endorsement of the state policy and national values insofar as they are congruent with basic humanist values and interests (Oommen 1986b). Fifth, it does not reject any cultural item be it ideology, technology, or sociology because of the locus of their geographical origin, but opts for creative confrontation and cautious synthesis of the alien and the native (Oommen 1983b: 111–36). Finally, it advocates disciplined eclecticism in theoretical orientations (Mukherji 1980) and contextualization (Mukherji 1945) as the cardinal principle of the sociologist's method.

It is thus clear that Indian sociology is gradually transcending inward-looking traditionalism, imitative cosmopolitanism, and virulent nationalism. It is cautiously proceeding with the judicious blending of the national with the global, rejecting the liabilities and retaining the assets in both. However, even as Indian sociology is absorbing the relevant corpus of knowledge produced elsewhere, one fails to see any reciprocal response from other nations, continents, societies, or civilizations. This is the Achilles heel of the ongoing process of the internationalization of sociology.

The foregoing case study of South Asia is presented to highlight the possible dangers associated with the process of internationalization of sociology, if it is launched prematurely in ex-colonial developing countries. Authentic interationalization implies equality in exchange among the interacting units. As it stands, imbalance in exchanges across 'nations' are too glaring both because of the underdevelopment of national traditions in sociology in the case of several developing nations and/or due to the restricted flow of sociology from these countries to the developed ones. Therefore, the process will have to be initiated with great caution and circumspection. Let me list the main reasons for the advocacy of this approach.

First, internationalization, given the present predicament of sociology, would in effect mean the spread of western sociology to non-western countries. This is more dangerous than colonial transplantation of sociology in that it is easier to avoid, distance, or fight something which is perceived to be part of the colonial baggage. When the flow takes place under relatively free political conditions, the acceptance of the concerned item is apparently voluntary. The hidden persuasiveness of the product captivates and coerces the mind of the consumer. That is, intellectual colonialism is an intimate enemy and it is extremely difficult to extricate oneself from its seductive grip.

Second, while westernization is instantly recognized as a current which flows from the West, internationalization, although a camouflage for westernization, passes on in a more respectable garb. This gives apparent autonomy to the non-West which is misleading. However, it is possible to transcend this misconception by recognizing that internationalization as it stands is essentially a western construction. It is then possible to develop a non-western construction of internationalization. That is, the content of internationalization needs to be viewed from the perspective of the dominant as well as the dominated partners. Such an exercise is an imperative for authentic internationalization because the perspective of the dominated is their sole epistemological privilege. No amount of empathy and transnationalism of the dominant can produce an equally authentic and rooted understanding of the victim.

Third, internationalization with its firm fountainhead anchored in the West would necessarily reproduce intellectual claustrophobia far beyond the boundaries of its current production space. This is so because internationalization emanating from the West is not obliged to accept and accommodate the sociologies of the other worlds—East, South, or the Third. Naturally, the process would remain one-sided, partial, and fractured. On the contrary, internationalization emanating from the developing regions invariably incorporates the sociology of the First and even of the Second worlds.

Admittedly, such a process would give birth to a more wholesome and holistic perspective in sociology.

Fourth, internationalization inspired from the West would necessarily be a search for an enlarged market for western sociology. Such a situation is likely to produce two dangers: non-westerns becoming the carriers of obsolete western perspectives and orientations on the one hand, and over-enthusiastic consumers of the new western paradigms, the intellectual fads of the West, on the other. Immersed in the consumption of the discarded items on the one hand and coping with the new fads on the other, the developing societies will fail to nurture and develop their own perspectives and orientations. Therefore, the kind of internationalization in vogue is a sure invitation to perpetuate the artificiality and sterility of non-western sociology and the blocking of its emerging autonomy.

Finally, internationalization to be authentic and fruitful should consciously design for a multidirectional flow of sociology, particularly strengthening the flow from the weak to strong centres. The project should not simply aim at 'educating' the non-westerns but *learning* from them. Such a replenishment would at least partly help western sociology to avert its coming (or has it already arrived?) crisis. Indeed, western sociology requires a judicious *glasnost* and cautious *perestroika*. On the agenda of internationalization of sociology these should be important items which would render the process authentic and meaningful.

7

Sociology for One World
Towards an Authentic Sociology

❖

The theme, 'Sociology for One World', is indeed in tune with the new imageries—in fact illusions—projected in the context of the emerging 'post-modern' society wherein information and technology are seen to be standardizing human life and problems everywhere and transforming the world into a 'global village'. Global sociology is the sociology of the global village! According to this paradigm, global sociology is the sociology produced at the centre and the periphery produces only regional sociology.

However, it is often forgotten that the imagery of post-modern society barely fits and is largely inappropriate to the bulk of humankind, given the acute imbalances in the distribution and spread of critical resources, technology, and information. If the illusion is allowed to be internalized and is not consciously challenged it will camouflage and perpetuate the genuine debilitating differences within and across societies and cultures.

Therefore, a meaningful discussion of the theme, sociology for one world, should ask and answer a few basic questions. How has the discipline of sociology defined and conceptualized the world? Is the world one or many? What is the authentic unit for sociological investigation? What is the purpose of sociology? Whose interest should sociology serve?

Before I proceed any further, I should enter a few caveats. First, I do not think it is tenable to characterize human society either as unity or as multiplicity. It is more rewarding to characterize society as an event, a process, an interhuman reality; a conceptualization which can account for the autonomy of as well as the reciprocity between structure, culture, and agency. Second, while recognizing the universality of human reasoning, it is necessary to insist that production of knowledge particularly in social science, calls for an empathic understanding of the object of knowledge in which intuition and sociological imagination play a significant role. Third, sociology for one world is an aspiration and not an accomplishment. Therefore, our analysis is bound to be largely normative and prescriptive.

Sociology as it is practised in Europe, its original abode, is a study of modern industrial (and now of course the post-modern, post-industrial) societies. To quote Gellner:

In the twentieth century, the essence of man is not that he is rational, or a political, or a sinful, or a thinking animal, but that he is an industrial animal. It is not his moral or intellectual or social or aesthetic, etc., attributes which make man what he is; his essence resides in his capacity to contribute to, and to profit from industrial society. The emergence of industrial society is the prime concern of sociology (1964: 35).

Not only that, 'Sociology ... is the off-spring of modernity and it bears the birthmark of modern parentage. Its mission is to understand the specificity of the modern world to which it belongs' (Heller 1987: 391). Further

... it is no longer sensible to speak of 'modern societies' in the plural ... Modern society is ... a world society in a double sense. It provides one world for one system; and it integrates all world horizons—as horizons of one communicative system. The phenomenological and structural meanings converge. A plurality of possible worlds has become inconceivable. The world-wide communicative system constitutes one world which includes all possibilities. (Luhman 1982: 298)

As sociologists of Europe study their own society which is 'modern', social anthropology had to be defined as a study of other cultures (Beattie 1964) which are traditional. It is well known that anthropology as a discipline arose and flourished in the context of western conquest and colonization; and it came to devote itself to the study of primitive, peasant, or pre-industrial societies (Lévi-Strauss 1966). But this historical accident has been invoked to claim superiority for social anthropology (Dumont 1966: 23) (see Chapter 2 for an elaboration).

The point at issue here is not the claimed distinctiveness or the assumed superiority of one or another discipline, not even the conventional but irrational rivalry between sociology and social anthropology but its consequence for the object of analysis: the human society gets acutely fractionated into two—the primitive and the modern, the agrarian and the industrial—a distinction not always sustainable. Thus, social anthropology as it got institutional-ized in the academies of the 'colonies' and came to be practised by the 'natives' instantly became sociology for two reasons. First, the native researchers were studying their own societies. Second, they did not view their societies as primitive or traditional; in fact these epithets were dismissed as pejoratives invented by western anthropologists and sociologists.

At any rate, with the gradual disappearance of the simple, 'primitive' societies, anthropology itself started studying peasant and modernizing 'complex' societies. The shift in its substantive concern necessarily called for a shift in the traditional techniques of data collection too. Understandably, anthropologists gradually took to the hitherto disparaged quantitative techniques convention-ally associated with sociology. These innovations and the instinct of survival displayed by social anthropology is to be widely welcomed and appreciated. But the rationale behind maintaining the academic distinction between sociology and social anthropology and its impli-cations for humankind and human society are scarcely articulated.

Fortunately, the beginning has been made in this context, al-though unfortunately it has not gathered adequate momentum. Those who questioned the artificial separation between sociology and social anthropology did so not only because the distinction is academically unsustainable but also because it creates an unac-ceptable division between the modern and the traditional, and the industrial and agrarian societies (see Eisenstadt 1965; Fallding 1968; Srinivas 1966; and Chapter 2 in this volume).

There is yet another reason, a deeper and more disturbing one, why the conventional distinction between the two disciplines should be abandoned without any hesitation. With the publication of Henry Maine's *Ancient Law* in 1861 and L.H. Morgan's *Ancient Society* in 1887 the foundation for the great rupture between the 'modern' and

'primitive' societies was laid and for one-and-a-half centuries social
scientists built their theories on that basis. Almost all the founding
fathers—Marx, Weber, and Durkheim included—of social sciences
endorsed the view that the difference between the primitive and
the modern societies is irreconcilable. In fact, sociology thrived by
postulating and nurturing dichotomous constructions of human
society. Gradually, the 'unalterable division of labour' between
sociology and social anthropology crystallized and primitive society
became the special concern of the latter and modern society that
of the former. To sustain itself in the chosen area of its interest
social anthropology had 'invented the primitive society', to recall
the evocative phrase of Adam Kuper (1988).

... modern society was defined above all by the territorial state, the mo-
nogamous family and private property. Primitive society therefore must
have been nomadic, ordered by blood ties, sexually promiscuous and
communist. There had also been a progression in mentality. Primitive
man was illogical and given to magic. Modern man, however, had invented
science (ibid.: 5).

Further,

The ideal of primitive society therefore provided an idiom which was ideally suited for debate about modern society, but in itself it was neutral. It
could be used equally by right or left, reactionary or progressive, poet or
politician—primitive society was the mirror image of modern society—or,
rather, primitive society as they imagined it inverted the characteristics of
modern society as they saw it (ibid.: 240).

The logical corollary of the invention of primitive society was the
invention of the human other—the savage other, the black other,
and the ethnographic other—each of which has specific connotations
and references in the western tradition. Anthropology, the study of
the human other, became an instrument in the hands of western
Judeo-Christian tradition to understand itself. As Pandian argues:

In the Judeo-Christian orientation the self is dichotomized into a divinely
sanctioned true self and a divinely rejected untrue self. Anthropology
seeks to synthesize the true self and the untrue self, inventing and creating the human other who enacts the human possibilities of the self that
are excluded from the Western tradition ... anthropology is a Western
cultural phenomenon generated by the Judeo-Christian cultural structure.
Modern anthropology was born out of the need in the West to reconcile

the true self and the untrue self in comprehending the unity of the self (1985: 124–5).

The invention of primitive society and the construction of human other (primitive man) logically implies the invention of modern society and modern man. Even as one may argue that the latter notions emanate out of the experiential base of western man and society, the tendency inherent in epistemological dualism manifesting itself in dichotomous constructions is bound to create neat and tidy conceptual creatures. Modern man and society are such entities because the temptation to juxtapose the modern with the primitive is loud and clear.

In the light of the discussion so far I suggest that the academic Berlin Wall between sociology and social anthropology can be demolished. Only then its corollary, the unjust vivisection of humanity into modern and primitive, industrial and agrarian, etc., can be done away with. This is the first prerequisite for building an authentic sociology.

It is, however, imperative that the genuine diversity of human society should be recognized and nurtured as a pre-condition for pursuing an authentic sociology. The fact that one has to prescribe it as a prerequisite is itself paradoxical in a world and at a time when vigorous movements and mobilizations are afloat to preserve the diversity of nature; the preservation of both plants and animals. It seems the contemporary world puts the cultural diversity of homo sapiens at a low premium! However, the advocacy for the preservation of societal diversity should not be misunderstood as an argument for cultural relativism. The present concern is to question the prevalent assumption and practice in regard to the preservation of cultural diversity.

The maxim, one nation one state, is based on the assumption that each culture, that is, nation, should have its own state to sustain itself. The assumption was attempted to be translated into practice in West Europe, the cradle of modern nation-states. The doctrine and its practice played conceptual havoc and perpetuated analytical anomie in contemporary social science. As it stands, social scientists of all hues invariably equate nation (society/culture) with state (polity) (see Bauman 1973; Oommen 1997b).

The popular assumption that 'nation-states' are natural human collectivities is unsustainable. In fact, quite a few of them are artificial entities and what is usually referred to as nation building is nothing but an attempt to transform these artificial entities into 'natural' units. To put it pithily, if global-society is an abstract notion and a conceptual dope, the state-society is an artificial entity and often an empirical monster. If so, where does one look for and pitch oneself in one's effort to identify an authentic unit of sociological analysis? I suggest that civilizational-society provides a viable anchorage and is an authentic unit for sociological analysis which would save sociology from both false universalism and false nationalism. It is necessary to spell out the rationale behind this choice. But before I take up this discussion it is advisable to refer briefly to a particular variety of false internationalism.

False universalism claims the whole world as its arena of operation ignoring civilizational specificities, false 'nationalism' insists that each state should have its own brand of sociology, and false internationalism often latches itself on to religion and/or language. Thus the sociologies of the French, German, English, Spanish, or Portuguese speech communities are sought to be built on the erroneous assumption that there exists a common denominator among the sociologies produced by them. It is true that in those state-societies which share a common language there exists 'communicative facility'. Nevertheless, it is a limited advantage confined to the context of communication. Perhaps an illustration would lend clarity to the discussion.

The French-speaking sociologists are drawn from three different contexts. First, those who are from the ancestral homeland of the French-speaking people, the French nation, which incidentally is not confined to the political entity called France; native French speakers are citizens of several countries. Second, migrants who are settled away from Europe, that is, an ethnie which was transformed into a nation such as the French Canadians. Third, the French-speaking states of the ex-French colonies, for example, of Africa. While one can legitimately expect considerable flow of communication across the three groups of French-speaking sociologists, to search for a uniformity or similarity in the sociology produced by the three groups would be a wild goose chase. Not only that there is an association of French-speaking sociologists but they also meet separately at the time of the World Congress of Sociology organized under the auspices of the International Sociological Association. There are similar associations for Spanish and Portuguese-speaking sociologists.

There is a more problematic version of internationalism, that which is anchored to religion. Since there has been a systematic and concerted effort to Islamize knowledge by a section of intellectuals particularly from Muslim-majority states, I shall continue the discussion with special reference to Islam. Ahmed, an anthropologist from Pakistan, defines Islamic anthropology thus:

The study of Muslim groups by scholars committed to the universalistic principles of Islam—humanity, knowledge, tolerance—relating micro village tribal studies in particular to the larger historical and ideological frame of Islam. Islam is here understood not as theology but sociology. The definition does not preclude non-Muslims (1987: 56).

Defined in terms of humanity, knowledge, and tolerance and inclusive of non-Muslims, one fails to understand the distinctiveness of and the need for an Islamic anthropology! The pertinent comment by a Pakistani political scientist puts the matter in proper perspective.

If Islamization of knowledge means simply that social sciences should serve a higher moral purpose, abandon their moral stance and be guided by universal moral considerations, then obviously there should be no serious intellectual problem. But if it means that every religious community and nation should have a separate social science then obviously this will create intellectual anarchy and constitute a serious obstacle to the realization of the goal of universality. (Inayatullah 1989: 627)

The logical corollary of Islamic anthropology or sociology would be Buddhist, Christian, Jewish, and Hindu sociologies! While one cannot deny the influence of religion in shaping the production and consumption of knowledge, to divide humankind based on religions and to carve out exclusive constituencies for different disciplines goes against the all-encompassing and humanist orientation of knowledge itself.

———

For building an authentic sociology it is enough that we avoid untenable divisions of humanity into primitive and modern societies, dispense with artificial and abstract units of investigation, or avoid false universalism, internationalism, and nationalism. We must also take into account the continuity between the past and the present of societies on the one hand, and the dualism which pervades all societies on the other.

Human society is divided not only spatially and culturally but temporally as well. Humankind is in a position to cope with the spatial wedge today largely because of the revolutions in transport and communication. In fact, one of the justifications for and the promise of 'Sociology for One World' should be located precisely at the intersection between society and technology. This intersection and the process of modernization which it abets and accelerates tend to standardize culture, at least a large segment of it, the world over. And yet, we find an incessant search for roots among peoples because of the anxieties created by the ruthless standardizing tendency of modernization. That is, precisely because modernity is a cauldron of cultures, it prompts the search for tradition. This search is a travel in history, even in myth, to establish one's link with the past and to assert one's collective identity. This search for roots is engulfing the whole world. 'It seemed that, all of a sudden, the "developed" world was catching the tribal malady of the Third World, much to the surprise and chagrin of both liberal and socialist ideologues. In Europe, what had seemed to be dormant and moribund national problems became reactivated ... ' (Van der Berghe 1983: 246). This belies the notion of a modern world society.

The abstract notion of sociology for one world is apt to ignore societies not only as cultural-spatial entities but also as temporal entities. Sociology, that is, the 'history of the present' is inextricably bound with history, 'the sociology of the past'. The notion of one world should therefore be conceived without endangering the spatial, cultural, and temporal specificities of societies. Civilization necessarily connotes the historical roots of culture and society and hence the importance and plausibility of civilizational-society as authentic units of sociological investigation.

I emphasize this point because sociology, defined and practised as the study of modern society in the contemporary West, often tends to the 'retreat of sociologists into the present' to recall the pregnant phrase of Elias (1987). This is not a good omen for building an authentic sociology.

The plea to link the present with the past should not be misunderstood as an effort to glorify or decry the past. The past, that is history/tradition, has both positive and negative elements in it and no society is exempt from this mix. As Rabindranath Tagore observed, 'Europe is supremely good in her beneficence when her face is turned to all humanity; Europe is supremely evil in her malfeasant aspect where her face is turned only upon her interest, using all her power of greatness for ends which are against the infinite and eternal in men' (1937: 67).

What is true of a whole civilization is also true of its constituent units. Jawaharlal Nehru wrote about two Englands: 'the England of Shakespeare and Milton, of noble speech and writing and brave deed; of political revolution and the struggle for freedom, of science and progress', and also of the other England, '...of the savage penal code and brutal behaviour, of entrenched feudalism and racism' (1956: 285).

In a similar vein one can speak of the two Indias: the India of poverty, illiteracy, untouchability, superstition, fatalism, gender oppression, and the India of the great cultural heritage and pluralism, of the tolerance of religious and linguistic diversity, of cultural symbiosis; of two former Soviet Unions: of nationalist oppression, authoritarianism, and regimentation but also of great strides in science and technology, of emancipation of women, of glasnost and perestroika; of two United States of America: of the American creed, American revolution, the tradition of freedom and enlightenment but also of Black oppression and slavery, of extermination of Native Americans, of military designs and Star Wars programmes (see Joshi 1975).

It is therefore obvious that each culture and civilization has its assets and liabilities. The ingenuity of a people largely depends on coping with this dualism, the Janus-faced reality. Their dynamism and creativity will be revealed in their ability to discard the liabilities without apology and in nurturing the assets with care. For this, one has to pursue a strategy of selective retention of the assets and rejection of the liabilities in the system (Oommen 1983a).

To be authentic, sociology for one world should be utterly devoid of xenophobia and jingoism. This calls for the recognition of the assets in other cultures and civilizations. The oneness of the world is to be reflected in its rich and variegated past and present, in its cultural diversity and pluralism. Tagore listed the grave but relevant issues that the western civilization grappled with, although it has not yet overcome them:

The conflict between the individual and the state, labour and capital, man and woman, the conflict between the greed of material gain and the spiritual life of man, the organized selfishness of nations and the higher ideals of humanity; the conflict between all the ugly complexities inseparable from giant organizations of commerce and state and the natural instinct of man crying for simplicity and beauty and fullness in leisure—all these have to be brought to a harmony in a matter not yet dreamt of. (Tagore 1937: 55–6)

Tagore (ibid.: 57) advised his fellow Asians to apply their eastern mind, spiritual strength, and love of social obligation to evolve a new path of progress. Similarly, while admitting that there is something positive in all civilizations and cultures, Mohandas Karamchand Gandhi insisted: 'I want the cultures of all lands to be blown about my house as freely as possible. But I refuse to be blown off my feet by any' (1948: 298). This is the principle which informs the strategy of selective retention of the assets in one's civilization and judiciously fusing it with the desirable elements, be it technology or ideology, of other cultures.

There is one more danger that the abstract notion of sociology for one world carries with it: the possibility of ignoring intrasocietal differences, disparities, and discriminations which exist in all societies. Even in the most homogeneous of all societies the differences based on age, gender, and class exist. While the discrimination and oppression based on the first two are camouflaged through the mellowing effects of family and kinship, class exploitation is much more naked and hence widely commented upon. Describing the conditions of the poor in eighteenth century England, Disraeli gives a gripping account:

… two nations between whom there is no intercourse and no sympathy; who are ignorant of each other's habits, thoughts and feelings, as if they were dwellers in different zones, or inhabitants of different planets; who are formed by different breeding, are fed by different food, are ordered by different manners and are not covered by the same laws, the rich and the poor (1945: 23).

Although this description may not hold true for all 'nations' of the world today, it captures the situation prevalent in many. Similarly, gender oppression and injustice is present and practised in most societies. As we move from the relatively homogeneous to heterogeneous societies we have to reckon with new differences and disparities. The inhuman discrimination and oppression practised in multiracial and multicultural/national societies against the weak and minority groups should not be allowed to be swept under the carpet in our eagerness to establish a sociology for one world. To put it pithily, the world is not yet one and hence we cannot have a sociology for one world. That is to say, inter- and intrasocietal differences, disparities, and discriminations should not be lost sight of in our enthusiasm to establish a sociology for one world.

I have suggested above that the civilizational-society is the appropriate unit of investigation for nurturing an authentic sociology. It is time to list the reasons for this advocacy.

First, the ongoing process of modernization tends to standardize human culture everywhere. As Lévi-Strauss laments ' ... humanity has taken to monoculture, once and for all, and is preparing to produce civilization in bulk, as if it were a sugar beet' (1961: 52). This trend and tendency should be reversed. Recognizing the specificity of particular civilizations and a commitment to preserve it is a necessary first step. That is, celebration of diversity is the necessary, nay, inevitable, first step in moving towards a sociology for one world.

Second, in spite of the wide currency of the term nation-state and the universal tendency to treat it as natural, available evidence shows that most of them are artificial entities born out of historical accidents. If most of them are small in size and do not have any cultural specificity, a few are multicultural mega systems. Given the fact that many nations are vivisected across state boundaries and irredentist movements question the very legitimacy of several states, one cannot treat such state-societies as viable units for sociological analysis. It is time we emancipate sociology from the epistemological trap into which it has fallen, the trap we have laid for it by equating polity and even economy with society.

Third, the notion of 'one world' is not only abstract, but it tends to ignore the intersocietal and intrasocietal differences, disparities, and discriminations. This is particularly problematic from the point of view of the dominated, the oppressed, and the exploited. Hence the advocacy of sociology for one world may go against the humanistic orientation of sociology as a discipline. It is important to insist that the project, sociology for one world, should address the task of recognition and celebration of diversity and not its integration. Integration is not only intimidating but also oppressive from the perspective of the weak; integration undermines their specificity and identity. Therefore, the attempt at integration undercuts the very diversity sociology for one world should preserve: operation successful, patient succumbed.

Having noted the rationale of recommending civilizational-society as the unit of sociological investigation, let me list the advantages too. While the relationship of culture and society with economy, polity, technology, and environment should form the subject matter of sociological studies, the focus ought to be on culture and society. Without such a focus the discipline is often reduced to one which deals with residual aspects left out by other disciplines. Civilizational-society provides the much needed focus for sociology.

The basic nature of civilizational-society is not affected by the short-term rise and fall of polities or even economies encapsulated within it. While such events and processes often happen within a civilizational matrix, the creation of a new economic order or a political system does not basically alter the lifestyles, belief systems, or even work habits of the people. That is, the notion of civilizational-society encapsulates a long time-span and helps focus on the durable aspects of human society to bring back the much neglected historical dimension of sociology.

The fact that a civilizational-society can (and often does) encapsulate different economic, political, and technological systems within it undermines many of the critical assumptions implied in constituting societies/nations in the contemporary world. In fact, sociological investigations in the last hundred years or so were primarily addressed to the task of understanding states/nations which are believed to be 'societies'. Because of this fallacy of misplaced concreteness, the very possibility of asking meaningful questions has been aborted. For example, the question, what happens to a society, culture, or civilization when it gets vivisected between different states or economies is not even posed, let alone answered. Examples such as the two Irelands, Koreas, Punjabs, Bengals, etc., rush to one's mind. The manner in which questions are formulated in contemporary social science has relegated sociologists to the background. Civilizational-society is an instrument capable of rehabilitating sociologists to their rightful place.

Civilizational-society recognizes the dignified co-existence of different cultures and lifestyles, religions, and languages. It does not plumb for an arrangement wherein particular types of economy, polity, and culture are taken to be necessarily and always co-extensive. That is, the notion of civilizational-society unambiguously attests pluralism, a strong tendency in contemporary world-society. In turn, it recognizes that all systems have their share of assets and liabilities and advocates the judicious fusion of the desirable elements in all civilizations and the rejection of undesirable aspects.

While endorsing cultural pluralism as its basic tenet, the notion of civilizational-society rejects the pernicious doctrine of cultural relativism without apology. The idea of cultural relativism is not only untenable in the contemporary world in which societies are constantly exposed to alien influences, but the notion of the pristine purity of a culture and the need for its maintenance can lead to the practice of racism, slavery, untouchability, gender oppression, and the like. In pursuance of the strategy of selective retention of the assets in a culture and selective rejection of the liabilities in it, civilizational-society consciously promotes cultural symbiosis as the kernel of societal reconstruction and development.

Authentic sociology ought to be synthetic, not insular or alienative; a synthesis of traditions, lifestyles, and cultures. The notion of civilizational-society provides the possibility of the co-existence of different nationalities and cultures. But this co-existence ought to be dignified and egalitarian, not domineering and authoritarian. It should not be geared to the displacement syndrome—the displacement of peasantry by proletariat, of the rural by the urban, of the weaker nationalities by the dominant ones—but to accretion and co-existence, not to the insulation or assimilation of different cultures and categories but to their constant interaction and cross-fertilization.

Keeping these considerations in mind, the acceptance of civilizational societies as units of analyses is the first necessary step to build an authentic sociology. The tradition of cognizing 'societies' in terms of particular races with specific cultures having a common market and polity has played havoc with humankind and human society. This has been happening in spite of the fact that: there are several multicultural and/or multiracial state-socieites; there are several states for the same race or culture; and several states may have a common market or military arrangement. It is time that sociology does away with the great rupture between reality and concepts. To opt for civilizational-society as the unit of analysis, as against global-society on the one hand and state-society on the other, is to be concrete and natural at once; to endorse cultural pluralism and humanism simultaneously.

8

The Trajectory of Globalization
and Its Implications for
Social Research

There is no consensus about the starting point of globalization although many agree that the process accelerated with the demise of the tripartite division of the world occasioned by the dismantling of the Second World. However, several authors, Karl Marx, Immanuel Wallerstein, Roland Robertson, just to mention three, locate AD 1500 as the starting point of globalization. There are others who pitch it later. For example, for Anthony Giddens, modernity is the theme song of globalization and the 1800s marked its beginning. According to Tomlinson, globalization began as recently as the 1960s with cultural planetarization. But as Nederveen Pieterse points out, these views imply that the history of modernity/globalization began with the history of the West and therefore these views are not only geographically narrow but also historically shallow (1994).

The manner in which the world is conceptualized in social science has been changing in the last two centuries. The most prominent of these are dichotomies such as traditional and modern societies, the Old and the New Worlds, and the Orient and the Occident all of which are products of colonialism; the trichotomy of the First, Second, and the Third Worlds is an offshoot of the Cold War and the currently fashionable One World is the gift of the structural adjustment programme. I shall discuss the problems in accepting these conceptualizations of the 'world' and some of the implications of these conceptualizations for social research.

The proclivity to divide the world into modern and traditional as well as Old and New is a product of the geographical explorations which started in the fifteenth century and the era of colonialism which followed it. In fact, according to most contemporary historians, 1492 marked the beginning of modernity although modern times and modern mentalities did not begin to appear until the 1520s. This period of transition was marked by three elements: sustained contact between different parts of the world such as Europe and America, Europe and Asia, Europe and Africa; the shift of the centre of modernity within Europe from the south to the north; and 'rupture of mentalities' which may be traced to a 'geo-cognitive' revolution of the world (Tiryakian 1994: 137). But this rupture of mentalities got articulated in social science only by the latter half of the nineteenth century.

With the discovery of the New World—the Americas, Australia, and New Zealand—the notion of the Wild Man, the Savage Other, and the Primitive Man surfaced. First descriptions came through Spanish and Portuguese explorers. When seven American aborigines were brought to Europe by Columbus, astonishment was expressed that they were different from Negroes because aborigines were sooty in colour. Given the tradition of social anthropology to study 'other cultures', these categories became the natural objects of research.

According to the monogenetic hypothesis implicated in the Christian doctrine of creation, mankind was the product of a single creative act, at a single moment in time and at a single spot on earth's face. Of one blood and common inheritance, human beings were physically, ethnically, and socially homogeneous. In contrast, the polygenetic theory upheld the view that mankind was the outcome of plural creative acts, at plural moments in time, and at plural locations. To uphold Christian monogenesis was anti-slavery, but by endorsing the secular polygenesis slavery could be rationalized (see Hodgen 1964). Finally it is polygenesis which prevailed facilitating the stigmatization of the savage. Indeed, the secular theory as against religious doctrine came handy for the colonizers. And early anthropology unambiguously upheld the secular view to the advantage of colonialism.

The descriptions about the savage were both negative and positive. One could hold on to either view. The French Catholic was inclined to endorse the negative description and hence would hold the view that the Spanish conquest of the Americas was a blessing for the wild man to be brought to true religion and through that to civilization. On the contrary, the Huguenots stressed the positive endowments of the wild man and would accuse the rapacious Spaniards for endangering the innocent and noble Indians. With the founding of the 'New France' in Canada, a distinctively new French description got endorsement through the good offices of the Jesuits. 'The Indians thus became representative figures of simple virtue, superior in every way to Europeans, save in their ignorance of revelation, and this defect would soon be made good by the labours of missionaries' (Symcox 1972: 227).

The inhabitants of America were 'wild', 'savage', 'barbarous', and 'bestial' as well as 'simple', 'peaceful', 'innocent', and 'uncorrupted by the evils of civilization'. But ' ... the seventeenth century Englishmen were raised on the belief that without religion and a notion of the Deity, men would live like "Savage Beasts"' (Ashcroft 1972: 150). Thomas Hobbes, having described the natural state of man as one of 'a war of all men against all men', referred to American Indians as an illustrative case, whose life is characterized as 'fierce, short-lived, poor and nasty'. That is, even if the savages were noble, being a people without history, religion, and state they needed to be civilized. If they resisted, physical liquidation was the answer. The institution of the modern state is the primary subject matter of political science and it had its theoretical foundation in the social contract theory. Thus, the modern state was introduced as an instrument of the civilizing mission. But by the time the state was instituted in the world of savages, the object of the mission disappeared!

In 1787, Australia's population was entirely aboriginal, but after 200 years of colonization in 1988 it became a mere 1 per cent. The estimates of Native Americans at the time of European contact vary between 2 to 5 million, but after 500 years of European occupation it dwindled to a mere 250,000 (see Snipp 1987). Half of these populations live in 260 reservations meant for them, the remaining are 'integrated' into mixed localities. As Jarvenpa observes: 'Reservation and reserves [have] perpetuated social segregation, administrative paternalism and lower-class status to the Indian people' (1985: 29).

One looks in vain in the entire New World for a 'nation-state' governed by the noble savage: they have been physically liquidated/reduced/dispersed, politically and culturally emaciated. The civilizing mission left hardly any trace of the 'savage other'. Their conceptual liquidation is complete and they are utterly powerless and have been incorporated into the 'world system' with pariah status. One cannot ignore the fact that social science in general and anthropology, political science, and history in particular, did contribute towards the initial marginalization and the ultimate liquidation of the 'savage other'.

The story of the Black other is somewhat different and greatly complicated. First, Africa, the dark continent was part of the Old World; it was also fairly well populated unlike the New World. Second, part of Africa was encapsulated within the ancient Egyptian civilizational region. Third, the colonizers' religion, namely Christianity had to face stiff competition from Islam, another world religion, belonging to the Semitic trio. Therefore, two identities had to be stigmatized: racial (Black) and religious (Islamic). Finally, there were two Africas: pagan and Arab, the former primitive and the latter civilized. Both Black Africa and Islamic Africa stimulated research in social anthropology, history, and political science.

The French philosopher Francois Bernier was the first who attempted a biological classification of the human race in 1648 and he held the view that blackness is essential for the African; the Brachocephalic African was adjudged as inferior to the Dolicocephalic European. Voltaire, the French satirist, held that whites were superior to Negroes (adjective freely used earlier) as the Negroes were to the apes and the apes to oysters. David Hume, the British philosopher, was categorical in his view that Negroes and, in general, all the other species of men were inferior to the whites.

That is, the Black other was invented in the sixteenth century and persisted through the seventeenth and eighteenth centuries. By the nineteenth century, typical physical features, intelligence, and culture got linked and a biological model of humanity was constructed. A whole new discipline called anthropometry emerged. Measurements of the various parts of the body, be it length and shape of nose, texture of hair and/or Cephalic Index were done and it has been argued that there is a relationship between these physical features and one's intelligence, capacity to build institutions, and create culture. The argument was that, those who are Black (and of course, derivatively, those who are Brown and Yellow) lacked mental capacity, intelligence, and hence needed to be civilized. This is the reason why the civilizing mission became the motto of colonialism in Africa.

Convinced that the Africans were incapable of self-rule, Europeans apportioned Africa at the Berlin Conference held in 1885 in the most haphazard vein, completely shattering the integrity of the 'nations' of Africa. The notion of national self-determination by the people was inapplicable to Africans because being peoples without history, they were not nations in colonial Europe's perception. Having accepted the western anthropologists' certification that African society was stateless, the colonizers set out to plant modern states in Africa. Invoking the Weberian notion that state is the only institution endowed with the legitimate authority to handle violence, European colonizers appropriated the right to control the African people. But the paradox that the colonial state is a wholly illegitimate institution was ignored by the European colonizers.

Today racism is derecognized in the constitutions of most democratic states. The United Nations Educational, Scientific and Cultural Organization (UNESCO) made Herculean efforts to demonstrate that while race is a fact, racial superiority, that is, racism is a myth. It is true that people do differ in terms of their physical appearance, but to attribute history, culture, and intelligence to specific physical features is nothing but a figment of the imagination. And yet enormous research was done to uphold this 'fact'. While racism is formally condemned what may be called 'everyday racism' persists with a vengeance in the western countries to this day (Essed 1991). Construction of identity based on race and the practise of racism was reinforced by the research of physical anthropologists and social scientists (see Duster 1990).

In the European Christian view, slave trade and Arab Muslims were closely bound together. And Christianity was projected as the emancipator of the slave. But this view was not endorsed by African Muslims. To them Islam was an attractive religion precisely because it was an African religion. However, the Christian intrusion was justified by missionaries as god's design.

This view was endorsed even by 'secular' leadership. For example, W.E. Gladstone in an article entitled 'Aggression in Egypt' published in 1877 wrote: 'Mohammedanism now appears, in the light of experiences, to be radically incapable of establishing a good or tolerable government over civilized and Christian races ... ' (quoted in Daniel 1966: 348). That is, Muslims were incapable of ruling justly or even competently. Daniel comments: 'The Europeans thought that their imperial achievement was the result of their superior moral culture, and often, that it was the result of their superior religion' (ibid.: 467). This explains the need for othering Islam in general and the Black African Muslim in particular.

Three factors have facilitated to gain control over Muslim Africa: the claim that Christian material civilization is higher; the claim regarding superiority of the moral system of Christianity; and the application of a double standard of judgement (ibid.: 480). Thus Islam was accused of encouraging male sensuality, ill-treating women, and approving slavery and these provided the rationale for the civilizing mission to be launched in Muslim societies. But the policy was not uniform; where Islam posed a threat it was propitiated. Thus, England treated Islam as an ally in fighting both Napoleon and Hinduism and pursued friendship with Turkey and Persia. That is to say, Islam was constructed and/or deconstructed as an other in different sites insofar as this device helped to control it. In these endeavours social science knowledge was of immense help.

The strategy had to be different in the case of South Asia. South Asians could not have been dismissed as peoples without history; they had a long and enduring civilization. The Aryan myth further complicated the situation because it claimed a shared ancestry between Indians and Europeans (see Poliakov 1974). Admittedly a new set of factors needed to be invented to stigmatize Indians. The institutionalized inequality of the caste system, oppression of women, and the presumed inadequacy of the Indian knowledge system came in handy.

Having castigated the ancient Indian knowledge system, Macaulay wanted to create ' ... a class who may be interpreters between us and the millions whom we govern ... a class of persons Indian in blood and colour, but English in tastes, in opinions, in morals and intellect' (quoted in Worsley 1984: 52). And Macaulay did accomplish his mission. According to one commentator, educated Bengalis prided themselves on the use of wine and champagne, pipes, and beef steak. Everything Indian looked primitive and barbarous, dirty, and odious (Misra 1961). There indeed arose an ideological battle between

Anglicists, who patronized colonial administration and the Orientalists who wanted to revive the Indian tradition. Even Indian Marxists
endorsed the beneficial aspect of English education. According to
one evaluation neither Chanakya, the author of the *Arthashastra*, nor
Vyasa, the immortal composer of the Mahabharata could arm the
Indian economist with theoretical tools to solve modern economic
problems (see Desai 1948). Thus colonization of the Indian mind
by the British was a splendid success.

The Oriental peoples of Indian and Egyptian civilizations have
been substantially marginalized because of their inability for self-
governance according to the colonizers. In 1810, Chateaubriand,
a French, justified the conquest of the Orient and he wrote:

Of Liberty they knew nothing, of propriety they have none, force is their
god, when they go for long periods without seeing conquerors who do
heavenly justice, they have the air of soldiers without leaders, citizens
without legislators, and a family without a father. Hence they should be
conquered and colonized. (Quoted in Said 1991: 172)

Exactly 100 years later, in 1910, Balfour, who founded the Asiatic
Society of India, observed:

Western nations as soon as they emerge into history show the beginnings
of those capacities for self-government. You may look through the whole
history of the Orientals, and you will never find traces of self-government.
All their great centuries have been passed under despotism. All their
great contributions to civilizations have been made under that form of
government, under despotism. Conqueror has succeeded conqueror, one
domination has followed another, but never in all the revolutions of fate
and fortune have you seen one of these nations of its own motion establish
what we from the western point of view call self-government. (Ibid.: 32–3)

That was the justification for subjugating the Orient so as to civilize
it. Social anthropology, which was earlier conceived as the study of
'other cultures', is also a child of imperialism and it has invented
'primitive man', the pre-literate society, and the stateless people
(see Chapter 9).

What one witnesses here is an attempt to create marginality through
conceptualization and European thinkers, irrespective of their ideological differences, endorsed this conceptual construction. Karl Marx,
the great revolutionary, Durkheim, the functionalist, and Weber,
the rationalist, in spite of the fact that they were so different in their

ideological orientations have all contributed to the marginalization of not only the savage, the Black, and the Muslim but also the Orientals.

The colonial connection prompted studies by the scholar administrators and European missionaries. They undertook numerous studies to understand the bewildering ethnographic variety they confronted in the colonies. Needless to say their motivations varied—efficient administration of colonies, quenching intellectual curiosity, facilitating proselytization. Apart from anthropology, anthropometry, linguistics, and Lexicography also received a boost. The monumental *Linguistic Survey of India* (17 volumes) undertaken by George Grierson was the first systematic survey of Indian languages. Further several Indian languages got their first grammar books and dictionaries from European missionaries. It is no exaggeration to suggest that most of the languages of the subaltern peoples—tribes and peasantry—owe their identity to the colonizers.

It is far from my intention to suggest that stigmatizing identity and construction of the Other is always done by the Europeans vis-à-vis the Africans and Asians. There was considerable 'othering' among and between the Europeans, although these did not persist. Similarly, the stigmatization of the only surviving superpower of the world by French intellectuals as recent as the early twentieth century is indeed incredible. When opinion was sought from André Maurois, the French professor, regarding the acceptance of a visiting professorship at Princeston University by one of his young friends, Maurois advised:

My dear child ... don't do such a thing! You won't come back alive. You don't know what America is all about. In that country ... men at forty, die of overwork, ... women leave home early in the morning to participate in universal restlessness .... Human beings do not have social life. All they ever talk about is money .... Did you read ... the description of Chicago's slaughter homes? ... And, what about those stories in the newspapers, the ... outlaws, who commit murder in broad day light, with the complicity of police themselves? ... Please give up this trip (quoted in Jean-Philippe 1993: 1–2).

The French intellectual's negative attitude toward the US was in existence for long. Tocqueville concluded on the basis of newspaper reports: 'In America, the majority raises very formidable barriers to liberty of opinion' (1956: 261). And today it is widely claimed that the US is the most successful democracy in the world. What is the background of these Democrats? Paul Marand pronounced: 'In the course of history, Mother Europe has sent to New York the children she wanted to punish—for being Huguenots or Quakers, poor or Jewish, or simply being younger sons. Today those children are grown up; they are at the center of the Universe' (Jean-Philippe 1993: 18).

To be sure French articulations about the US varied across time; both positive and negative views were expressed, but they were largely negative. The US was constructed as the other, indeed a formidable other, of Europe. According to some, the neo-liberal thrust which lies behind the genesis of the EU and its consolidation through a single market and a single currency were forged not out of any idealism, but to enable it to compete effectively with the US and Japan (see Sandholtz and Zysman 1999).

The construction of Jews as the other in Europe, particularly in Nazi Germany, is so well known that I need not elaborate on that. Bauer's description of the plight of Jews is telling.

In elaborating their concept of Jews as non-human, the Nazis described them as parasites … , viruses or loathsome creatures from the animal and insect world (rats and cockroaches). As a parasitic force, the Jews corroded and would ultimately destroy the cultures of their host nations. (1982: 89)

This provided the rationale for the holocaust and for flushing the Jews out of Europe. But enthused by the Zionist movement the establishment of the tiny but strong state of Israel provided them with the required clout. Today the Jewish state of Israel, supported by the sole superpower, is at the centre of the world. The erstwhile Jewish other has not only been destigmatized but has been put on a high pedestal. Can anybody deny that social science scholarship did not facilitate this process?

It is necessary to recall here that the 'standard of civilization' in international society, a step towards globalization, was fixed by the West. These standards reflected the norms and values of the European civilization rooted in the mores of Christendom (see Gong 1984: 14–15). The standard is a mixture of objective and explicit as well as subjective and implicit elements. To practise the latter set in a civilization outside the West necessitated their internalization and institutionalization. This invariably meant creating disjuncture between the past and the present of the non-western civilizations which adopt these standards. Some of the non-European states such as China, Japan, or the Ottoman Empire already had their standards. Therefore, to accept the new standard meant to ignore and marginalize their standards.

The standard was formulated by the middle of the nineteenth century but it was questioned by the early twentieth century. As Sir John Fisher pointed out in 1921, ' ... the conception of "Civilized Society" as a community of nations or states distinct from the rest of the world no longer corresponds with the main facts of contemporary life' (quoted in Gong 1984: 85). The events in the first half of the twentieth century revealed that the so-called civilized states were indulging in utterly uncivilized actions. So much so, historian Collingwood (1942) was constrained to observe that the Germans represented the fourth great barbarism, after the Saracens, the Albigenian heresy, and the Turks.

The point to be noted is that globalization which started in 1500 recognized only the strong; those who were willing to fall in line; or those with some strategic value. The non-European states to be recognized first as having the standard of civilization were: the two strong states, the Ottoman Empire and the Chinese state, Japan and Siam (Thailand) which undertook the required internal reforms (Siam was not colonized also because it was kept as a buffer state between the British and French colonies to minimize conflicts), and Abyssinia (Ethiopia), a centre of pre-colonial Christianity, the only African country not colonized during the scramble of Africa at the end of the nineteenth century (see Gong 1984). It seems that to escape colonialism one should possess appropriate resources—the capacity to pose a threat, willingness to adapt European norms and values, of strategic value to avoid conflict between European states, and/or shared religious sentiment. The invisible hand of social research was present in all these.

Colonialism ended with World War II, and the Cold War persisted barely for 45 years, that is, during 1945–89. We find a shift from the old strategy of constructing others, a shift from specific social categories such as savages, Blacks, Muslims, Africans, Asians, Orientals, and the like; a movement from several dichotomies to one trichotomy—the First World, the Second World, and the Third World. If civilizing mission was the motto of the colonial era, modernization became the motif during the Cold War. Here we come across a new complication because there is a contestation between two modernities, that of capitalist democracies of the First World, and that of socialist regimes of the Second World. The Cold War was a contest to annex the modernizing Third World into one of these modernities.

Why was such a contestation necessary? Because capitalist modernity was 'natural' and total and socialist modernity was 'enlightened' but segmental. To quote political scientist Pletsch,

The Third World is a world of tradition, culture; (culture in the bad sense of the term, that is, religion), irrationality, under-development, over-population, political chaos and so on. The Second World is modern, technologically sophisticated, rational to a degree, but authoritarian and repressive and ultimately inefficient and impoverished by contamination with ideologically motivated socialist elite. The First World is purely modern, a haven of science and utilitarian decision making, technologically efficient, democratic, free, in short, a natural society unfettered by religion and ideology (1981: 574).

One can discern three constructions here: 'we' of the First World, 'they' of the Second World, *and* 'the' Third World which is different from the two other worlds. The Second World is partially good: technologically efficient and advanced, but they do not have multiparty democracy, civil society, or a competitive market. When it comes to the Third World, it is negative in all respects. That is, as we come to the Cold War period, there is a new construction. 'Others' of the colonial period have either been completely deconstructed as in the case of the savage other, or have been reconstructed as in the cases of the Black other and the Oriental other. Instead the three Worlds were put in a hierarchy, the First at the top, the Second, which was partially modern, in the middle, and the Third utterly unmodern, at the bottom.

As Pletsch notes, two methodological consequences for social science followed from this categorization. First, the belief that there exist neatly distinguishable entities such as politics, economics, and society and these should be studied by separate groups of social scientists. Second, there emerged a new academic division of labour.

One clan of social scientists is set apart to study the primitive societies of the Third World—anthropologists. Other clans—economists, sociologists and political scientists—study the Third World only insofar as the process of modernization has begun. The true province of this latter social science is the modern world, especially the natural societies of the West. But again, sub clans of each of these sciences of the modern world are specially outfitted to make forays into the ideological regions of the Second World. (Pletsch 1981: 579)

In addition to the confusions and flawed perceptions that the three-world schema has created for social science as a whole, it also devastated particular disciplines by narrowly defining their scope. This is especially true of sociology and social anthropology (see Chapters 2 and 9). The favoured disciplines of the Cold War era were sociology, development economics, international relations, all of which were viewed as instruments of modernization, economic development, and political stability.

The competition for the Third World between the First and the Second Worlds was also supported through a reconceptualization of the others of the colonial era. This was necessitated by several reasons. First, the Third World consisted of Africa, Asia, and Latin America, the last being racially and culturally proximate to Europe and hence the irrelevance of the civilizing mission as far as the European settler societies were concerned. Second, while all the three continents experienced European colonialism, Asia and Africa had retreatist and Latin America had replicative colonialism (see Chapter 6). While the common feature of the Third World was underdeveloped economy, the constituting units were vastly different historically, politically, and culturally. Third, both the US and the former Soviet Union wanted to create their independent knowledge bases about the Third World. Finally, as the intellectuals of the modernizing Third World came of age, they rejected much of the European formulations about their culture, society, and polity and the presumed reasons for underdevelopment (see Chapter 9).

The neo-orientalist mood was captured by the speech A.I. Mikoyan delivered to the 25th International Congress of Orientalists in 1950. He said.

... the peoples of the Orient create themselves their own science, elaborate their own history, their own culture, their economy; in this way, the peoples of the Orient have been promoted from being objects [matter] of history to the rank of creators .... The duty of the Orientalists in their work is to reflect objectively on the most important processes of the countries of Asia and Africa. ... (Quoted in Abdel-Malek 1963: 122)

This was a direct challenge to the universalism created and propagated by renaissance Europe. The way out was to absorb the erstwhile inferiors, those who were stigmatized as outsiders, under one social category. Globalization is an eminently suitable instrument for the same.

It is pertinent to recall here that 'nation-building' during the Cold War era led to stigmatization of the weak and minority nations within the national states. This is understandable, although not acceptable, in the case of capitalist nation-states wherein cultural homogenization was vigorously pursued. But even in the case of socialist multinational states stigmatization of the weak and minority nations was pursued with alacrity.

Engels had accepted the Hegelian distinction between 'historic' and 'non-historic' nations; the latter being counter-revolutionary needed to be denationalized or exterminated. The forces of enlightenment were represented by nations such as the Germans, Italians, Magyars, and Poles; Russian and Slavic nations represented the dark forces. The Mexicans were 'lazy' and the Slavic people were 'barbarians'. The two most 'scoundrelly nations on earth' were the Chinese and the Yankees, the former 'patriarchal swindlers', the latter 'civilized swindlers' (Marx and Engels 1964: 174).

Marx and Engels referred to the less developed nations as 'people without history', 'remains of nations', 'ruins of people', and their hope was to get attached to more 'progressive' nations, which were 'large', 'well-defined', 'historical', 'great', and who possessed 'undoubted vitality'. The support to the national movement of Poland was intended to administer a blow to Russia, 'the citadel of reactionary force' in Europe and they believed that 'the English working class will never accomplish anything before it has got rid of Ireland' (quoted in Wright 1981: 152). Contrary to the pronounced principle of equity to all nationalities, the power structure of multinational Soviet Union was very lopsided. For example, '... the 1917 list of the Council of the People's Commission (CPC) consisted of 15 persons of whom 14 were Slavs ... and one was a Georgian—Joseph Stalin' (see Moynihan 1993: 116–17). The process of stigmatization abetted by social science research came handy in rationalizing such domination.

Sun Yat-Sen was a great proponent of assimilation of national minorities. In 1921 he said that the non-Han people of China were destined 'to be melted in the same furnace to be assimilated within the Han nationality' (cited in Connor 1984: 67), although he changed his position later. In 1936, Mao Tse-tung pronounced that 'the Moslems must establish their independent and autonomous political power' (cited in Connor 1984: 67, 83) ignoring the communist notions of proletarian dictatorship or proletarian internationalism. It is clear that even the socialists were guilty of stigmatizing the small and weak nations. Admittedly, this profoundly affected the nature of social research in socialist countries.

With the dismantling of the Second World, the world has become one; there is now only one modernity, the capitalist modernity, and all can be equals. But to become equals the inhabitants of the erstwhile Second World and Third World should endorse certain values and adopt certain institutional arrangements. The Structural Adjustment Programme (SAP) wherein there ought to be a minimal state, a free market, and a vibrant civil society is the new prescription. Today's ideal society is one in which the state, the market, and the civil society co-exist and a division of labour between them is being accepted. If a country, nation, or people do not accept this prescription, they remain marginalized or excluded. Therefore, one no more hears about the civilizing mission of the colonial times or modernization project of the Cold War era but only of good governance.

During the colonial times, the stigmatized others were told that they were incapable of self-government and hence the justification of the colonial state. During the Cold War, the Third World democratic states were castigated for their being 'soft' and hence the need to establish modern 'hard' states (see Myrdal 1971). But now, the prescription is to roll back the state and create minimal states so that they can globalize swiftly. Governance is a more encompassing phenomenon than government; it embraces governmental institutions but it also subsumes informal, non-governmental mechanisms whereby those persons and organizations within its purview move ahead, satisfy their needs, and fulfil their wants (Rosenau 1992: 4). To globalize is to catch up with this prescription and there is no possibility to opt out.

The chief agent of this prescription is the erstwhile First World and within it the only surviving superpower, the United States of America. The US is aided and abetted by the Bretton Woods institutions. The real deficit of the Second World was the absence of

multiparty democracy; one party or 'peoples democracy' was stigmatized as totalitarianism. To be sure, in socialist regimes state took
over the market and civil society was sponsored by the state. That is,
structural differentiation, a prerequisite for modernization, was indeed absent. As for the Third World, its real maladies are primordial
collectivism, casteism, communalism, and corruption. But all these
persist in the First World also although their manifestations differ.

As is well known, Islamophobia is rampant and discrimination
against Asians and Africans persists, not to speak of gender oppression in the First World. So in the modernized West too, primordial
collectivism of which the Third World has been accused of for
long persists to this day. The point I want to make is that negative
attributes are not exclusive or an inherent feature of a group, community, or civilization. But it is a matter of labelling by the powerful
and the dominant, through a process of othering so that they can
be excluded from the mainstream. Much of western social science
has facilitated this process.

And yet there are many who endorse the unity of globalization.
For Wallerstein there is only one single world which in the final
analysis is a capitalist one. Even the communist state is merely a
'... collective capitalist firm as long as it remains a participant in
the capitalist market' (1979: 68). The building blocks of the world
system are put on a continuum consisting of countries on the periphery on the one hand, and core countries on the other. Clearly,
Wallerstein's model at the core is an economic one. There are others
who focus on particular aspects of the economy to define the world
as one. For example, Cox writes: 'The global economy is the system
generated by globalizing production and global finance' (1992: 30).

In sociology, the focus is on the 'intensification of world-wide
social relations which link distant localities ... ' (Giddens 1990: 64).
In anthropology, it is the spread of culture and lifestyles and in communication studies, it is the standardization of culture brought about
by mass communication which is seen as the kernel of globalization.
If the earlier dichotomous and trichotomous constructions of the
world cognized it in spatial and temporal terms, the current one-
world conceptualization perceives it in sectoral terms—economic,
cultural, political, social, and so on.

However, there are others who take a more inclusive view of
globalization, which ' ... refers to all those processes by which the
people of the world are incorporated into a single world society,

global society' (Albrow 1990: 9). If the world is one, logically, there could only be one unified social science. Pleading specifically the case for sociology, Margaret Archer writes:

I want to advocate a single sociology, whose ultimate unity rests on ac-knowledging the universality of human reasoning; to endorse a single world, whose oneness is based on adopting a realistic ontology; and to predicate any services this Discipline can give to this world upon accepting the fundamental unicity of Humanity (1991: 131).

It is necessary and useful to list the rationale behind Archer's ad-vocacy of 'a single sociology'. First, with the demise of positivism, sociology has become 'increasingly localized'. Second, the current celebration of diversity, tradition, locality, and indigenization are occurring through a retreat from 'international endeavours'. Third, the emergence of 'false universalism' such as (1) modernization theory which lays down a common teleological track for all societ-ies, (2) dependency theory which divides the world into the core and peripheries with the ultimate objective of 'modernising' the latter, and (3) post-modernism which is in effect a repudiation of 'modernity' (ibid.: 132–5).

The domain assumptions to which Archer anchors her argu-ment are, however, questionable. First, it is true that positivism has been vehemently criticized and its excesses have been exorcised but it is not true that positivism is dead. Those methodological orientations, which arose as alternatives to positivism, do retain certain aspects of it. Second, international endeavours and localized enterprises are not necessarily mutually exclusive; they can and do co-exist. Third, there is and should be a wide variety of moderniza-tions. Therefore, modernization becomes a false universalism only when it is equated with westernization. Finally, the juxtaposing of the universal (one world) with the traditional/local (many worlds) smacks of western epistemological dualism. Therefore, to build an authentic social science, that is, a social science which incorporates all varieties of human experiences, it is necessary to question the domain assumptions behind untenable divisions of the world into traditional and modern and/or into First, Second, and Third Worlds. Further, one must also avoid the unsustainable assumption that the world is one. I have argued elsewhere that:

... a world society discerned in terms of one culture, one civilization, one communication system and the like is not only not possible but not even desirable. It is not possible because world society is an aggregation of state-societies, the effective units of operation. Specificities of particular societies and civilizations emanate from geography, history, culture, political arrangement or level of economic development. That is, pluralization encapsulates the very conception of world society (Oommen 1995b: 266).

However, a 'world society' viewed in terms of shared technology and a common communication system does exist. But it encapsulates only a thin layer of human population and institutions. At any rate, when values are transplanted from one civilization to another, they lead to pluralization. For example, Buddhism in India and Japan, Islam in Iran and Indonesia, Catholicism in Italy and Brazil, Protestantism in the United Kingdom and the US differ. That is, globalization carries with it elements of diversification and hybridization; one world splits into many worlds. Islamic socialism, Japanese modernity, and Hindu capitalism are manifestations of these processes. To talk of unilinear modernization and the emergence of a world society is to ignore the 'globalization of diversity' (Nederveen Pieterse 1994: 165).

Finally, human society is divided spatially, culturally, as well as temporarily. But the revolutions in technology particularly in transport and communication facilitate humankind to cope with it. However, the relentless march of modernity unsettles many a traditional identity which prompts an incessant search for roots among peoples leading to revivalism and even fundamentalism and as Van der Berghe writes: 'The search for roots is a temporal retreat from the present from which none is exempt' (1983: 246).

This belies the existence of a 'modern' society even in the West; it seems that the advocacy of 'sociology for one world' ignores not only the cultural-spatial dimensions but also the temporal dimensions of societies (see Chapter 7). It is against this background that one should view the notion of multiple modernities, post-modernism, cultural studies, and global studies.

I emphasize this point because sociology, defined and practised as the study of modern society in the contemporary West as noted above, often tends to ignore the continuity between the pre-industrial agrarian past and the industrial present; the feudal past and the capitalist present; the capitalist past and the socialist/welfarist present imparting an artificiality to western sociology. Having allocated the pre-modern society to social anthropology (and/or history), the disengagement of the past from the present appeared to be natural and the assumption that transformation is necessarily and always a process of displacement of the old by the new became axiomatic. The recognition of the process of continuity would entail the acceptance of an accretion syndrome in social transformation and these in unison would at least partly help in correcting the cognitive distortion which has crept into western sociology, liberating it from its obsession with modern society.

9

The Pasts and Futures of Anthropology and Sociology
Implications of Shifting Locations

B oth modern anthropology and sociology[1] emerged in Europe but at different points in time and in different political circumstances to meet drastically different purposes. In spite of this, there has been considerable convergence between these disciplines outside Europe. To ignore their initial divergences and focus only on their subsequent convergences is to indulge in 'retreat into the present' (Elias 1987) relegating the specificities of their trajectories. At any rate, to project the 'futures' of sociology and anthropology it is necessary to recall their 'known pasts' which impact on and have implications for the shifting locations of these disciplines. Both sociology and anthropology had passed through two distinct 'locations'—the colonial state and the nation-state—and are at present in the throes of a third location, the 'post-national' globalizing world. I propose to argue that the processes implicated in the crystallization of these locations, namely, colonialism, nationalism, and globalism, have deeply moulded the career of these disciplines. To explicate the argument I shall attempt a broad but brief comparison of sociology and anthropology in three locations—western Europe, where they originated, and North America and South Asia, wherein they were transplanted.[2]

There is no consensus about the time of origin of academic anthropology (cf. Harris 1968; Hodgen 1964), but there is broad agreement on two counts: (1) anthropology flowered during the colonial period and (2) the essence of the anthropological perspective is to study the Other, because it enables a better understanding of one's own society. European anthropologists analysed three others—Savage, Black, and Ethnographic—who were different, racially and culturally, and were located at a great distance in time and space from Europe. The assumption regarding the temporal distance entailed a value judgement; the Others studied were believed to be located at a low ebb in the evolutionary chain. The allusion to spatial distance was a fact in that the others were 'elsewhere peoples' (Trouillot 2003) located at geographically distant sites far away from Europe. These two 'distances' in conjunction also facilitated the conception that the others are inferiors.

The Savage Other was assigned the lowest rung in the hierarchy of the great chain of being according to the Western/Christian doctrine of monogenesis that endorsed a common origin for all human beings. It is true that 'Savages' did exist in Europe, for example, the Samis of Scandinavia and the Highlanders of Scotland, but they were culturally absorbed into the European mainstream although with low esteem. But it is the discovery of the New World—the Americas, Australia, and New Zealand—which facilitated the assigning of Savages to distant locations, temporal and spatial, with very low status; the New World was perceived as the epicentre of Savages. While project homogenization launched by the institution of nation-state in western Europe facilitated the absorption of Savages, in the New World the colonizers recognized and maintained the racial and cultural differences between them and the Savages. But the fact that the native Red Indian was not perceived as racially inferior to the migrant white and the eventual recognition of 'Savages' as human beings with souls by Christianity and their conversion into that religion led to the conceptual liquidation of the Savage. According the H. White, 'the idea of the Wild Man [read Savage] was progressively despatialized. This despatialization was attended by a compensatory process of psychic interiorization. And the result has been that modern cultural anthropology has conceptualized the idea of wildness as the repressed content of *both* civilized *and* primitive humanity' (1972: 7, italics in the original).

The Black Other, with its territorial location in Africa, was the other Other in anthropology (Thornton 1983). Black Africa became the preferred site for fieldwork for European anthropologists. The Black Other, as an inferior Other, found easy acceptance in Europe. As Y.D. Nash notes, 'In English image black became a partisan word. A black sheep in the family, a black mark against one's name, a black day, a black look, a black lie, a black guard, and a black ball all were expressions built into cultural consciousness' (1974: 162–3). Probably this facilitated the export of Black Africans during the colonial period to the Americas. But their mode of incorporation determined their status at the points of arrival; if in the United States of America their initial incorporation was as slaves, in Brazil, thanks to the policy of 'racial democracy', they were conferred some dignity and equity (see Fernandes 1969). The differences in social status accorded to the Black Other in different locations—Africa, North America, and Latin America—has also impacted the discipline of anthropology in these spaces. Gradually, the focus shifted from Savage Other to Black Other (see Barker 1998).

Gradually, the biological basis of human superiority/inferiority anchored to race and the justification given to the practice of racism has come to be interrogated through research in physical anthropology in North America. The race-culture antinomy delinked race and culture; the attempt was to underplay the distinctions based on race and deny the practice of racism. At any rate, 'American anthropologists deliver inchoate messages about anthropological understandings of race and racism' (Shanklin 2000). In fact, the American Anthropological Association has already recommended to the US Government to eliminate the term race from the 2010 census because research in human genome shows that DNA of human beings is 99.9 per cent alike irrespective of their physical characteristics. This points to the gradual conceptual liquidation of the Black Other as a racial category. In contrast, the prevalence of cultural diversities is focused upon, perhaps over emphasized. As early as the 1920s, it was claimed that 600 separate cultures which can be grouped into seven cultural types existed in the USA (Wissler 1923). Perhaps this explains the metamorphosis of social anthropology into cultural anthropology in the process of its transplantation from Europe to North America.

The conceptual liquidation of Savage Other and the gradual disapproval of the notion of Black Other do not mean the conventional subject matter of anthropology has or will disappear; the Ethnographic Other has become the new focus.[3] The Ethnographic Other is a general and generalized Other and its specificity is based on culture/civilization rather than on race. But the process of othering can and did continue and the Oriental Other[4] (which is an Other in other social/human sciences too) at the civilizational level emerged (see Said 1991).

The stigmatization of the Orient was in tune with the inferiorization of the Savage Other and Black Other, which, in combination provided the justification for the civilizing mission launched by the West. And western anthropology played a significant role in this context. The rise of sociology in the West was in sharp contrast to this. The initial mission of sociology was to study the modern industrial society of Europe. 'The emergence of industrial society is the prime concern of sociology', wrote Ernest Gellner (1964: 35). Not only that, 'Sociology...is the offspring of modernity and it bears the birthmark of modern parentage. Its mission is to understand the specificity of the modern world to which it belongs' (Heller 1987: 391).

Imaginations can and do crystallize independent of location. And the wide variety of dichotomous constructions in sociology and social/cultural anthropology are often the product of wild imaginations bereft of the authenticity of social reality which these disciplines were expected to be engaged in. An eloquent example of that is the age-old community–society dichotomy which has numerous incarnations. Community could be a structure, a sentiment, or merely a designated territory, and it is often juxtaposed with society in sociology. But as Robert A. Nisbet observes, 'Community begins as a moral value, only gradually does the secularisation of this concept become apparent in sociological thought in the nineteenth century' (1966: 18). Community which engaged anthropologists is all encompassing, a 'cradle to grave' arrangement to recall the tempting phrase introduced by Robert Redfield (1955). The secularized version of community is society, characterized by 'secondary contacts over wide geographical areas' and 'considerable mobility', according to S.P. Hays (1989: 12), the staple of sociologists.

However, the 'eclipse of the community' did not occur, the primary group was 're-discovered' in the industrial-urban setting, and the tradition–modernity dichotomy was pronounced to be a misplaced polarity (Gusfield 1967). If so, the attributed estrangement between sociology and social anthropology in Europe seems to be the manifestation of academic vested interests. The intertwining between community and society is self-evident and one cannot be understood independent of the other. Pursuantly, sociology and social anthropology are inextricably bonded and they cannot be separated without harming each other. This became self-evident when these disciplines were transplanted outside Europe, to the analysis of which I will turn now. However, it is necessary to briefly advert to the implications of linking sociology with modernity and the nation-state at this juncture.

There are several implications of linking sociology with modernity and the nation-state. I shall list two self-evident consequences of linking sociology and modernity here, deferring the discussion on linking sociology with the nation-state to a later point. One, the non-modern societies will not witness the birth and flowering of sociology, which is a privilege of modern societies. In this rendition the division of labour between sociology and social anthropology is immutable, the latter eternally consigned to the study of traditional societies, an inadmissible proposition. Two, logically, sociology should wither away as modernity recedes into the background; with the forging ahead of globality, sociology will meet with its inevitable demise. It should be emphasized here that the historical conjunctions which facilitated the birth of particular disciplines in specific locations need not repeat themselves. Different circumstances do lead to the birth of particular branches of knowledge in different locations and then spread to other locations. The resilience of anthropology is an eloquent example of this phenomenon, it is alive and well in spite of the demise of colonialism. The continuous recasting of disciplines is an inevitable survival mechanism which is constantly happening.

The series of dichotomies—primitive/savage versus civilized, orient versus occident, traditional versus modern—receded into the background with the eclipse of colonialism and a trichotomy—First, Second, and Third World—emerged in their place with the onset of the Cold War. The conceptualization of these three worlds determined the new division of labour among social scientists. The three worlds were conceived differently: the First World was purely and totally modern; the Second World, technologically modern but politically non-modern; and the Third World was a world of tradition, irrationality, underdevelopment, over population, and political chaos. Project modernization replaced the civilizing mission of the colonial time and European social scientists changed their roles in this context (see Chapter 8).

The task assigned to the peoples of the Orient (read the Third World) by the Second World to produce their own knowledge system unsettled the self-assigned monopoly of Europe in this context. To challenge the area studies regime launched by the First World, the Second World too started producing knowledge about the Third World. The metamorphosis that occurred in the erstwhile colonies called for a new approach because they got differentiated into two: some parts of the New World—North America, Australia, and New Zealand—got incorporated into the First World, and the other part of the New World—Latin America—became part of the Third World. Because of its poor economic condition, Latin America could not launch a vigorous area studies' programme; rather it became an area to be studied by First World scholars. Given this, the relevant unit for the present comparison is North America because of its material affluence and the rapid progress the region made in the social sciences.

While both North America and South Asia were erstwhile European colonies, they vary drastically with regard to the type of colonialism they were subjected to: North America had 'replicative' colonialism and South Asia had 'retreatist' colonialism (see Oommen 1991). The colonizers reproduce their society, polity, economy, and culture on the site of replicative colonialism because the local elements are weak and marginalized, if not completely destroyed. In contrast, the colonizers retreat from colonies where they face stiff nationalist resistance and opposition. The local society and culture are largely retained, but economy and polity are superimposed. This produces a new amalgam of the local/national and alien/global. I suggest that the two situations differently impact on the transplantation of social sciences, here, social anthropology and sociology. In spite of the dismantling of colonialism, the perception about the subject matter of social anthropology and sociology drastically varied between West Europe, North America, and South Asia. Social anthropology is defined as the study of primitive peoples (Lévi-Strauss 1966) and/or the study of other cultures (Beattie 1964) in

Europe. In contrast, the North American sociologist Harold Fallding holds that 'cultural and social anthropology comprise neither more nor less than the sociology of simpler peoples. So I think one is entitled to claim all of it for sociology' (1968: 71). And, the South Asian social anthropologist M.N. Srinivas is equally forthright: '... the traditional but irrational distinction between sociology and social anthropology is so disastrous. A true science of society must include the study of all societies in space as well as time—primitive, modern and historical' (1966: 164).

However, North America retained the distinction between sociology and social anthropology, but it re-christened the latter as cultural anthropology, as noted above. Cultural anthropologists of North America studied the tribes, the First Nations, of their countries as well as peasants and tribes of the Third World, facilitated through the regime of area studies. In contrast, North American sociologists rarely studied tribes included in the Savage slot by their colleagues in cultural anthropology; they studied race-relations, that is, White–Black interactions without endorsing the notion of the Black Other. South Asian social anthropologists initially focused on the study of tribes but gradually started studying peasantry as well as urban centres. In contrast, it is rarely that sociologists of South Asia studied tribes, but certainly studied rural India and urban centres. These differing inclinations of social anthropologists and sociologists of South Asia indicate the persisting traditional influence of their respective disciplines on them.

We may recall here the distinction between tribal communities and peasant societies in social/cultural anthropology. Tribal communities are conceptualized as social structurally distinct and culturally autonomous entities. In contrast, peasant/folk society is a part-society constituting an important element in the wider civilization which has both rural and pre-industrial urban elements (Foster 1953). The popular notion of rural–urban dichotomy, which was later re-christened as 'rural–urban continuum' in Europe could not be applied in North America and South Asia; the rural segment in these regions had peasantry as well as tribes, which are distinct. To capture this complexity it is necessary to postulate a trichotomy—tribe, peasant, and urban (for an example from South Asia, see Oommen 1967a). This illustrates how the nature of empirical reality in specific locations calls for reformulation of concepts that have emerged elsewhere and shape the scope of particular disciplines.

How can one understand the differences in orientation of social/cultural anthropology in the three regions—West Europe, North America, and South Asia? As J. Fabian notes '...nineteenth century anthropology sanctioned an ideological process by which relations between the West and its other, between anthropology and its object, were conceived not only as difference but as distance in space and time' (1983: 147). But the Savages of North America, consisting of the pre-colonial inhabitants, became fellow nationals and co-citizens. Furthermore, in North America, anthropology is conceived as holistic and culture-centric. In contrast, sociology is society-centric and segmental, in that the different societal dimensions are analysed, ignoring the totality. The fact that North America's native Savages and imported Blacks were 'within people' studied by White anthropologists who are themselves 'outsiders' as compared with European anthropologists who studied 'elsewhere people', has facilitated this process through a role-reversal (cf. Mintz 1998). There is an interesting trichotomy emerging here: the White American anthropologist, a cultural and racial outsider, studied the American Savage who is a cultural and racial insider as well as the African-American Black who is also a cultural and racial outsider. And yet all the three are legal insiders, that is, citizens of the same country. These factors facilitated an agreed academic division of labour between cultural anthropology and sociology *within* North America, and consequently their peaceful co-existence.

But, the relationship between social anthropology and sociology is hostile in Europe; in fact, European social anthropologists looked down upon sociology (see Chapter 2). The superiority of social anthropology as a discipline that studied 'elsewhere' peoples through participant observation is articulated aloud. In fact, the North American sociologist Homans testifies to the stigmatization of sociology by British social anthropologists (1962: 113–19).

The situation in South Asia is also drastically different from that of western Europe; as in North America, the South Asian social anthropologists too study fellow citizens and co-nationals. But on two counts, however, the situation in South Asia and North America differ. One, in North America the indigenous population has dwindled substantially in the last 500 years and at present they constitute a mere 1 per cent of the national population in the United States of America. Of this 50 per cent are in reservations, areas recognized as their exclusive habitats and the other half are dispersed, marginalized, and impoverished (Jarvenpa 1985). The condition of the indigenous peoples in Canada is equally dismal (see Roosens 1989).

The situation of India's indigenous people[5] is in stark contrast to this; they are cultural and legal insiders like the Indian anthropologists who studied them. The 461 STs of India constitute 8 per cent (that is, over 80 million) of the national population and the majority of them live in their ancestral homelands. In fact, 70 per cent of them live in two enclaves in central India and north-east India and, of the 35 states and union territories of India, the tribal population is in majority in five wherein their political clout is evident (see Oommen 1989, for a comparison between the indigenous peoples of India and the USA). This is to say, if the traditional object of study of anthropology is an endangered species in North America, in South Asia, particularly in India, it is alive and well. This has serious political implications for the practice of anthropology. If in North America the anthropologist often takes on an advocacy role and pleads for the protection of human rights of the indigenous peoples, in South Asia the anthropologist is invariably inclined to plead for the protection of citizenship entitlements of the tribal population.

The second difference between North America and South Asia in this respect is also important for the practice of anthropology. While the cultural specificities of the indigenous peoples of North America are recognized, there is no evident enthusiasm to assimilate or integrate them into the national mainstream. In contrast, there are at least three distinct views regarding the relationship between the tribal and non-tribal peoples of India. If Verrier Elwin (1957), the British missionary-turned-anthropologist, advocated preservation of the cultural integrity of India's tribes, the Indian anthropologist D.N. Majumdar (1939) preferred cautious acculturation through mutual borrowing of cultural elements between tribes and non-tribes of India. In contrast, according to the Indian 'sociologist' G.S. Ghurye (1979 [1932]; 1963 [1943]), the tribes of India are but backward Hindus and the entire Indian population is gradually evolving into a single 'Indian race'. Indian Anthropologist B.S. Guha (1951) too attested the unity of the 'Indian race', but advocated a cautious approach. He wrote

The essential thing is to realize that the tribal and general population are inhabitants of the same country and their interests are closely interwoven for good or bad...The administration of primitive tribes should be so planned that the purpose is served by developing them as their own models and thought, but also gradually bringing them up as full and integral members of the country and participating like the rest in her joys and sorrows (Guha 1951: 44).

These differing approaches to tribes in North America and South Asia are bound to affect the discipline of social/cultural anthropology and pursuantly, the discipline of sociology in these regions. In West Europe the object of social anthropological analysis is a distinct and distant 'Other'; but the subject matter of sociology is the similar and proximate fellow nationals and co-citizens. In North America too, the indigenous peoples who constitute the object of study in cultural anthropology are distinct in cultural terms and distant on the evolutionary scale but proximate in space; they are fellow countrymen and co-citizens. As for the North American sociologist, the object of study is fellow citizens but drawn from a wide variety of ethnic groups and cultural contexts. In the case of South Asia, the impulse for integrating the tribal peoples, either through complete assimilation or through selective acculturation, into the national mainstream is strong and persisting. Consequently there is considerable overlap between the disciplines of sociology and social anthropology.[6]

Instead of recognizing the historical circumstances that led to the spread of anthropology and sociology, both of which originated in Europe, and the metamorphosis they have undergone in the process of transplanting to different locations, some writers tend to stigmatize the discipline of anthropology. I shall recall a sample of these articulations because they have negative implications for the practice of the discipline outside Europe. Kathleen Gough (1968), who taught anthropology in North America and did fieldwork in South Asia, famously remarked that anthropology is a 'child of Western imperialism'. Similarly, G.D. Berreman (1968), who also taught anthropology in North America and did fieldwork in South Asia, was concerned about using results of anthropological research against the people who were studied. West European anthropologist Claude Lévi-Strauss (1966) conceded that knowledge produced by anthropology legitimized colonial regimes.

A number of non-Europeans too hold negative perceptions about anthropology. While most of them refer to 'academic colonialism' of the West (read West Europe and North America) in general, a few have specifically referred to anthropology. For example, Talal Asad (1973) sees anthropology as a product of unequal encounter between the dominant West and the dominated Third World. And, the Sri Lankan social scientist Susantha Goonatilake (2001) has characterized anthropology in his country as 'a Eurocentric misadventure'. Whether one accepts or rejects these views, they have serious implications for the discipline of anthropology. In labelling anthropology as an instrument of domination by the West over the rest, anthropology's academic legitimacy erodes in the non-West.

Generally speaking, sociology is not subjected to such stigmatization as it is firmly anchored on the nation-state. But an unanticipated consequence of this is that sociology has become utterly state-centric. And, thanks to the conflation between state and nation, 'national sociologies' emerge and disappear with the rise and fall of sovereign states. In a book entitled *National Traditions in Sociology* published in 1989, there are two separate chapters on the 'national' traditions of West Germany and East Germany. If the book had been published after the fall of the Berlin Wall, there would have been only one national tradition in German Sociology! In the same book there is but one chapter on the national tradition of Soviet Union (see Genov 1989). Had the book been published after the dismantling of the Soviet Union, there could have been as many national traditions as successor sovereign states. Similarly, if the Indian subcontinent had not been partitioned there would have been only one Indian sociology; now we have three 'national' sociologies—Bangladeshi, Indian, and Pakistani—in the region. This means for every sovereign state there is a 'national' sociology!

There are several implications of this. Let me note just three of them. One, those nations which did not succeed in creating their own sovereign states will not have their sociologies, there is a French sociology but no sociology of Brittany; there is a Spanish sociology, but no Catalan sociology; there is a British sociology, but no Welsh sociology. The South Asian situation is more intriguing. Indian sociology encapsulates within it Bengali, Punjabi, Tamil, and several other sociologies none of which is conceded autonomy. To complicate matters, the sociology of Punjab is apportioned between India and Pakistan; that of Bengal, between India and Bangladesh; and Tamil sociology, between India and Sri Lanka. This is to say, the integrity of sociology as a discipline is mutilated because of its inextricable intertwining with the state, a western trap.

Two, to link sociology with nation-state is against the very grain of the discipline. The primary mission of sociology is to study the wide variety of social structures and cultural patterns. That is, sociology has a disciplinary vested interest in diversity, both social and cultural, which it shares with nations. In contrast, the western nation-states relentlessly pursued the goal of creating homogeneous societies. It is an unfortunate paradox that, in spite of their similarity in orientation to cultural diversity, sociology and nation are chained together to an institution, the nation-state, which pursues a goal inimical to their interests. For an authentic flowering of sociology, its co-terminality with the nation-state should be dismantled.

Three, sociology gets linked with the pathologies of state-sponsored nationalism, the three important manifestations of which are racism, religious fundamentalism, and linguistic chauvinism. And wherever sociology falls into the shadow of pathological versions of nationalism, it loses its humanistic value orientation. The way out for sociology is to consciously pursue emancipatory nationalism anchored to secularism, democracy, and humanism. For this, sociology should distance itself from the state and acquire and retain its autonomy, a task largely achieved by West European anthropology in the post-colonial era.

Traditionally, European anthropologists studied 'stateless societies', which is actually a conceptual nullity because no society ever existed without an authority system be it a tribal chieftain, council of elders, monarchy, democracy, and the like. But A.R. Radcliffe-Brown wrote in 1940, 'The state in this sense (that is having sovereignty and its own will) does not exist in the phenomenal world; it is a fiction of the philosophers. What does exist is an organisation, that is, a collection of individual human beings connected by a common system of relations...There is no such thing as the power of the state...' (1955 [1940]: xiii).

Whether the state is an empirical reality or not may be debatable but the government is, and the anthropologist needs to keep this in mind while studying societies. I am not arguing that western anthropologists always kept a conscious distance from the state, but suggesting that insofar as 'the power of the state' is not recognized as an empirical reality, it is not under the pale of their analyses. The relevant point here is, this is in contrast to sociology whose link with the institution of the nation state is explicit.

I have suggested that due to the passage from colonialism to the Cold War and their attendant goals of civilizing mission and moderniza- tion respectively, the disciplines of anthropology and sociology too are undergoing changes. With the disappearance of the tripartite division of the world—First, Second, and Third—and the emergence of the 'Global Age', the world has come to be perceived as one. The national sociologies are believed to be disappearing and the new refrain is 'global sociology'. This was clearly articulated in the XII World Congress of Sociology held in 1990, the theme of which was 'Sociology for One World: Unity and Diversity'.

In social/cultural anthropology such considerations are rare, the concern being the spread of culture and lifestyles which manifest not only in homogenization but also in pluralization, traditionali- zation, and hybridization, thereby recognizing cultural diversity as an essential aspect of the ongoing process of globalization (see Oommen 2005[a]). This is *not* in consonance with the conven- tional idea of recognizing cultural specificities of communities by anthropologists. And, globalization of cultural diversities give rise to global cultural flows conditioned by ethnoscapes, mediascapes, technoscapes, financescapes, and ideoscapes which rendered the world social reality fluid, according to Arjun Appadurai (1997: 27–47). That is, the tranquillity of the cultural world is disturbed by global cultural flows.

However, two points need to be noted here. One, the vast major- ity of human population does not experience any spatial mobility in spite of globalization. But, thanks to satellite communication, they are constantly exposed to alien influences at their own loca- tions. Two, the turbulence of migration started in the sixteenth century with geographical discoveries and colonialism that followed it. Although 40 to 50 million migrants left Europe between 1846 and 1924, 90 per cent of them went to the Americas. Furthermore, 12 million enslaved Africans were brought to the same region bet- ween the seventeenth and the nineteenth centuries (see Trouillot 2003: 30–1). These developments are prompting social/cultural anthropology to abandon the traditional notions of highly localized, boundary-maintaining, holistic, primordialist images of cultural form and substance as is evident from the works published in the 1980s and since (see, for example, Hannerz 1989; Marcus and Fischer 1986: 66–75; Thornton 1988). This is to say that anthropology as a discipline anchored on territoriality—the non-West, East, South,

Third World, or specific pockets within them—has disappeared.

The turbulence of large-scale migration which started during the colonial period continues and its impact has affected the disciplines of anthropology and sociology, albeit in different ways. During the colonial period Europeans migrated in large numbers to the New World—Americas, Australia, and New Zealand—and settled down, but the number of European migrants to South Asia, for example, was limited in spite of colonization of the region. On the other hand, large numbers of indentured labour were taken to several destinations from South Asia creating a new system of slavery (Tinker 1974). South Asian anthropologists and sociologists have studied for the first time their countrymen located outside their countries leading to the emergence of a new specialization; studies in diaspora provided graphic accounts of South Asian migrants settled away from their homelands.

With the eclipse of colonialism and the coming of post-colonial states the patterns of migration changed drastically. The new immigrants from South Asia went to West Europe and North America for higher studies, particularly in the fields of science and technology. The hope at that time was that they will return and contribute to the 'nation-building', process. But most of them did not and the talk about 'brain drain' became common by the 1970s and 1980s. The 'brain drain' spurred a large number of studies in sociology and anthropology and UNESCO sponsored some of them (see, for example, Atal and Oglio 1987).

Those who stayed back and worked in metropolitan countries after obtaining training were dubbed as anti-national and unpatriotic during the Cold War era but they are hailed as trail blazers in the emerging Global Age; those who were accused of causing brain drain are getting enlisted in the 'brain pool' of the world. The implications of the changing compositions of immigrants and attitudes towards them, for sociology and social/cultural anthropology, need to be noted here. First, the old practice of West European and North American scholars studying 'elsewhere' peoples and cultures is persisting, but shrinking fast. Second, the South Asian sociologists and social anthropologists are studying their own people located away from their homelands and this is assuming increased importance. Third, South Asian sociologists and anthropologists who have become citizens or residents of the countries in West Europe and North America study not only their ancestral homelands but also the societies in which they live and work. Fourth, a formidable fund of knowledge is being created by the 'the scholars in Diaspora' who often look at the social reality they study wearing a different lens. Finally, the emergence of multi-sited field research prompts the same researcher to traverse different field areas as against the conventional single field site (Marcus 1995). These developments are bound to change irreversibly the old conceptions such as 'the Other', the distinction between the emic and etic perspectives, centrality of participant observation as *the* method, and consequently the conventional distinction between sociology and social/cultural anthropology persisting in Europe.

Notes

1. Although the focus of this chapter is on sociology and social anthropology, in its origin and spread, anthropology as a whole consisting of physical anthropology, ethnography, ethnology, and pre-historic archaeology were bound together. Therefore, anthropology and social anthropology are referred to interchangeably in this chapter.
2. Although both North America and South Asia were largely British colonies (with the exceptions of Quebec in Canada or Pondicherry [now Puducherry] and Goa in South Asia), the types of colonialism they experienced drastically varied, which, in turn, moulded sociology and anthropology in these post-colonial spaces. This indicates the importance of locations to which they were transplanted.
3. It is not suggested that the focus of anthropology shifted successively from the Savage Other to the Black Other to the Ethnographic Other. But the centrality of one Other over another Other shifted gradually for the reasons indicated.
4. Although Said imagines the whole of Orient in the singular, I have suggested elsewhere that there are at least three possible Orients, each of which could be viewed with different attitudes and orientations by the West. The Near Orient, broadly the Egyptian civilizational region, was geographically the most proximate and predominantly populated by one of the peoples of the Book—the Muslims—and yet an object of stigmatization because of the prevalence of slavery and oppression of women. The Far Orient, the area of Chinese civilizational region, was geographically and mentally distant from Europe and yet the object of admiration for its technology, bureaucracy, and religion. The attitude towards the Middle Orient—the Indian civilizational region—was mixed: it was admired for its ancient civilization, Sanskrit language, and Aryan connections, but despised for the caste system and oppression of women (see Oommen 2005[a]: 160).

5. The preferred self-labelling by the tribes of India is *adivasis* (early set-
    tlers), but this unsettles the view that India was the original ancestral
    homeland of Aryan Hindus. Understandably, those Hindus who pursue
    the idea of creating a Hindu nation in India contest this claim. The
    Indian state and some anthropologists/sociologists too are averse to
    this claim by the 'tribal' population.

6. This overlap is taken cognizance of and the close collaboration of
    social anthropology with sociology is advocated. The rationale for this
    is articulated thus: '... in a country such as India which includes nearly
    30 million tribal people, 60 million Scheduled Castes and nearly 160
    million Other Backward Classes, sociology has to be taught in close
    association with social anthropology' (Srinivas et al. 1961: 26). This
    view endorses social anthropology's conventional interest in studying
    the underprivileged Other.

PART III

10

Y.B. Damle
The Teacher, the Researcher, and the Scholar

I have been asked to deliver a public lecture on 'The Sociology of Y.B. Damle' by the Department of Sociology of University of Pune. But for three reasons I refrain from doing so. One, it would have taken much more time than that was available to me given the short notice, for preparing the lecture. Two, I do not intend to attempt an exhaustive review of all the works by Damle but to highlight a few major trends. Three, given my affinity to Professor Damle as a person, as a teacher, and as a professional, such a topic sounds too formal. Therefore, I propose to speak on 'Y.B. Damle: The Teacher, the Researcher, and the Scholar'.

I was asked to alight at the Poona ('Pune' came into vogue later) Railway Station on a day of torrential rain in July 1958, on my way to the Tata Institute of Social Sciences (TISS), Bombay ('Mumbai' is a recent entry) for an interview for the diploma course in Social Service Administration (Dip. SSA., TISS). As I could not have reached TISS for my interview on time, I sought admission for MA Sociology in University of Pune. Before I started attending Professor Damle's lectures, Jayant Lele, whom I met by chance and who had just completed his MA course in sociology introduced me to Professor Damle. Now, after half-a-century, 49 years to be precise, I am invited to deliver the first Damle Memorial Lecture. Let me note at the very outset that the Damle factor was the single most important one, which sustained me in sociology. I feel deeply grieved as well as highly gratified on this occasion.

The widespread perception in Indian sociology is that Damle is a theorist and that too an incurable Parsonian and a committed Mertonian, and that he has not taken fieldwork seriously. I propose to dismantle this distorted perception and Damle himself comes to my help. In his review of sociological theory in India commissioned by the ICSSR he wrote thus:

Even though he [that is, Damle] has been greatly influenced by Talcott Parsons and Robert K. Merton, he has not made an extensive use of their theories except perhaps the reference group theory as developed by Merton ... Both Weber and Marx are found to be extremely significant for the understanding of Indian society by him ... One cannot say that he has been able to provide a particular framework. (Damle 1985: 62)

I am afraid even this self-assessment is not entirely correct. It is true that Damle did not succeed in providing a specific framework for the study of Indian society (in fact no sociologist of India has, so far). It is indeed true that he did invoke the Weberian framework in some of his studies, notably that of bureaucracy, but Damle hardly employed the Marxian framework in his research although Marx was taught in the MA Course in sociology at Pune in the revised syllabus he introduced. Damle did press into service the pattern variables of Parsons and Merton's reference group theory but he had much more extensively and frequently invoked Parsons rather than Merton. I need to justify these observations and for that it is necessary to attempt a review of his role as field researcher and theorist. But before that it is befitting to situate Damle in terms of the academic milieu in which he had to function.

Damle started teaching and research at University of Pune at a time when there was a general trend to shift from anthropology to sociology in India. Let me recall just three examples from western India. In Bombay, when the leadership of the Department of Sociology changed from G.S. Ghurye to A.R. Desai, the dominant orientation shifted from British social anthropology to Marxian sociology. Similarly, in the MS University of Baroda, the dominance of social anthropology diminished when I.P. Desai succeeded M.N. Srinivas. In both these cases the shift in orientation was characterized by *sequentiality*. But at Poona the shift was more tortuous because it was characterized by *simultaneity*; indeed two different orientations co-existed with tension within the same department, ultimately leading to its bifurcation. But it needs to be underlined here that Damle de-anthropologized sociology in Poona.

Irawati Karve, the anthropologist, pursued the European tradition of anthropology; not only social but also physical anthropology. She taught a course on Social Biology to the students of MA Sociology which dealt with biological bases of society, eugenics and euthenics, and race and racism among other topics. Karve's researches ranged from anthropometric measurements of castes, to kinship organization in India, to Hindu society. In contrast, Damle taught mainly American sociological theories. Abandoning raw empiricism, Damle invariably undertook research studies which attempted to apply concepts and theories to specific empirical situations in India.

However, it is difficult to argue that he formulated a grand theoretical framework to study Indian society as Parsons did or a set of theories of the middle range as Merton attempted. At the same time Damle was continuously engaged in empirical research and hence, it is appropriate to designate him as an empiricist. I use the term empiricist positively and not pejoratively. In my understanding, an empiricist is constantly engaged in comprehending social reality with the help of concepts and theories, but does not necessarily interrogate or reformulate them.

⸻

Damle was a very conscientious and serious teacher and his concern for teaching was clearly articulated in his writings (see, for example, Damle 1986: 101–12). But it cannot be said without the fear of being contradicted that he was an eloquent speaker although he was an effective communicator. At any rate, in the 1950s and possibly in the 1960s, teaching was not very demanding in University of Pune. Damle taught the MA students only on one day in a week, for two hours at a stretch. Attending these routine lectures was mandatory and attendance was taken. But Damle conducted a weekly seminar, at his own initiative, usually on an afternoon. While there was no coercion to attend these seminars most of the students did participate in them. The idea was to motivate students to familiarize themselves with modern sociological theories and concepts which in effect meant the writings of Parsons and Merton, which did not figure prominently in the syllabus of University of Pune those days. In fact, the promptings to read Parsons and Merton came to Damle through Professor M.S. Gore who completed his PhD from Columbia University, USA. Damle told me of this several times. He was a lecturer at the Delhi School of Social Work when Gore was the principal there.

Students, particularly those who were doing a PhD under Damle and the brighter MA students were asked to present papers in the weekly seminars. This provided a great motivation for them to read Parsons and Merton. If you visited his residence in the 1960s you would have come across a group photograph with the caption: 'The Parsonians'. Incidentally I am not in the photograph because I left Poona soon after my MA in 1960.

Damle was very keen that his PhD students should apply modern sociological theories to primary data collected from specific empirical situations and/or to the available secondary data. In either event he insisted that world class examiners were appointed to evaluate the dissertations. According to the then existed rule, of the two examiners one should be a foreigner, which usually meant a sociologist from the United States of America. Dr M.C. Sekhar who was the first to register with him worked on: 'Social Change in India: The Planning Decade'. He applied the Parsonian pattern variables to understand the direction of social change in India and his foreign examiner was Talcott Parsons. Dr V.V. Gourisurudu worked on the 'Phenomenon of Anomie' and S.N. Eisenstadt examined his thesis. Dr K.C. Alexander applied Merton's reference group theory to comprehend social mobility among Pulayas, an ex-untouchable caste of Kerala. His foreign examiner was R.K. Merton. I worked on the Bhoodan-Gramdan movement and the title of my dissertation was 'Charismatic Movements and Social Change'. My foreign examiner was Edward Shils. Dr A. Ramanamma's thesis was on 'Position of Women in India' and her foreign examiner was Margaret Cormick. This practice of Damle is in stark contrast to the tendency on the part of many research supervisors to 'manage' PhD for their students by appointing obliging examiners. Indeed, Damle was a professional par excellence. However, I understand that the practice of appointing foreign examiners was discontinued later in University of Pune because of administrative reasons.

It may also be noted that Damle's PhD students worked on a wide variety of topics although Indian sociology was obsessed with caste, family, and village those days. According to the list I obtained, 35 students completed their PhD under his supervision, the first of these in 1964 and the last in 1994. In the span of 30 years 30 students from University of Pune and five students from SNDT, Bombay completed their PhD with him. The topics they worked included, in addition to those mentioned above, the following: Education in a Cross-cultural Setting, Impact of Development Programme on Rationality, Role of Bureaucracy in Development, Social Organization of Indian Army, Regionalism in Bombay, Labour Commitment, Inter-generational Conflicts, Industrial Sociology, Rural Banking, the Legal Profession, and the like. The wide variety of topics on which Damle's students worked is a standing testimony to his academic versatility.

I want to make an observation about Damle's relationship with students at this juncture. He was rather distant from the MA students, although a student could meet him at the time set apart for the purpose, usually in the afternoon, on two days in a week. The University Grants Commission did not prescribe this norm those days. As for the research students, he was close and informal and rather liberal in bestowing praise and extending recognition. Let me recount two personal instances, one communicated orally and the other in writing. In the early 1990s we were co-participants in a seminar at the Department of Sociology, Bombay University. The theme of the seminar was 'Ethnicity and Nation Building' and I was one of the speakers at the inaugural session. After the session we were walking together to the place of our residence and he remarked: 'Oommen, I felt like a mere school master when I was listening to you'.

In October 2002, my colleagues at the Jawaharlal Nehru University organized a seminar to felicitate me. Professor Damle was invited and he agreed to attend. Unfortunately, Mrs Damle passed away a few days before the seminar and understandably, he could not attend the seminar. But he sent a message titled: 'An Ode to Professor Oommen' and wanted it to be read out at the seminar. Professor Damle was indeed profuse in his praise and went to the extent of designating me 'the Charvak of Indian Sociology' and observed that I am as prolific as Professor G.S. Ghurye, his revered teacher. I am recalling these incidents with considerable embarrassment but the intent is to convey a teacher's compassion for his student rather than the student's competence.

I referred to de-anthropologization of sociology in Poona at Damle's initiative. When I was doing MA during 1958–60, the department was under the spell of Professor Irawati Karve. Very little sociological theory was taught at that time and the bias was in favour of social anthropology. A decade later in 1969–70 the 'Revised Syllabus of MA Sociology' looked distinctively different. Not only was a paper on Durkheim, Marx, and Weber introduced but there was also a paper on Talcott Parsons and Robert K. Merton. When I was a student nothing was taught as Research Methodology but a full paper on it was there by 1969–70. 'Hindu Social Institutions' was retained but with different 'prescribed readings'. The paper on 'Indian Ethnography' disappeared and its replacement was 'Rural, Urban and Tribal Social Structures'. Thus it is evident that the revised syllabus was not simply sociological but also modernized and Americanized. This should surprise none because by this time 'modern sociology' and 'American Sociology' became synonymous, not a positive development in all respects.

◆

Now let me turn to Damle's theoretical contributions, which are of two types. One is his abiding interest to develop a theoretical framework for the study of Indian society (see, for example, Damle 1965: 32–52; 1989: 1–14). Sociology was introduced in Indian universities by the 1920s and until political freedom arrived Indian sociologists were obsessed with nationalism. After the arrival of independence the orientation was to highlight the past glory of India, which explains the fascination indology had for Indian sociologists at that time. The fact that several of the pioneers were either trained in Sanskrit (such as G.S. Ghurye) or uncritically endorsed the importance of Sanskrit (such as D.P. Mukherji) explains the undue importance assigned to tradition. The sociology of the past was portrayed as the sociology of the present as reflected in the then studies of family and kinship, caste and religion, cultural history, and so on. This was countered by social anthropologists trained in the British tradition (for example, M.N. Srinivas) through an excessive emphasis assigned to intensive fieldwork. But both approaches emphasized stability of Indian society as against the rapid changes that were taking place. This is the context, which prompted Damle to plead for the simultaneous understanding of stability and change, continuity and discontinuity. And yet it is paradoxical, but true that he was passionate about the Parsonian framework, which constantly harped on system stability and integration.

Although Damle recommended the adoption of the Parsonian framework which gave equal importance to personality, culture, and society, he cautioned that, 'individual' being a conceptual nullity in the traditional Indian society, society and culture should be given greater importance. In western theory, a la Durkheim, the individual is nothing but a spark in the collective current in societies in which mechanical solidarity prevails but s/he gains autonomy through the emerging division of labour in industrial societies characterized by organic solidarity. But the paradox that the caste system had the most elaborate pre-industrial division of labour and yet, the Indian individual lacked autonomy was not taken cognizance of, let alone explained, by Indian sociologists, including Damle. However, Damle did point out that the central tendency in Indian society in the 1960s was the superimposition of the new structures and values occasioned by industrial urbanization, modern education, secularization, modern communication, and the like on the traditional structures and values. Thus, social change in India was brought about through accretion and not displacement, unlike in the West, according to Damle although he did not invoke these phrases. And yet, he was prone to apply the Parsonian pattern variables somewhat mechanically, which were anchored to western epistemological dualism (see Damle 1965: 46–51)

There are several other research papers in which his concern for the relationship between social theory and social reality (see, for example, Damle 1989: 145–57; 1993: 1–27) is articulated. The broad position that he has taken is that Indian social reality is amenable for analysis with the help of Western (read American) theoretical frameworks. I have designated Damle as an 'academic cosmopolitan' elsewhere (see Oommen 1983b: 111–36). But I suggest that it is more rewarding to recognize the specificities of particular societies and the need for amending and altering the theoretical frameworks whether they are formulated elsewhere or in the same society earlier to capture the crux of the evolving empirical reality. The engagement between theory, concepts, and data should be recognized as creative and continuous.

The second strand of Damle's theoretical writings started at the very beginning of his career with his PhD thesis under the supervision

of G.S. Ghurye at Bombay University. Defying the then existed dominant tendency of producing PhD dissertations based on analysis of
ancient texts and/or fieldwork, Damle opted to make a comparative
analysis of three polities—Britain, India, and Soviet Union—based
on secondary data. It was an enquiry into the relationship between
stratification and income. Based on this study he formulated the
proposition that social stratification and income are not directly linked
but they are indeed related to each other through socially valued
skills (see Damle 1955). The three polities compared vary vastly in
that they are democratic-class (Britain), authoritarian-class (Soviet
Union), and democratic-caste (India), and hence the proposition
has wide applicability and theoretical power. But this line of enquiry
was not pursued by anybody in India, including Damle.

Damle's well known research paper which applied reference
group theory to analyse mobility within caste (Damle 1968: 95–102)
is another example of the same strand of theoretical writings. He
attempted to invoke Parsonian pattern variables in this case too,
as noted earlier. But it did not yield much theoretical dividend.
Merton's unit of analysis in reference group behaviour is the individual who functions in American society, characterized by acute
individualism. The mechanism adopted is anticipatory socialization,
that is, gradually internalizing the norms and values of the group in
which s/he aspires membership. It is an individual–group dynamic.

In contrast, given the fact that the Indian individual has little
autonomy (this is acknowledged by Damle as I have pointed out
above) and it is the lower castes which aspire to move upward by
adopting the norms and values of the upper castes, the dynamic
involved is an inter-group one. Admittedly, M.N. Srinivas's formulation of sanskritization can be justifiably described as the Indian
variant of anticipatory socialization (see Srinivas 1956: 481–96).
By so doing the power of reference group theory could have been
considerably enhanced. Unfortunately, Damle has not attempted
this and Srinivas has ignored reference group theory. To my mind
this was a missed opportunity for Indian sociologists/social anthropologists for extending the frontiers of social theory.

There are several other instances when Damle attempted to
invoke a Parsonian framework to the study of Indian social reality (see, for example, Damle 1967: 250–80). In undertaking these
and other studies the impression one gets is that the theoretical
frameworks are endorsed uncritically and hence do not contribute

much to theory construction. But he had indeed filtered empirical data he analysed through theoretical frameworks.

——◆——

I hope you will recall that I began this lecture by noting that the perception regarding Damle as a theorist is not exactly correct. On the other hand, there is ample evidence to suggest that he was an empirical researcher to the core in that he was continuously engaged in apprehending Indian social reality. I could list 18 research projects (and the list may be incomplete) that he has undertaken in and around Poona during the half-a-century of his active academic life.

These research projects are: 'Communication of Modern Ideas and Knowledge in Indian Villages'; 'Harikatha: A Study in Communication'; 'Auxiliary Nurse Midwife: A Study in Institutional Change'; 'Inter-group Relations in Rural Communities in Maharashtra'; 'Social Structure of the Intellectuals: A Study of College and University Professors in Pune'; 'College Youth: Elite in the Making'; 'Students and Their Parents Living in Different Settlements: A Study on Impact of Socialization'; 'Social Science Press in India'; 'Bureaucracy and Agricultural Development'; 'Perception of Modernization by College Youth in India'; 'Studies in the Sociology of Education: Maharashtra Report'; 'Holocaust in Marathwada'; 'Citizen Participation in Rural Development and Urban Administration'; 'A Study of the Impact and Implications of Protective Discrimination in Education'; 'A Study of Factory Workers: Motivation and Alienation'; 'Scientists in Academics and Industry'; 'Science for Social Action'. Perhaps his last project was an analysis of Dr B.R. Ambedkar's writings published in Marathi in the journals *Mooknayak* and *Bahishkrit Bharat.*

I am sure that you will agree with me that Damle's continuous involvement with a variety of field projects is indeed incredible. The indefatigable energy required for this stupendous task and his frail physique were a mismatch. Of course he collaborated with others, mainly his former students. I have noted only one collaborative project with Professor Irawati Karve, his senior colleague in the department, which was a study of inter-group relations in the villages of Maharashtra. Other prominent collaborators were M.C. Sekhar, P.H. Reddy, A. Ramanamma, Jacob Aikara, and U. Bambawale, all his former students.

Damle did collect considerable amount of empirical data for each of these projects and monographs were produced based on them. Some of these are published but mainly by the Deccan College Institute of Post-graduate Studies. As is well-known, academic institutions in India are printers but not publishers, in that their mechanism of marketing is poor and hence their products do not reach a wide audience.

This partially explains the inverted perception to which I referred to in the beginning; that Damle is a theorist and not a field researcher. Most of his field studies are not known to readers beyond the sociology circles in Pune or, at best in Maharashtra, and hence, the recognition Damle got is not commensurate with the quantity and quality of his contributions. Contrarily, the few theoretical research papers he wrote were published in reputed academic journals and/or in books edited by well-known academics and published by established publishing houses.

Permit me to make a suggestion before I proceed further. His unpublished research monographs can provide important baseline data to understand the process of social change occurring in India, particularly Maharashtra. I can illustrate it best through a couple of examples. The study of college and university professors in Poona in 1968 revealed that 80 per cent of them were Brahmins and there was not a single professor of SC origin.

Similarly, his study of scientists in academics undertaken in 1985 report that 75 per cent of the MSc students were upper castes and of which 44 per cent were Brahmins. The OBCs were only 4 per cent and the SCs and STs a mere 2.5 per cent. As for the students of the IITs, 72 per cent were high castes of whom 46 per cent were Brahmins. While 10 per cent were of OBC background there was none from the SC/ST category. Finally, 82 per cent of the science teachers were upper castes, 57 per cent being Brahmins. OBCs constituted a meagre 3 per cent whereas there was no one from the SC/ST categories.

The importance of these crucial data should be seen against the hue and cry raised by upper caste students in the context of the present government's initiative to provide for 27 per cent quota in institutions of higher education. We should be grateful to Damle that he had provided us with the required benchmark data which demonstrate that even after 35 years (that is, in 1985) of the reservation policy being in operation, its impact on SC/ST categories is

virtually nil, and those of the OBC background are scarcely beginning to benefit. Viewed against this fact, the banner under which
the students of upper caste origin are protesting—viz. 'Youth for
Equality'—is an insult to the very notion of equality. I only hope
that the Department of Sociology, University of Pune, will re-visit
these empirical studies, which will be of crucial significance for
informed public debate and balanced policy decisions.

It is my contention that Damle did not get the credit which he
amply deserved for the enormous empirical research work he did
but he has been over evaluated for the theoretical slant he took.
It is time that I provide the requisite explanation for the position
that I have taken. First, the lack of recognition that I am referring
to is a reflection of the tension between the different styles of doing sociology in India from the 1950s onwards and they persist
even to-day. This has three aspects: theoretical, methodological,
and substantive.

Much of the sociological and social anthropological studies
done in India in the 1950s to 1980s, when Damle was academically active, were rarely moulded by theoretical frameworks. If
they were, these frameworks were drawn mainly from European,
particularly British, social anthropology. Damle's insistence on
invoking the theoretical frameworks of American sociologists, as
against those of British social anthropologists, although innovative,
did encounter considerable resistance and even stigmatization. For
example, I recall an article published in the *Economic and Political
Weekly* dismissing Parsonian sociology as mere empty verbiage,
which was a reflection of the then existing academic mood in
India. The methods in contention those days were indology and
participant observation. Damle's approach was methodologically
eclectic; his sources of data included surveys, observations, content
analysis, and informal interviewing. Substantively, the pet themes
of research those days were village studies, caste, religion, family,
and kinship; the projects undertaken by Damle that I have listed
above transcended these conventional themes. He was a deviant
on all the three fronts—theory, method, and themes of research.
Deviants—that is, innovators—are disadvantaged by the time-lag
between their work and the recognition they get.

Second, he moved rather swiftly from one research project to
another without consolidating the previous ones in terms of deft
editing and processing for publication, to the level acceptable by

reputed publishing houses. Most of his monographs are in-house publications by the Deccan College which are in very limited circulation.

Third, while he was a popular seminarist, Damle himself did not organize any national, let alone international, seminars. Similarly, to the best of my knowledge he did not edit any book. These two activities—organizing seminars and editing books—are often closely related as the first leads to the second, and these in unison create one's professional network. That is, to be in circulation, to stay in touch in the academic circles, it is often necessary to be an academic entrepreneur. Damle was not cut out to initiate and sustain an academic network leading to production of knowledge.

Fourth, generally speaking, those who are widely read in contemporary sociology are those who produce books and research papers through creatively reviewing and synthesizing the vast body of available literature (the classic case in contemporary sociology is that of Anthony Giddens). In India also, there are a few such authors who command wide readership. Damle did not undertake any such project, except one: *Caste, Religion and Politics in India,* the only book of his published by a commercial publisher. He did undertake an elaborate review of caste studies in India, which was published in the prestigious journal *Current Sociology,* an official organ of the International Sociological Association, for which he did not get the much deserved credit. Since the story of this project (narrated to me by Professor Damle himself) informs one of the intricate relationship between the academic power structure and knowledge production it is rewarding to recall it.

T.B. Bottomore was the editor of *Current Sociology* in the late 1950s and each issue of the journal focused on the review of studies done on a particular theme and the editor invited a reputed scholar to do the review. M.N. Srinivas was the natural choice to be invited from India given the theme involved, namely, a review of studies on caste. Srinivas in turn asked Damle to do the review, which was indeed a mark of recognition for him. Damle did the work and took the review with him when he went to Lucknow to attend the Sociological Conference. He showed the manuscript to Bottomore without knowing that the latter had commissioned Srinivas to do the work. Bottomore promised Damle that he will sort out the matter with Srinivas and the review would be published in *Current Sociology* under the authorship of Damle. However, finally the review was published under the authorship of four authors: M.N. Srinivas, Y.B. Damle, André Béteille, and Savitri Sahani, with some editorial changes. But the review was also published elsewhere under the sole authorship of Damle (see Damle 1961). If one reads both the versions one can easily discern the differences between the two and assess Damle's contribution to the review. And yet, for those who read only the *Current Sociology* version Damle was one of the four authors!

Finally, the ideological camp to which one belongs may often be instrumental in getting acceptance and recognition, particularly in the social sciences. In the Indian context there are three such camps: the political left (the CPML, CPM, CPI, RSP, etc.), the political right (the BJP and its affiliates), and the political middle (the Congress). Damle belonged to none of these camps but he did not hesitate to take a political position when required, as was evident from his activities during the internal emergency during 1975–6. If anything, he was a quintessential liberal as can be discerned from his Ambedkar Memoral Lecture (Damle 1999: 7–39).

Friends, I started with a personal note, let me also end in a similar vein. One of the motivations for me to accept the invitation to attend the seminar on the 'History of Sociology in India' organized by Professor Sujata Patel was to come to Pune so that I can meet Professor Damle. I was told that he had agreed to contribute a paper to the seminar. I came to know about his critical illness from Professor S.K. Srivastava of Banaras Hindu University, who is currently engaged in editing a book entitled *Tradition, Modernization and Globalization.* He told me that Professor Damle had agreed to contribute a chapter for the volume. Thus, he had two unfinished assignments on hand while he passed away; he was working even as he was dying! We were indeed fortunate to have such a committed scholar in our midst. We may not see one of his kind for some time to come.

11

Disjunctions between Field, Method, and Concept
An Appraisal of M.N. Srinivas

Mysore Narasimhachar Srinivas (1916–99) is admittedly the most widely read and recognized 'sociologist' of India. The fact that the ISS, in collaboration with the ICSSR had instituted a memorial lecture to honour Srinivas is a standing testimony to his standing in Indian social science. Memorial lectures are occasions to celebrate the contributions of the remembered personality. However, let me also state at the very outset that the spirit which informs this memorial lecture is the Durkheimian assertion that a discipline can forget its pioneers only at its peril and yet, unless it transcends them no progress is possible.

The three acknowledged teachers of Srinivas are G.S. Ghurye, Radicliffe-Brown, and Evans-Pritchard, the first an Indian sociologist and the second and third British social anthropologists. While Ghurye is widely acknowledged as one of the founding fathers of Indian sociology, his ambivalence to sociology and affinity to anthropology is not so well-known.[1] Ghurye has substantially contributed to the 'anthropologisation of Indian Sociology' (see Savur 2011: 3–28).

M.N. Srinivas did his PhD from Bombay University under the supervision of G.S. Ghurye. He then registered for a DPhil at Oxford University under Radicliffe-Brown but completed the dissertation under Evans-Pritchard. Both doctoral dissertations were written based on the same material, namely the ethnography of the Coorgs.

Radicliffe-Brown wrote, after a meeting of anthropology teachers from Oxford, Cambridge, and London, 'The comparative study of institutions of primitive societies was accepted as the task of social anthropology, and this name was preferred to sociology' (1952: 276).

The 'fields' of sociology and social anthropology were clearly distinguished in Europe; by common consent sociology was the study of one's own society which was reckoned as 'industrial', 'modern', and hence 'advanced'. In contrast, the task of social anthropology was to study 'primitive' societies. Srinivas was initially trained at Bombay University where the preferred 'method' those days was mainly indological. For social anthropologists in Britain the field was primitive societies and the method they prescribed to study them was participant observation. Srinivas attempted an innovative combination of studying one's own society through the method of participant observation. This creative leap he made has far-reaching implications for sociology in India, which is one of the two themes of my lecture.[2]

—✦—

The notion of one's own society as conceptualized by Srinivas has a broad as well as a narrow referent. According to him '... any Indian working in any part of India or with any group, is working in his own society defining the society in purely political terms' (Srinivas 2002: 577). He refers to polity and society interchangeably; in fact, often the reference is to subcontinental India and not even 'political India'. This conflation of polity/country with society is particularly problematic in South Asia. For example, one finds the existence of Tamil society not only in India but also in Sri Lanka, and of Punjabi society not only in Pakistan but also in India. Bengali society is vivisected between India and Bangladesh and Naga society between India and Myanmar, and so on. Additionally, how about the Indians in the diaspora, whose stock is continuously increasing? The conflation of polity and society, of state and nation, is so common that most social scientists are impervious to its consequences (see Oommen 1991: 67–84) and Srinivas is no exception to this.

On the other hand, Srinivas's narrow conception of one's own society is indeed vexatious. Referring to the neighbourhood in Mysore city where he grew up, he notes that the culture of College Road inhabited by Brahmins was different from that of Bandikeri (literally, bullock-cart street), the locality inhabited by shepherds who lived barely 50 yards from College Road. He reports that he got his first 'culture shock' from this neighbourhood. Srinivas goes so far as to note: 'Bandikeri was my Trobriand Island, my Nuerland, my Navaho country and what have you' (2002: 579). But the problem of specifying the boundaries of one's own society does not end here; the cultural diversity of College Road itself was substantial because the Brahmin residents there are drawn from different linguistic groups and belonged to different Hindu 'sectarian' groups. Srinivas asserts: 'The point I am making is that I could have found "the other", not only in my backyard but even next door' (ibid.: 580).

Srinivas rightly holds that studying one's own society is as difficult as studying the Other. His reasoning goes thus: 'I am a Sri Vaishnava Brahmin by birth, but it will take me years to do a proper anthropological study of a Sri Vaishnava Community, and a life-time to master the complex theology and ritual of different groups and subsects among them' (ibid.: 586). If so, the social anthropologist would need a long time to study not only the Other, be it the Bandikeri shepherds or Trobriand Islanders, but also 'one's own society', defined in the narrowest possible terms. In the case of Srinivas, it was the Sri Vaishnava Brahmin community into which he was born. Srinivas is right in discarding the much-touted distinction in social anthropology between studying the Other and the Self.

However, obliteration of the distinction between the Other and the Self, the merging of the two fields, poses several serious questions for the method. First, can one really merge all the Others? Is it not that there is a continuum of the Others beginning with one's neighbourhood, one's linguistic region, one's country, and the distant Other, be it of the Navaho Country or Nuerland with two polar points? If the degree of otherness varies, the intensity required for field observations too is bound to vary. Second, if one is studying one's own society defined in the narrowest possible terms (for example, Sri Vaishnava Brahmins in the case of Srinivas), is not participant observation a contradiction in terms because the observer and the participant are rolled into one? Third, if one is to understand the theology and rituals of a religious sect, is it not necessary to carefully analyse the texts (oral or written) so as to understand the gap between prescription and practice? Will intensive fieldwork in itself sufficient? Is not study of texts also essential?

Including the study of the Self and not only the Other within the ken of social anthropology has a logical consequence: namely, that the study of the individual self, and not merely the societal self, can also become the unit of research! And Srinivas did reach this logical destination when he proposed the following 'field' for anthropological investigations. He asks: 'Why cannot an anthropologist treat his own life as an ethnographic field and study it? ... The life of every individual can be regarded as a "case study" and who is better qualified than the individual himself to study it?' (2002: 593). If these proposals are accepted, not only does the 'field' of social anthropology expand exponentially but the methods of social anthropology, too, have to multiply because it has to study the distant Other, the immediate Other, one's own society, and even the individual self!

Srinivas did recognize that, 'What is one's own society is always difficult to define' (Srinivas et al. 1979: 3). In the case of India, with such stupendous religious, regional-linguistic, and social (caste) diversity, it is indeed intriguing to define one's own society. And yet he pleaded to undertake '... the field study of *typical villages* in different linguistic areas in our country' (Srinivas 1955b: 21; italics mine). It seems to me that a rationale and an acceptable notion of what is one's own society in the Indian context is indicated here. These are linguistic regions to which people belong and one's mother tongue is usually the language of that region which considerably facilitates intensive fieldwork. When one refers to villages in Karnataka, Kerala, Gujarat, Punjab, Bengal, Tamil Nadu, and so on, one is referring to villages in such 'societies'.

Such an understanding avoids the conflation between polity (India) and society (Tamil Nadu) and the consequent confusion that emanates from it. Thus the observation that '...most Indians know only a tiny segment of it (that is, culture) and this is frequently confused with the culture of the country' (Srinivas et al. 1979: 3) makes profound sense. Yet, Srinivas holds that '... the study of a village or a small town or a caste provides a strategic point of entry for the study of Indian society and culture *as a whole*' (Srinivas 1972: 158; italics mine). This quantum leap from the village to the country is mistaking the part for the whole. The tendency to treat the unit of one's field work as a microcosm of the macrocosm which is India (and often the subcontinent) is indeed problematic given the mind-boggling diversity of India for two reasons.

One, as Srinivas himself admits, the cultural difference between College Road and Bandikeri in Mysore City, two adjacent neighbourhoods, was substantial. Indeed, they were two different worlds for him. Second, in spite of his suggestion to study typical villages from each of the linguistic regions, Srinivas does not accept typical villages as an empirical reality. He insists: 'The few who do take the trouble of searching for the "typical" field discover that there is no such thing...' (Srinivas et al. 1979: 7). This indeed fits in with his stumbling on Rampura: '...the time at my disposal was so short that I had to start my work at the earliest possible opportunity, and Rampura was the only village I could get a place to stay' (Srinivas 1979: 20). While appreciating Srinivas's disarming sincerity, it is difficult to endorse his ambivalence about the typicality of the unit of research; ambivalence because he 'selected' Rampura in 1948 for sheer pragmatic reasons and yet, in 1955 he recommended the study of typical villages from each of the linguistic regions while in 1979, he asserts that typicality of village is a mirage! Situational exigency cannot be the basis of abandoning a well-established principle.

All of Srinivas's field research was done in India and the first major fieldwork was done in Coorg, which was not part of his 'society', and hence an ideal site for participant observation. But he admits that the Coorg study was not based on intensive fieldwork (Srinivas uses the two expressions, participant observation and intensive fieldwork, interchangeably). He writes:

In fact, my first major fieldwork, viz., in Coorg, was severely affected by my coming down with a serious abdominal ailment during the first few weeks of my stay in Mercara. I took months to recover and had to abandon the ideas I had entertained of spending several months in a Coorg village. I got a chance to experience field research only in 1948 when I spent over ten months in Rampura, a village 22 miles from Mysore...(1979: 19–20).

I want to underline here a serious disjunction, which exists between 'field' and 'method'. Rampura was very much a part of the society to which Srinivas belonged, not withstanding the cultural differences between urban and rural areas within the same regional–linguistic region, which is a universal phenomenon. In contrast, the Coorg society was not a part of Hindu society, it was 'a tribal society' moving in the direction of Hinduization when Srinivas was studying it. In fact, that movement provided the rationale to reinforce the notion of sanskritization, which he noted earlier (see Srinivas 1942).

By common consent, *Religion and Society among the Coorgs of South India*, was/is a masterly ethnographic account and yet it is *not* the product of participant observation, which calls for intensive study of a small society for two to three years (Srinivas 1955b: 21). On the other hand, Rampura was a part of his society which he studied through participant observation and on the basis of which he formulated the concept of dominant caste. Viewed thus it seems that participant observation is not a necessary condition for producing brilliant results. I have argued long ago that the substantive concerns of a discipline, the nature of society one investigates, and the purpose for which the research is undertaken conjointly determine the appropriateness of the techniques of data collection one employs (Oommen 1969: 809–15) and hence, I do not intend to pursue the argument here.

Srinivas recognizes two problems which confront the social anthropologist who is engaged in the study of his/her own society. S/he is '...likely to be influenced by his social position, not only in his observations but also in the problems he selects for study' (1972: 154). Gender bias in the selection of themes for research existed everywhere, until recently, irrespective of disciplines, whether one studied one's own society or the other. It required the feminist movement to overcome this bias, and viewing problems through the gender lens is providing the much-needed balance in the very selection of problems for study.

Indian society was viewed from the perspective of the upper-caste male at least until recently. There was an interesting conjunction between indology and the male perspective because women did not have access to sacred texts. The non-Brahmin perspective was subjected to a cognitive black out. The field-view is an asset here but the impossibility of upper-caste male researcher to penetrate the worlds of women, untouchables, and some of the religious minorities still lingers. The advocacy of a bottom-up perspective is an essential corrective (see Oommen 2004[a]: 161–75). It is important to underline here that it is not enough that the problems are looked at from the earthworm's eye-view, that is, with empathy, but the earthworms (that is, the lowest groups) themselves need to study the problems, an impossibility in rural India, at least until recently.

The complaint that Indian sociology is but Hindu sociology persists. The few beginnings made to study non-Hindu groups are welcome but grossly inadequate considering the size and diversity of the non-Hindu population. But the scarce attempts to study Indian social reality from the perspective of religious minorities are invariably dubbed as 'anti-national' and 'communal'. Thus an unintended and indeed unjustifiable juxtaposition between national sociology versus communal sociology comes into being (see Oommen 1983c: 92–133). The persisting bias in selecting problems for research, be it based on gender, caste, or religion do not augur well for Indian sociology. The social location of the researcher further complicates matters thereby bringing about a rupture between field and method.

Srinivas hold the view that '...sociology and social anthropology ought to be field oriented in India if not become "field sciences"' (Srinivas et al. 1979: 2). This reaction is understandable viewed in terms of the Indological orientation, which prevailed in the Department of Sociology of Bombay University where Srinivas got his initial training. In fact the advocacy of the field-view as against the book-view helped considerably to de-indologize Indian sociology and we are indeed indebted to Srinivas for this. But field-fundamentalism is as problematic as text-extremism. Let me illustrate this with special reference to the study of caste system in India.

If a researcher undertakes a comparative field study of the institution of caste among Hindus, Sikhs, Christians, and Muslims in India without taking into account the relevant texts of the respective religious communities, it could be highly misleading. While the similarity of some of the caste practices, including the practice of untouchability across religious communities could be captured through field work, the facts that the norms and values of Hinduism sanction the caste system, those of Sikhism have challenged them, and those of Islam and Christianity totally disapprove them will not be brought out through fieldwork. To argue that the fieldworker is expected to have knowledge of the relevant texts before s/he starts fieldwork is to acknowledge the importance of textual knowledge. To suggest that what is relevant for the fieldworker is only to understand people's behaviour without bothering about the norms and values prescribed in the text is to ignore the seminal distinction between 'ought' and 'is' in the study of human society. At any rate, it will not be possible to make sense of verbal articulations and behaviour of the respondents/informants if the fieldworker is unfamiliar with the texts which are the sources of norms and values. As Levy aptly remarks:

The distinction between ideal [read, prescriptions in the texts] and actual [read, what is observed in the field] structures is one of the most vital and useful tools of analysis of any society, any time, anywhere. In one form or another, men have been aware of it since time began for them. It is, however, so obvious and such a humble distinction that many social scientists either neglect it or overlook its importance (1966: 26).

Those who look upon sociology and social anthropology as 'field sciences' are apt to ignore the ideal structures and those who ignore the field and confine to textual analyses, written or oral, will not have adequate familiarity with actual structures. These one-sided approaches can only provide distorted understanding of social reality. This is particularly true of Indian civilization region with an uninterrupted history of some 3,500 to 5,000 years. That is why I suggested quarter of a century ago, 'Render unto the Text that which is the Text's and Render unto the Field that which is the Field's. The constructed estrangement between the Text and the Field, value and fact, does not exist; it is largely an artifact of scholastic craftiness, a manifestation of intellectual trade unionism' (Oommen 1983b: 116).

According to Srinivas, the deep division between rural people and urban academics dictates the 'special significance' of field-orientation for Indian sociology and social anthropology: 'Intellectuals in this country tend to be drawn from upper and middle strata living in urban areas, and are usually ignorant of rural India and the culture of the people inhabiting it. They are unaware of the need to study it with respect and humility' (Srinivas et al. 1979: 2).

I am afraid this observation is factually incorrect because not an inconsiderable proportion of Indian intellectuals are drawn from rural India. Even if it were correct on the eve of independence, by the time it was articulated in 1979 the situation was fast changing. At any rate it is not based on any empirical evidence. I shall let that pass but the statement has nothing in it which is specific to India. Intellectuals all over the world used to be largely from urban upper and middle classes, although the situation is gradually changing everywhere. Similarly, ignorance about rural people and their culture is indeed widespread among urban dwellers in almost all parts of the world and the latter may hold the former in contempt. Finally, given the above conditions the intellectuals rarely recognize the need to study the rural people and their 'culture with respect and humility'; this is not an Indian peculiarity. But there are three grave problems in the context of field research in rural India and Srinivas did recognize them (see Srinivas 1979: 19–28). The problems are the notion of purity and pollution, the exclusion of women from public space, and externalization of non-Indic religious communities, particularly Muslims in North India.

The Indian researchers drawn from ritually clean caste backgrounds, irrespective of their religious identity, cannot interact with ease with 'untouchables', particularly in rural India, as they are constrained by the disapproval imposed on them through the code of conduct prevalent in villages. Srinivas prescribed: 'Ideally the anthropologist should be able to empathise with the Brahmin and the untouchable...' (2002: 583). The desirability of this prescription apart, the issue is what happens if the researcher indulges in behaviour which violates the prescribed code of social conduct. There is indeed a serious conflict between desirability and possibility and some researchers have reported about the adverse consequences for their research endeavour if and when they violate the local norms (see Srinivas et al. 1979). The way out of this impasse seems to be to view the village with the lens of the untouchables, and to live and interact with them. But this remedy is rarely prescribed and, if prescribed, hardly executed. In either event, viewing the village from top or bottom will imperil the holistic picture an avowed goal of participant observation.

Equally tortuous is the male researcher obtaining accessibility to women respondents/informants in the field. Generally speaking, village women are not expected to interact even with men of the village, save a few close kin, not to speak of strangers. This rule applies in the reverse too, although it is not observed as strictly. Thus a woman researcher may have greater access to male informants/respondents as compared with a male researcher to female informants/ respondents. This inaccessibility, however, varies across regions, religions, and castes.

Finally, just like the social architecture of the Indian village is determined by the purity–pollution line (those who are above and below the line are residentially segregated), ghettoization based on religion is common, particularly in some parts of India. The acceptability of a researcher of Muslim background visiting the areas inhabited by caste Hindus and vice-versa is very low. Thus, all the three factors—the practice of untouchability, the exclusion of women from the public sphere, and ghettoization of religious communities—put severe limitations on participant observation in village India. As and when it is attempted, the possibility of obtaining a holistic view of village life, one of the main advantages of participant observation, would scarcely be accomplished.

Participant observation, the method, which emerged in the context of European anthropologists studying colonies, is recommended not only to study tribal and peasant communities by Indian anthropologists, but assumed to be appropriate to study all varieties of 'fields'. For example, of the 15 chapters in *Fieldworker and the Field* which report on fieldwork in India, 10 are on non-rural 'fields', five on urban India, and five on complex organizations (see Srinivas et al. 1979). The unstated assumption appears to be that participant observation as a method can be profitably invoked in all varieties of field situations.[3] This evidently implies that there is no relationship between the nature of the 'field' investigated and the type of 'method' employed; a multiplicity of field situations can be investigated through one method. This advocacy of 'method-monism' comes as an unpleasant surprise because Srinivas himself had acknowledged earlier that 'They (social anthropologists) should also realize that there is a vast range of problems where the intensive method is either not applicable at all or needs to be supplemented with other techniques' (Srinivas 1962: 143). It is intriguing that after 17 years, in 1979, the year in which *The Fieldworker and the Field* was published, his position became rigid. Mercifully, he reverted to his earlier position and recognized '... the need for methodological catholicity and resilience, and an ability to choose the appropriate method for tackling a particular problem' (Srinivas 1994: 13).

The information types, which need to be obtained from the field, are basically three: frequency distribution, incidents and histories, and institutionalized status and norms. The efficiency of 'methods' varies depending upon data-types. For example, the best method to understand frequency distribution is enumeration (census) and samples. As for incidents and histories, the most appropriate method is observation. Finally, to get a proper understanding of institutionalized status and norms, the best method is interviewing the informants. But no method is completely adequate by itself for collecting data regarding any information type. Thus, although data regarding institutionalized status and norms is best collected through interviewing critical informants, that data need to be supplemented through observation. That is, adequate and appropriate data collection invariably requires the employment of a plurality of methods, which is a long settled issue in sociology (see Zelditch Jr 1962: 566–76) and practised even in India (see, for an example Oommen 1987b: 185–202).

In this context, the persisting and pointless controversy regarding the superiority of data-type, qualitative versus quantitative, should be taken note of. Different disciplines collected different types of data depending upon the demands on them and this, in turn, required different styles of data collection. These traditions are historically evolved and the practitioners of different disciplines followed them without much questioning. For example, the demands of the welfare state compelled economists to collect quickly massive quantitative data from huge populations either through census and/or from samples. In contrast, social anthropologists were required to collect qualitative data from small pre-literate communities, which was a time-consuming exercise. But over a period of time, unfortunately, these styles of data collection came to be accepted uncritically by academics instead of understanding the limitations of the data they analyse, either directly collected by them or collected by the paid investigators. The mutual profound disrespect between economists and social anthropologists has disastrous consequences for Indian social science.

Srinivas spent 13 years at the Delhi School of Economics (1959–72) and might have experienced the condescending attitude of economists towards the discipline of social anthropology. The economists look down upon micro studies, qualitative data, and participant observation.[4] Perhaps as a response to that, Srinivas wrote a paper which is a scathing criticism of survey research packed with biting sarcasm (1975: 1387–94). He rightly castigated the research/academic entrepreneurs who preside over large-scale surveys as directors and the division of labour between data gatherers who occupy the lowest position in the hierarchy, the data analysts who are in the middle, and the theory-builders who have no idea whatsoever about the manner in which the data are collected and/ or analysed. In contrast, the social anthropologist who collected data directly had a great command over his/her data in discrete details and there existed no hiatus between data and theory, Srinivas argued. However, he admitted of knowing '...anthropologists staying in five-star hotels and being driven by chauffeurs to their villages where they checked the work of their research assistants, issued instructions for the next stage of work, and returned in the evening to the cool of their air-conditioned hotel rooms' (Srinivas 2002: 545). If so, research entrepreneurs and the division of labour between those who collected data and those who theorized are common to both the disciplines.

Srinivas criticized survey research mainly on three counts: incompetence of field investigators, their dishonesty, and the danger of faking data. Yet, it cannot be asserted that these deficits do not afflict participant observation. Incompetence of researchers has nothing to do with the techniques of data collection. One comes across incompetence among survey researchers as well as participant observers. Similarly there are honest and dishonest researchers both among survey researchers and participant observers. As for faking, human ingenuity for it is stupendous; humans are capable of faking everything. The point is how to formulate questions, the response to which cannot be faked.

Let me conclude my observations on the relationship between field and method. Social anthropology emerged in the colonial context and its field was the study of the Other. The context disappeared and there is no rationale for clinging to it; Srinivas rightly argued for the study of one's own society as the new and/or additional field of social anthropology. Participant observation was an appropriate method to study the Other but to study one's own society, one can resort to a plurality of methods.

—◆—

So far I have discussed the disjunctions between field and method in social anthropology and often indicated the lack of fit between them. Presently I propose to analyse the relationship between these two, that is, field and method on the one hand, and concept formation on the other. Fieldwork, particularly participant observation, can only be undertaken in specific locales and settings—villages, parts of towns and cities, complex organizations—but it can be creative only if researchers make quantum leaps into concept formation and/or theory building. Srinivas is justly famous for the concepts of sanskritization and 'dominant caste'. The notion of sanskritization, it is widely believed, has been formulated based on fieldwork in Coorg. When Srinivas did his fieldwork among the Coorgs they were cognized as a 'tribe' eager to be a part of Hindu society and sanskritization was the means to achieve that goal.[5] But this understanding is not entirely correct.

Srinivas acknowledges that the idea of sanskritization was already present in its incipient form in his master's degree thesis (Srinivas 1942) which was based '...primarily on a study of earlier published work on Mysore' (Srinivas 1972: 149). The process of sanskritization followed by non-Brahmin castes of Mysore region manifested in banning divorce and widow remarriage, approbated norms among Mysore Brahmins. Similarly, at the time of the Coorg study, Srinivas did not formulate the notion of dominant caste, although he acknowledges the possibility of Coorgs becoming a dominant caste. He writes: 'Occasionally, a group originally outside the Hindu fold, such as the Coorgs...may become dominant by virtue of their numbers, wealth and martial prowess' (Srinivas 1955a: 7). But the notion of dominant caste was explicitly formulated based on intensive fieldwork in Rampura to unfold the co-existence of two 'hierarchies'—ritual and political.

The points relevant for the present analysis are the following. One, Srinivas, a Mysore Brahmin, was studying his own society when he was studying marriage and family in Mysore and in the village of Rampura; two, the first study, being based on published data collected by others, was not based on intensive fieldwork, let alone participant observation, but the second study was based on intensive fieldwork; three, it is not necessary to study other cultures in order to understand better one's own society as several distinguished European social anthropologists argued;[6] four, concepts as popular as sanskritization (which was implied in the study of marriage and family in Mysore) and dominant caste (which was noted in the study of the Coorgs) were not necessarily anchored to intensive fieldwork and five, given the above, mystification of participant observation and study of other cultures as the unique selling points of social anthropology are dispensable ideas.

I have dealt with the problems associated with the concept of dominant caste long ago and shall not repeat them here (see Oommen 1970a: 73–83). For the present I shall confine my attention to the concept of sanskritization. Srinivas initially conceived sanskritization as an endogenous micro process to understand social mobility within the Indian society, thereby exploding the long established myth that the caste system is static. Initially only

Brahmins were thought to be emulated but later he discovered that twice-born non-Brahmin groups can also be role models for lower castes. But the atypicality of the field can constrict the reach and scope of a concept. Srinivas admits this: 'My model of sanskritization was derived...from both the Brahmins and Lingayats. I did miss the Kshatriya and Vaishya models...because Mysore region lacks the Kshatriya and Vaishya castes whose style of life is markedly different from that of Brahmins and Lingayats' (Srinivas 1972: 150).[7]

This observation of Srinivas points to the imperative need for selecting representative unit/s from the field instead of pronouncing that no such thing exists. If the Mysore region did not have Kshatriya and Vaishya groups of appropriate social standing, other regions could have been selected for observation. If indeed Kshatriyas and Vaishyas too did exist in the Mysore region, all the four groups—Brahmins, Kshtriyas, Vaishyas, and Lingayats—would have provided role models for sanskritization, enhancing its scope and rendering the concept more powerful. Thus, Srinivas successfully rebutted the tendency to equate sanskritization with Brahminization. Even so, it needs to be underlined here that all the role models are twice-born groups or the groups which experienced substantial upward mobility through reform movements and whose status is equivalent to twice-born groups, as illustrated by the case of Lingayats. The OBCs of Mysore were neither a source nor an obstacle to sanskritization, although they were leading a powerful protest movement for caste quotas at that time. That is, the agents of sanskritization can't but be upper castes. The castes in the OBC category can become dominant castes as they are above the pollution line. But the untouchables cannot ever become dominant castes. Thus viewed, we get three broad layers of caste-clusters—upper castes, OBCs, and SCs—the last being cumulatively dominated, ritually, economically, politically, socially, and culturally.

It is against this background one must situate the cohesive role claimed for sanskritization by Srinivas (2002: 221–35). Along with sanskritization, which is an endogenous process, Srinivas identified as sources of social change in modern India exogenous processes such as westernization/modernization and secularization. While the untouchables may take recourse to these exogenous processes, there is no scope for them *within* Hinduism to achieve upward mobility. Even the non-religious route is not accessible to them because, as

Srinivas reports, 'I have not come across the untouchables being dominant anywhere' (1955a: 7) and 'The untouchables are never wealthy...' (ibid.: 35). Yet he asserted: 'Sanskritization is beginning to transform the culture of Hindu castes from the Brahmin to the Harijan...It is enabling the lower castes and the groups marginal to Hinduism to occupy a high place in the structure of Hindu society...to the decrease of structural distance between various castes. This is likely to result in greater cohesion among Hindus' (Srinivas 1962: 108).

There is hardly any empirical evidence to confirm this because it is not sufficient that untouchables attempt to sanskritize themselves but it is necessary that those who are above the pollution line should accept them, the prospects of which are bleak; sanskritization is dysfunctional for them. For example, the Smiths of Karanataka did not succeed in their efforts to sanskritize. If all the three routes to upward mobility—sanskritization, political power, and material prosperity—are inaccessible to untouchables, they cannot be 'integrated' into Hindu society.

If, for one-sixth of Hindus, the concept of sanskritization is alienating in its content, if not intent, is there a way out to render it relevant? I suggest that if sanskritization is conceptualized as anticipatory socialization on the part of a group or community and if it is visualized as an Indian variant of reference group behaviour (Merton 1957), it can be done; because anticipatory socialization can be functional or dysfunctional. The critical difference between the two modes of anticipatory socialization lies in the unit which takes to it; in the case of sanskritization it is an inter-group dynamic but in the version elaborated by Merton it is an individual–group process. This clearly illustrates how the social structural features of the 'field' one investigates condition concept formation. However, this does not mean that one cannot transcend the limitations of concepts in the light of field experiences and reformulate them.[8]

As is well known, parallel thinking is common in the scholastic world and the scope of concepts and power of theory increases if they can be applied to a variety of empirical situations. I suggest that with increasing upward social mobility occurring in contemporary India among ex-untouchables—independent of sanskritization as formulated by Srinivas—and the increasing individualism in Indian society as a whole, particularly in the urban setting, individuals and groups who aspire to narrow the gap between ritual and secular status may resort to sanskritization. Sanskritization can thus become an instrument of coping with status incongruence. Additionally, sanskritization can also be conceived as a process of protest; given the increased freedom of behaviour available, individuals and groups may be emboldened to take to the norms and values of upper castes in a spirit of defiance and not necessarily because it will lead to upward mobility. But this mode of 'sanskritization' will not bring about cohesion in society. The points I want to make are two: one, as the characteristics of the 'field' changes, the concepts which emerged out of fieldwork done earlier can be and should be reformulated and two, as and when concepts are invoked to understand a variety of empirical situations, both the potentialities and limitations of concepts will be unfolded (see, for an illustration, Oommen 1987a: 15–34).[9]

Other than sanskritization, Srinivas does not mention any alternate or parallel form of endogenous source of mobility. But that there existed several such processes which undermined the over-arching character and cohesive role of sanskritization is certain: Islamization (latterly Arabization) and Tamilization being two examples. Since Islamization is outside the pale of Hinduism, I shall not discuss it. But Tamilization is very much within the ken of Hinduism (although not sanskritic Hinduism), and hence I shall briefly advert to it. The cognitive blackout of Tamilization goes against the very grain of India and Hinduism's diversity; it promotes a monistic Hinduism.

Sanskritic Hindusim has been an important and perhaps the most dominant version of Hinduism and because of that it is assumed that everybody is eager to fall in line and sanskritize. But as Hart writes:

...the role of Aryan culture in Tamilnadu has been overestimated...All classes of South Indian Brahmins follow mostly Dravidian customs; that the 'sanskritization' made so much of by some anthropologists is, in the case of Tamilnadu at least, for the most part the adoption of Dravidian customs which have always belonged to the upper class; and that where Aryan elements have entered into this process, they have been radically altered to fit Dravidian norms (1975: 58–9).

In the same vein, Berton Stein observed that the Tamils invoked the symbols of Tamilakam from at least the first century BCE and suggests that the Tamils had a 'unique culture' (1977: 11, 25). Tamilakam connotes the home of Tamil language, culture and/ or people and symbolizes the distinction between Tamils who are internal to Tamil Nadu and contrasts them with the 'external other', the Aryan Hindus, who follow sanskritic Hinduism. Tamilakam thus became a political symbol. Tamils, as other linguistic groups, are also divided into a number of endogamous status groups (*kudi* or *kulam*). They follow diverse Hindu sectarian traditions as well as Jainism, Buddhism, Islam, and Christianity. Thus, Tamil unity is anchored to Tamil culture and language irrespective of religious variations. There is no evidence to suggest that sanskritic Hinduism encapsulated Tamilakam.

It is true that a large number of protest movements against Brahmin priesthood (not Brahmins as such) and *varna* hierarchy, and by implication, against sanskritic Hinduism crystallized but eventually, either got marginalized or absorbed into Hinduism. The prominent examples are Buddhism and Jainism of the sixth century BCE, which emerged in north India and Lingayat movement, which crystallized in the twelfth century CE in south India. But the Tamil literary tradition began before the Tamils came into contact with Sanskritic/Aryan Hinduism. And in contemporary India the Tamil movement was propelled mainly by language and not religion, although the undercurrent of non-sanskritic Hinduism (Dravidian Hinduism) was always present. This has been reported by historian Irschik (1969), political scientists Hardgrave (1965) and Barnett (1976), and Spratt (1970), a journalist, among others.

In the nineteenth century several ancient Tamil texts which were hitherto available only in private libraries appeared in print and became accessible to substantial number of educated, wealthy non-Brahmin *jati* groups. The Tamil scholars who did extensive research on these sources argue that Shaiva Siddhanta was the essence of Tamil religion before Brahmanic priesthood made its inroads. The leaders of the Tamil (Dravidian) movement of the twentieth century labelled Shaiva Siddhanta as Dravidian religion, juxtaposing it with Aryan/Sanskritic Hinduism and invoked it as an electrifying source of mobilization (Irschik 1969: 292–5). The Tamil purity movement identified Brahmins as Aryans and as custodians of the sanskritic civilization. The non-Brahmins were identified as Dravidians and as the carriers of Tamil civilization and Brahmins were perceived as the sole agents of sanskritization.[10]

Even an exaggerated scope attributed to sanskritization cannot completely enlist SCs, STs, OBCs, Sikhs, Muslims, Christians, and even Tamils (Dravidian Hindus) as *agents* of sanskritization and the last three (Muslims, Christians, and Tamils) may not even aspire to undergo sanskritization. The points I am making are: (1) that unless sanskritization is re-conceptualized so as to take it out of the groove of Aryan Hinduism it cannot encapsulate Dravidian Hinduism; (2) unless it is defined as the Indian version of reference group behaviour it cannot be applied to SCs, STs as well as religious minorities and (3) therefore, sanskritic Hinduism which excludes these groups from its ambit does not promote cohesion in Indian society. It is not sufficient to suggest that the scope of sanskritization is constantly expanding but it is also necessary to demarcate the boundaries within which the concept is functional, and to identify the eligible aspirants who are likely to adopt it. As it is conceptualized by Srinivas, sanskritization cannot but be cognized as an instrument for perpetuating upper caste hegemony by those who are the perennial role-models and tools of cultural homogenization, producing, if successful, a coercive equilibrium because it does not address the issue of ritual inequality between the agents of sanskritization and the sanskritized. Admittedly, sanskritization cannot be a tool of creating consensual equilibrium, that is, authentic cohesion informed of ritual equality.

Srinivas did not deal with methodology as such although he frequently refers to the method in social anthropology. However, he discusses several issues in methodology such as objectivity, empathy, and the like. Methodology refers to philosophy of social science, which poses questions such as: is social science a 'science' in the same sense as material and life sciences? Is 'objectivity' possible in social science and if yes, in what sense? What is the relationship between theory, concepts, and data? (see Chapter 2 of this volume). In contrast, discussions on method deal with specification of units of study, sampling, techniques of data collection, and modes of analysing data. Needless to say, methodology and method are interrelated. My present interest is to understand the methodological orientation of Srinivas.

Social scientists drastically differ in their methodological orientations. For example, Durkheim gave primacy to society and hence his methodological orientation may be designated as societal determinism. Similarly, Marx's methodology is often labelled as economic determinism. In contrast, Weber's obsession with individual action prompted analysts to designate him as a methodological individualist (see Benton 1977). The tendency to conflate state and nation and treating the nation-state as a self-contained unit of analysis is referred to as methodological nationalism (see Smith 1979). Following the same trail, the methodology pursued by Srinivas to understand Indian society may be designated as 'methodological sanskritic Hinduism'. This qualifier to Hinduism is crucial because he did not take into account Dravidian Hinduism, as I argued above. But for purposes of brevity and elegance I will refer to his orientation as 'methodological Hinduism'.[11]

It is crucial to recall here Srinivas's understanding of Indian unity. He writes: 'The concept of the unity of India is essentially a religious one' and 'As the idea of unity of India has its origin in the Hindu religion, non-Hindus are excluded from it...' (1962: 105, 107). Further, 'India is the sacred land not only of the Hindus but also of the Sikhs, Jains and Buddhists' (Srinivas 1980: 2). This vision, which absorbs even Indic religious minorities into Hinduism and by implication postulating them as cultural insiders and those of non-Indic origin as cultural outsiders is precariously proximate to that upheld by the Rashtriya Swayamsevak Sangh (see Golwalkar 1939; Savarkar 1929). The pertinent point to be noted here is that non-Indic religious communities are outside the pale of Indian unity as Srinivas conceptualized it.[12] I have argued above that it is impossible to encapsulate the 'untouchables' and Tamils into the fold of sanskritization. Similarly, followers of non-Indic religious groups also cannot be within the fold of sanskritic Hinduism. These groups and communities together make well over 40 per cent of India's population. The cohesion that sanskritic Hinduism is capable of producing excludes them.

In spite of the above limitations, Srinivas holds that: 'All India Hinduism was synonymous with sanskritic Hinduism' (1972: 149). There is also a sequential determinism in his writings which connotes an inevitability of sanskritization. As the Brahmins were rapidly westernizing, castes ritually lower to them but above the pollution line were sanskritizing; the implied stages are pre-sanskritization, sanskritization, and westernization. But this sequential determinism may lead to cognitive blackouts in the field. Thus, although the Coorgs were more westernized than Mysore Brahmins when Srinivas was doing fieldwork, he failed to observe the phenomenon. And in spite of the fact that Coorgs were more westernized than Mysore Brahmins, Srinivas found that they were eager to sanskritize! The implication seems to be that westernization is necessary but not sufficient; sanskritization is absolutely inevitable as a stepping stone to westernization for upward social mobility. Finally, the possibility of a group skipping sanskritization and directly westernizing is not logically admissible within this framework, although Srinivas notes: 'It is possible that Westernization may occur without an intermediate process of Sanskritization' (2002: 217). But empirical evidence to support the possibility of westernization skipping sanskritization is not collected and presented by Srinivas.

Srinivas upholds the centrality of Hinduism in grafting tribes on to Hinduism as exemplified by the Coorg case, in facilitating status mobility of OBCs as manifested in reform movements and in boosting the aspirations of even ex-untouchables to move up in Hindu society. That is, even an expansive version of sanskritization can only be conceived as a mechanism of 'integrating' Aryan Hindu society because Srinivas did not pay attention to the challenges posed by Tamilization. This is the rationale behind designating his orientation as methodological Hinduism, which is an anachronism in secularizing India. I am not suggesting that secularization is necessarily displacing sanskritization; the two can and do co-exist. However, as the 'secular space' expands the 'sacred space' is likely to shrink. Perhaps Srinivas was aware of this and hence, he suggested in 1956, 'The moment it is discovered that the term is more a hindrance than a help in analysis, it should be discarded quickly and without regret' (see 2002: 218). We need not follow his advice literally but we need to reformulate the notion of sanskritization so that the disjunction between the concept and the fast changing field, the empirical situation in India, is attended to.

Let me conclude by affirming that M.N. Srinivas did bring in a breath of fresh air into Indian Social Science and we should celebrate his life and works. At the same time, we should not hesitate to stand on his shoulders to see far ahead, to recall Isaac Newton's aphorism. In doing so we need to abandon the ambiguity which persists in India between social anthropology and sociology, fully endorsing anthropology's unique contribution; de-mystify participant observation but giving credit the method amply deserves to collect qualitative data and provide critical insights; graduate on to macro studies without sacrificing the advantages of micro studies and give due credits both to qualitative and quantitative data. The quicker we traverse these tracks the faster will Indian sociology forge foreword.

NOTES

1. A Sanskritist by training Ghurye, was sent to England by Bombay University in 1920 to do PhD in sociology so that he could start the Department of Sociology on his return after training. The recommended research guides for him were L.T. Hobhouse and Sidney Webb, both sociologists. But Ghurye defected to anthropology and opted for W.H.R. Rivers, as his supervisor, without seeking any prior approval from the Bombay University. And, only in January 1923, a few months before the submission of his thesis, Ghurye informed the Registrar of Bombay University of this unauthorized shift to anthropology. Ghurye was suitably 'punished' for this 'aberrant' behaviour by the University of Bombay (see Savur 2011: 10) for details.

2. It is not my point that metamorphosis of a scholar trained in one discipline to another is not possible or will not take place. G.S. Ghurye trained in Sanskrit becoming a 'sociologist', S.C. Dube trained in political science becoming a social anthropologist, Ramakrishna Mukherjee trained in anthropology (including physical anthropology) becoming a sociologist are well-known Indian examples.

3. Incidentally, this is contrary to the rationale provided for the study of rural India through intensive fieldwork. But even when urban India and complex organizations are the objects of study, participant observation is the prescribed method!

4. I have no hard data to prove this. But Srinivas's account of 'Sociology in Delhi' (2002: 623–40) certainly suggests this. However, let me provide some anecdotal evidence to indicate the stigmatization of sociologists/ social anthropologists by economists. Dr A.M. Khusru, who was at the Institute of Economic Growth, used to remark that sociologists were those economists who found their arithmetic difficult during their school/college days. Nasim Ansari, an agricultural economist, at the Agro-economic Research Centre, which was located on the same campus as that of the Delhi School of Economics narrated to me with great relish an imaginatively constructed incident. In an international conference on inflation, in the Delhi School of Economics, a couple of eminent sociologists from the Department of Sociology too were invited. When they were called upon to speak in the course of the conference, they asserted authoritatively that there was no inflation in their respective villages, contrary to what the economists thought!

5. Incidentally, it may not be out of place to recall here that the ongoing Codava movement insists that the Coorgs have a unique identity as

distinct from the 'Kannada society' to which they were latched while creating the state of Karnataka, formed on the basis of linguistic identity. The Codava movement claims that they have a distinct language, legal system, customs, and territory and, hence, are entitled to a separate provincial state.

6. Srinivas took Edmund Leach to task in several of his papers for holding such a view (see, for one example, 1972: 148). But he ignores the view of several others who hold the view that sociological understanding can be promoted better by social anthropologists who study other cultures than sociologists studying their own societies. For example, see Barnes (1959: 15) and Dumont (1966: 23), elaborated in Chapter 2.

7. Whether Lingayats can be viewed as a model for sanskritizing groups is doubtful. They rejected priestly authority, Vedic sacredotalism, and sanskritic beliefs (see Venugopal 1977: 239). But I shall ignore this.

8. I don't know whether Merton and Srinivas knew each other's works. As far as I know only Y.B. Damle attempted to analyse mobility in India's caste system invoking Merton's theory of reference group behaviour. But, unfortunately, he did not refer to sanskritization as the Indian variant of reference group behaviour (Damle 1968: 95–102). It is a pity that useful cross-pollination of ideas does not always take place.

9. According to Weber, charismatic leadership is a system-changing force but my field experience revealed that it can as well be a system-stabilizing force. That is, fieldwork can help conceptual reformulations (see Oommen 1972b).

10. Although sanskritization is claimed to be a process much broader than Brahminization, the principal agents of sanskritization are indeed Brahmins (see Srinivas 1956: 481–96).

11. There is scope for misunderstanding here and the mischievous may exploit it and therefore I need to make the following clarificatory remark. I am not referring to Srinivas's religious disposition but only indicating the implications of the concept of sanskritization.

12. The persisting deep wedge between Indic and non-Indic religions, is an important obstacle for the unity of India (see Oommen 1986a: 53–74). Therefore the project of creating cohesion in Indian society will have to be anchored to secular norms and ideas anchored to citizenship and not to sanskritic Hinduism.

12

Scheduled Castes, Scheduled Tribes, and the Nation
Situating G.S. Ghurye

G ovind Sadashiv Ghurye (1893–1983) is arguably the most prolific Indian anthropo-sociologist[1] and also probably the most written about scholar in this field. There are at least two known PhD theses on Ghurye's work, one of which resulted in the publication of a book (Pramanick 2001) and the other led to the publication of a few research papers (Venugopal 1986, 1993, 1996). Further, there are three well-known felicitation volumes published to honour Ghurye: a volume was brought out on his 60th birthday (Kapadia 1954), another volume was presented to him on his 80th birthday (Pillai 1976), and a centennial festschrift was also published (Momin 1996) after his death.

Ghurye's scholarship is encyclopaedic, straddling caste and race, family and kinship, religion and nation, civilizations and communities, and Rajput architecture and human sexuality; indeed, he was an academic amphibian who was at ease in many worlds of scholarship. Most of his colleagues, contemporaries, students, and admirers have articulated their views and commentaries on Ghurye's analysis of castes and tribes, two seminal themes which were his lifelong passion. However, I suggest that the SCs were subjected to cognitive blackout and the STs were victims of cognitive dissonance in Ghurye's writings. And none of his commentators have taken note of this, which provides the justification for the theme of my lecture. Further, in relentlessly advocating their assimilation/integration into the Indian 'nation', Ghurye held a notion of nation that is utterly West European. This contradicts the famous pronouncement of D.P. Mukerji (1954), that Ghurye was the only 'Indian sociologist' of his time, while others were merely 'sociologists of India'.

———◆———

Ghurye's first book, published in 1932 and titled *Caste and Race in India*,[2] is also his most celebrated book, which has been revised and updated several times. Its fifth edition was published in 1969 and reprinted in 1979, the edition I am referring to in this lecture. The book has one chapter titled 'The Scheduled Castes' that is exactly 30 pages long (pp. 306–36) in a book with 476 pages. While the Indian caste system is the most widely commented upon social phenomenon, the practice of untouchability to which SCs were subjected to was and continues to be the most abominable in human history, shaming even slavery and racism, partly because it was sanctioned and legitimized by a set of religious doctrines. The moment such a statement is made, efforts to dissociate caste system and by implication untouchability from Hinduism, invoking the distinction between *smriti*s and *shruti*s, claiming that the latter oppose the caste system, are in vogue. It is also argued that in the event of a contradiction between the two, shruti shall prevail over smriti (see, for example, Nadkarni 2003). The point at issue here is not one of correctness of doctrines, whether they exist in smriti or shruti, but one of practices in the life-world. The lived reality in Indian society is that untouchability is practised even today, particularly in rural areas, and people who practise it and who are its victims believe that Hinduism and untouchability are inextricably intertwined.

The term SC is an administrative coinage and terms such as *Chandala*, exterior caste, Harijan, dalit, and so on have been in currency, each of which had a different origin.[3] The SCs form '… the fifth order in the four-fold society of Hindu theory of caste', according to Ghurye (1979 [1932]: 307). He admits that 'Ideas of purity, whether occupational or ceremonial, which are found to have been a factor in the genesis of caste, are at the very soul of the idea and practice of untouchability' (ibid.: 307).[4] And, '… the breed of the Chandala is a degraded one and is ranked with that of dog and the pig' (Ghurye 1979 [1932]: 309). The concern here is that the Hindu doctrine of creation refers only to four *varnas* and, if so, how does one account for the *panchamas*, those of the fifth order?

According to ancient Hindu texts, the Chandalas are the progeny of the most hated of the reverse order of the mixed unions, that of the Brahmin female and a Shudra male (ibid.). But, according to Ghurye, '...the more plausible explanation would be that the Chandalas were a degraded group of aborigines' (ibid.: 52). Be that as it may, there were other groups such as Svapachas and Mritapas like Chandalas '...who had to live outside the limits of Arya villages and towns' (ibid.: 312). A number of questions need to be asked and answered if one were to endorse this textual explanation of the origin of untouchables. One, how did the differentiation between the different types of untouchables—Chandalas, Mritapas, Svapachas, and others—come about? Are these distinctions based on the differences in the status of their Shudra/aboriginal fathers? Two, is it that the Brahmin women had so much freedom those days to have illegitimate sexual relations with Shudra men? Three, if they did, was this so well-known to the community so as to sift out the progeny based on paternity, assuming that the Brahmin women had their legitimate Brahmin husbands? Four, if the answer to the above question is in the affirmative, what was the mechanism through which the children of Brahmin females through legitimate and illegitimate unions were separated and grouped together so as to form different castes? Five, why were the deviant Shudra males in question not done away with, given the then prevailing hegemony of the Brahmins? Six, was it not the practice to ostracize the deviant Brahmin females from the family and community? Unfortunately, Ghurye did not pose any of these questions, let alone answer them.

These and several other questions can be answered only if one gets a field-view of the phenomenon under investigation. There is no evidence of Ghurye having done fieldwork to understand the phenomenon of untouchability. This is not to argue that the text-view is irrelevant, since the religious texts sanctioned and legitimized the practice of untouchability, ensuring its persistence till this day. The texts prescribe norms and values, but only the field study unfolds human behaviour: the former prescribes 'the ought' and the latter unfolds 'the is'. And the rupture between 'the ought' and 'the is' needs to be understood. Hence, the dictum: give unto the text that which is the text's and to the field that which is the field's becomes crucial, as I argued quarter of a century ago (Oommen 1983b).

Ghurye refers to Namashudras of West Bengal, an untouchable caste, who numbered 3,20,000 according to the 1951 Census. They have experienced occupational change and a considerable number of them now follow the various learned professions. Yet their social position as a caste continues to be very low (Ghurye 1979 [1932]: 317). This indicates the bi-dimensional status system in Indian society: ritual and secular. Thus, an 'untouchable' may achieve high status in the secular status system, but would retain his low status in the ritual status system. The incongruence between these two status systems is of crucial importance to understand the limited possibility of upward social mobility the SCs can achieve in the caste hierarchy. And, Ghurye's silence in this context is, indeed, disappointing.

Ghurye divided untouchables into two: 'pure' and 'impure'. The untouchables become pure through abjuring 'beef and such other anathematic diet' (ibid.: 322). This is precisely what M.N. Srinivas christened sanskritization (1956). However, sanskritization was scarcely functional for the purpose of achieving a higher ritual status for the untouchables (see Chapter 11). Further, Ghurye admitted '… that the legislative measures against untouchability can at best produce a few dents in the solid wall, whose demolition requires the operation of an active sentiment of the people at large' (1979 [1932]: 330), and he provides several examples of resistance against the changes attempted to eradicate untouchability. Ghurye concluded: 'While these gruesome events reveal the persistence of the occasional but darkest feature of the situation of the Scheduled Castes, daily and routine life of the village registers fair amount of segregation and contemptuous treatment offered by the people at large' (ibid.: 335). Given this conclusion, Ghurye's advocacy of assimilation of untouchables into Hindu society seems to be a wild goose chase.

Apart from the chapter titled the 'Scheduled Castes' in *Caste and Race in India*, there is an article titled 'Untouchable Classes and their Assimilation in Hindu Society' published in the journal *The Aryan Path* in 1933 (see Ghurye 1973: 316–23). The reproduction of this article in the 1973 book probably points to Ghurye's firm conviction that assimilation of untouchables into Hindu society is a feasible proposition. Ghurye wrote:

According to the orthodox theory of Hindu social organization these classes form the fifth and the outcaste section. They are given the appellation of untouchables because they are believed to impart pollution to members of higher sections if they touch them. But in the orthodox theory on the subject this characteristic of imparting pollution by touch belongs really to the fourth section of Hindu society. The fifth section that is now called untouchable is supposed, both in theory and practice to pollute members of the other sections even if they stand at a certain distance. Thus, it will be realized that the so called untouchables are, in practice, really unapproachables. It is this unapproachability that creates the main difficulties in the path of their assimilation in the Hindu society (1973: 316–17).

It is clear that by 'assimilation' Ghurye meant transformation of the status of 'unapproachables' who belong to the fifth order to the status of 'untouchables' drawn from the fourth varna! Ghurye endorsed the 'inherent connection between the spirit of castes and untouchability', and admitted that 'Removal of untouchability, therefore, intimately depends on the disappearance of the spirit of caste' (ibid.: 317). To achieve this, Ghurye advocated four steps: one, removing the individual's disability which hampers a better and cleaner living; two, enabling these classes to cultivate a cleaner and moral mode of life; three, to encourage those of other sections to have freer social intercourse with these people; and four, 'undermine and eradicate the exclusive spirit of castes' (ibid.: 319).

To achieve this truly revolutionary task, Ghurye advocates an administrative approach by setting up a central organization with its provincial and local committees to adjudicate disputes that arise between ritually pure and impure castes. Additionally, providing modern technology and adequate training to the untouchable classes is also an important step prescribed by him. Finally, ensuring employment to these classes, particularly in offices situated in towns and villages will facilitate the process of eradicating the practice of untouchability, according to him. In sum, Ghurye advocates change of status in the secular dimension of untouchables to assimilate them into the Hindu society. On the other hand, he wanted to leave undisturbed the ritual dimension.[5] Thus, he suggested:

We must try to see the various items in the campaign against untouchability in their proper perspective and not exaggerate the importance of temple entry so as to divert our attention from the other items. Free access to Hindu temples is only one of the rights and it is not the most important means for assimilation of these classes in the Hindu society (1973: 320).

Ghurye wanted 'to prepare the minds of populace at large to look upon untouchability as both undesirable and impractical' (ibid.: 321). And to achieve this objective it is necessary to start an extensive propaganda preaching against untouchability. But in the process '... we must not be drawn into a controversy over the existence or non-existence of the doctrine of untouchability in the Hindu Dharma Shashtras' (ibid.). It is clear that Ghurye wanted to 'assimilate' the untouchables into Hindu society without disturbing the ritual status system seminal to it and without interrogating the Hindu *dharmashastras*, which provide legitimacy to caste hierarchy. I have referred above to the bi-dimensional nature of the status system in Hindu society and there is enough evidence to show that, while the status of ex-untouchables has gone up in the secular context, it does not lead to a concomitant change in their ritual status. This calls for the need to locate the core institutional order in a society and the kernel of that institution.[6] The dominant view when Ghurye wrote this article in 1933 was that the caste system constituted the core institutional order of Hindu society and ritual status was the kernel of caste hierarchy. Therefore, the advocacy of assimilation of untouchables into Hindu society leaving the ritual dimension of the caste system intact was untenable.

I propose to conclude the discussion on SCs by calling attention to a possible strategy for social change. Given the bi-dimensional nature of the status system in Hindu society and because ritual status is its kernel, two possible strategies can be invoked. One, start with the soft-spot in the system: the soft-spot in the case of Hindu society is constituted by the secular dimension consisting of education, employment, political representation, access to economic resources, and the like. In contrast, measures such as temple entry, inter-caste marriages, etc., are more change-resistant as they erode the ritual superiority of the higher castes. And, therefore, a strategy for social change to eliminate untouchability may start with the soft spots, namely, the secular dimension, but ultimately the sanctity of ritual dimension should be questioned (Oommen 1968). Alternatively, one may attack the Hindu dharmashastras so as to de-legitimize the caste system and the practice of untouchability that it entails.[7]

Ghurye, however, was not advocating either of these approaches and, therefore, it is difficult to comprehend the process of assimilation of untouchables into Hindu society he had visualized. He even held: 'Reserved representation is not necessary; it is harmful in so far as it tends to perpetuate the distinction based on birth' (1979 [1932]: 290). This observation is not simply curious but also amusing because the caste system is all about perpetuating distinctions based on birth. And, reservation is conceived as an instrument to unsettle it at least partially. His main concern was that the policy of reservation will tear asunder Indian society through inter-caste strife and it will unleash caste patriotism. It seems that Ghurye preferred the coercive equilibrium institutionalized through upper-caste hegemony rather than a consensual equilibrium that will gradually evolve based on social justice and equality. Inevitably, inter-caste conflict is a small price to be paid for the structural change of the caste system.

Ghurye reposed great faith in the 'noble' Constitution of India that promised equality to all including the ex-untouchables. However, he refused to recognize that, in order to put into practice this ontological equality, the state had to provide for equality of opportunity, as it is a shell without substance unless equality of conditions is created. The instrument of reservation or protective discrimination is nothing but an attempt to create this condition so that those who are placed in grossly iniquitous conditions are enabled to compete with the traditionally privileged. However, this is not to deny the possibility of inequality in outcomes when the policy of reservation is implemented. To cope with this problem it is necessary to take out the emerging creamy layer among the traditionally underprivileged, so that the benefits can vertically flow to the less fortunate among them.

However, Ghurye's hope that 'certain exigencies of modern life will force high caste Hindus to change their attitude and practice to some extent' (1979 [1932]: 295) has not come true. And he asserted that '...social and religious privileges and disabilities of caste are no longer recognized in law and only partly in custom. Only the depressed classes are labouring under certain customary and semi-legal disabilities' (ibid.: 302). This sounds rather unrealistic viewed in the context of the latest available empirical evidence regarding the practice of untouchability (Shah et al. 2006).

I have suggested that Ghurye's analysis of SCs is characterized by a cognitive blackout and this for the following reasons. First, the limited space (barely 40 pages taking into account the chapter on 'Scheduled Castes' [Ghurye 1979 [1932]] and the article in *The Aryan Path*, together) devoted to the analysis of SCs. Second, his considerable reliance on ancient Hindu texts and not having done any fieldwork among the untouchables to unfold their life-world. Third, the excessive optimism he reposed in the forces of modernization to weaken the caste system and the practice of un-touchability. Finally, his underestimating the strength of the ritual dimension and religious doctrines in perpetuating the practice of untouchability.

The second category with which this lecture is concerned, namely, the STs, was the subject matter of Ghurye's second book, published in 1943, titled *The Aborigines-so-Called and Their Future*. The book was enlarged and published in 1959 with the title *The Scheduled Tribes*, and its third edition was published in 1963. Unlike caste, which is widely acknowledged as a unique Indian social category, tribe is a universal socio-cultural collectivity found in Africa, Australia, Asia, the Americas, and Europe. Two basic features distinguish tribes from castes: they have their definite territories (homelands) and languages. In contrast, several castes jointly share a common territory and a common language. In India, linguistic regions have specific castes. Both castes and tribes may share a common religion; the SCs could be Hindus, Buddhists, Muslims, or Christians. Similarly, the STs may abandon their original primal vision, usually designated as animism/naturism, and embrace one of the 'world religions'.

Just as Ghurye wanted the SCs to be assimilated in Hindu society, he wanted to integrate the STs into the Indian society and polity. In this context, he differentiated the encysted tribes of central India from the tribes of North East India that belonged those days to Assam; the first category was to be integrated through Hinduiza-tion, and the second to be politically incorporated through strong administrative measures of the Indian state. *The Aborigines-so-Called* deals with the encysted tribes, and the issues relating to the tribes of North East are discussed in the book *The Burning Caldron of North-East India*, published in 1980.

The Aborigines was written as a response to Verrier Elwin's *Loss of Nerve* published earlier in 1941. Elwin advocated insulation of tribes from the Hindus surrounding them which eventually most anthropologists supported, although some had argued for gradual and mutual acculturation of the Hindus and the tribes, as Majumdar already did (1939). Elwin wanted to create National Parks for the tribes so that they are protected from the depredations of Hindus.[8] Contrarily, Ghurye thought that the contact of tribes with Hindus will gradually enhance the former's status and earn respectability for them. Ghurye provided the rationale which informs his position in the Preface to the second edition of the book, titled *The Scheduled Tribes*, published in 1959. He wrote,

Most of the contemporary nations are composite wholes formed of many ethnic stocks which had their own separate cultures before the nation-making epoch...The process of assimilation of smaller groups of different cultures into larger ones or less homogenous cultures has been steadily going on...This process of assimilation was upset with the appearance of the British on the scene. It is the problem of these peoples (that is, tribes) which is the subject of this essay. (1959: xiii–xiv)

Ghurye is, by and large, correct in the above observation in that most countries in the world followed this track. But there are two issues, that of size and the social milieu of the 'nations' that he ignored. Of the 220 member states of the United Nations, 54 per cent have a population of five million or less. In contrast, at the time Ghurye wrote the above lines, India's population was approximately 500 million. More importantly, the cultural complexity of India's population was much greater than any country in the world, including the USA. While Indians lived mainly in their original homelands, the US population was drawn from all over the world. Above all, some of the tribes—Bhils, Gonds, Santals—numbered three to five million each.

In social anthropology, peasant society is conceived as a part-society, part of a civilization; tribes are autonomous and 'independent' entities. Ignoring this, the Indian Constitution envisaged SCs, which are part of the Hindu society, and STs, who are independent of it, as belonging to one category under the rubric of 'Backward Classes'. Unfortunately, Ghurye endorsed this in his eagerness to create a composite 'nation' (see Ghurye 1959: x–xi). As a sociologist who respected empirical details, Ghurye should have recognized the difference between castes and tribes. The idea of core institutional order would have come handy in this context also. As noted above, the core of Hindu society is caste hierarchy, the kernel of which is ritual purity. This is not applicable to tribal society; a common ancestral homeland and a shared language are the specific features of tribal societies all over the world.[9] Thus viewed, the conventional rural–urban dichotomy is inapplicable to India; rather, a trichotomy of urban, rural, and tribal segments becomes pertinent (Oommen 1967a).

I suggest that the fatal flaw of Ghurye in this context should be located in his endorsing the view held by British Indian Census Commissioners (although he severely criticized them on many counts) that animism and Hinduism are not very different (see Xaxa 2008: 76–7). Although this perspective favoured Ghurye's enthusiasm to integrate tribes into the Hindu fold, given the colonizers' proclivity to stigmatize everything Indian, it could also be seen as an attempt to demean Hindus and Hinduism. At any rate, the similarity between Hinduism and animism was usually located in the context of religious practices of lower-caste Hindus and tribal groups. Thus, this could be seen as a triple-barrel gun: (i) keep the lower castes where they are within Hinduism by clubbing them with tribes, (ii) attempt incorporation of groups such as SCs and STs into the Hindu fold, and (iii) maintain the superiority of upper castes as upholders of sophisticated Hinduism, conceding the hegemony of Brahmins as norm-setters and value-givers. What I am suggesting is that, by deflecting attention from the core features of tribal society—territorial concentration and linguistic specificity—and latching on to religion as its core dimension, Ghurye's analysis of the tribal question in central India suffered from cognitive dissonance. For example, he noted that the Ranchi district had 80 per cent tribal population, but only 53 per cent spoke non-Aryan languages, and 2,80,000 were Christians (1963 [1943]: 127). The assumptions are (i) tribes cannot have Aryan languages as their mother tongues, and (ii) if they embrace Christianity, they cease to be tribes. Both are incorrect.

An important implication of invoking Hinduization of tribes leading to the eclipse of their tribal identity needs to be noted here. If one applies the same process to other territorially anchored linguistic communities, the absurdity of the argument will become self-evident. Will Maharashtrian Hindus cease to be Maharashtrians if they embrace Buddhism? Will Malayali Hindus cease to be Malayalis if they convert to Christianity? Is it that Kashmiri Hindus ceased to be Kashmiris because they adopted Islam as their religion? These questions can be extrapolated and applied to tribes too. The Nagas of India are predominantly Christians, but they still remain Nagas irrespective of the religious faith they follow. Ignoring multiple identities shared by collectivities and privileging a single identity, Ghurye and most Indian sociologists and social anthropologists believed that Hinduization of tribes would result in a total transformation of their identity from tribes to Hindus! This issue is now being raised by some scholars (see, for example, Xaxa 2008).

The other cognitive dissonance found in Ghurye's analysis of STs relates to the antiquity of settlers in India. He asserted '... science and history do not countenance the practice of calling these tribes aborigines' (1963 [1943]: 13). But a few lines above he hypothesized: 'If the Rigveda Aryans came later than others, they made up for the lost time by energizing the local people, creating a high culture and making India their permanent home' (ibid.: 13). That is, the Aryans came to India,[10] they did not come to an empty space and that there were some pre-Aryan inhabitants in India was conceded by Ghurye. But the belief that Aryans created a high culture cannot erase the facts that the Aryans were immigrants who intruded into India and the Dasas and the tribes were the original inhabitants of India. Ghurye argued: 'To adjust the claims of the different strata of Indian society on the ground of the antiquity or comparative modernity of their settlement in India is a frightfully difficult task which if undertaken, will only let loose the forces of disunity' (ibid.: 13).

This is not a tenable academic or scientific position, but rather an explicitly political or activist one. I am not suggesting that an academic should not take a political or an activist position, but arguing that the activism of an academic should be buttressed by scientific analysis. The role of an analyst is indeed to undertake frightfully difficult tasks and, based on that analysis anchored to history and reason, persuade all concerned to recognize the merit of his/her argument and strive for unity among and welfare of people which is a political task. Instead, Ghurye took the shortcut and left the task unattended because it was 'frightful'. Although this can bring temporary and superficial truce, as and when the wounded history unfolds itself, the emerging middle class from among the victimized collectivities will rise in protest. This is precisely what is happening in the tribal world of central India through the agency of Naxalbari movement. And Ghurye did recognize the fact that 'In all these areas the respective tribes were no doubt the earlier settlers reclaiming the land from the jungles...There can be no room for doubt that a number of the so-called aboriginal tribes had lost their land to the Hindus' (1963 [1943]: 24, 25). And yet, he advocated Hinduization of these tribes that could have only transformed them into pauperized Hindus, and this is precisely what happened.[11]

Why is it that most Indian sociologists, including Ghurye, did not apprehend the tribal issue in its proper perspective? I suggest that this is so because they did not take cognizance of the distinction between different varieties of colonialism. In his attempt to understand the dominant relationship of England vis-à-vis Ireland, Scotland, and Wales, Michael Hetcher (1975) characterizes the latter three as 'internal colonies' within United Kingdom. The homelands of tribes too could be conceptualized as internal colonies within India.[12] Instead, the prevailing mood was (and this persists obstinately to this day) to conceptualize tribes, particularly of central India, as 'backward Hindus' who should be absorbed into Hindu society.

There is yet another, and perhaps more relevant, distinction in the context of external colonialism; replicative and retreatist, which I have made in another context (see Oommen 1991). In social science writings retreatist colonialism is widely recognized. Thus, European colonizers retreated from Asia and Africa after having ruled for a couple of centuries or so. But in the case of the New World—the Americas and Australia—the Europeans settled down, replicated their own societies and marginalized the natives (aborigines) through genocide and 'culturocide'.[13]

When the Aryans arrived in India, the Dravidians and aborigines were the occupants of the then Indian territory. The Dravidians were forced to go to south India and they carved out a separate space, but the aborigines receded to the hilly tracts, and through their 'superior cultures', to which Ghurye alluded, Aryans have subjected the tribes to culturocide. Since the phenomenon occurred in the hoary past and as the notion of colonialism was absent in human cognition those days, nobody referred to the Aryan advent as colonialism. However, viewed in the context of what had happened in the Americas and Australia, one can legitimately refer to what the Aryans did as replicative colonialism. Thus, the Indian tribes were subjected to replicative colonialism in Ancient India and to retreatist colonialism by the British, along with other Indians in modern India. After the British retreated, tribal settlements became internal colonies in independent India, a repetition of what happened in several parts of the world. Such a perspective will help us understood the structure of deprivations of the Indian tribes.

Ghurye wanted the tribes of central India to be culturally assimilated through Hinduization. In contrast, the tribes of North East India had to be politically integrated. The British policy of scheduling tribal communities and areas introduced through the Government of India Act, 1935, was an obstacle to achieve the task of integration. According to Ghurye, the purpose of the Act was to prevent the emergence of independent India as a unified 'sovereign state' and as a 'well-knit nation in the making' (1973: 110). A year later he wrote: 'The North-east India (Bharat) appears to be on the peak of a volcano which may erupt at anytime and break the integrity of the country as we find it in the Constitution of India 1950 and its subsequent amendments' (1974: 160). Fortunately, this pessimistic prognosis did not stand the test of time.

Ghurye did not advocate Hinduization of North East tribes probably because of the substantial presence of Christianity among the Nagas, Mizos, and Khasis, and also because some of the tribes or their sections were already Hinduized or had become Buddhists. But he was opposed to the tribes being referred to as *adivasis*, be they of North East, who became part of India only 100 years ago, or those of central India, who were part of India for thousands of years. To Ghurye, 'The usage of this word [adivasi] has done incalculable harm and doing so, to the cause of bringing about some kind of harmony among the many races and peoples, some of whom have been inhabiting this country for more than four thousand years' (Ghurye 1980: 29). Admittedly, Ghurye's principal anxiety was political unity of India, as he visualized it, rather than to the facts of history. If one cannot ignore the claims of those inhabiting the country for 4,000 years, is it not reasonable to respect the claims of those who inhabited the country for 20,000 years? The point at issue here is not longevity of habitation but equity and justice, both of which were/are denied to the adivasis in India.

To understand Ghurye's advocacy of assimilation of SCs into Hindu society, Hinduization of the STs of central India, and political integration of the STs of North East India, one has to comprehend the notion of nation implicit in his writings. Ghurye had not only conflated state and nation, but also society and nation-state that was/ is widespread in social science.[14] Ghurye fits neatly into Zygmunt Bauman's conceptualization:

> The term society as used by well-nigh all sociologists regardless of their school loyalties is for all practical purposes, a name for an entity identical in size and composition with the nation-state. [Further] with hardly any exception all the concepts and analytical tools currently employed by social scientists are geared to a view of the human world in which the most volu- minous totality is a society, a notion equivalent for all practical purposes to the concept of the nation-state. (Bauman 1973: 43, 78)

The idea of nation-state, as it was conceived and translated into practice in West Europe after the Treaty of Westphalia concluded in 1648, wanted to create culturally homogeneous societies; 'for each nation its own state' was the dictum. Homogenization of the nation-state witnessed enormous violence (see Oommen 1997b: 135–59), and yet the project did not achieve its target. And, as Charles Tilly observed, 'Only a tiny proportion of the world's dis- tinctive religious, linguistic and cultural groupings have formed their own states, while precious few of the world's existing states have approximated the homogeneity and commitment conjured up by the label "nation-state"' (1994: 137).

Therefore, to treat state, nation, and society as one entity was and continues to be an untenable proposition, particularly in the case of India which encapsulates one-sixth of humanity and has incredible cultural diversity. The Indian Constitution, to which Ghurye referred frequently and with ample admiration, did not visualize the creation of a homogenous society. Its first sentence reads: 'India is a union of states.' The Constitution did not privilege Hinduism as the national or official religion, in spite of the fact that 82 per cent of Indians are Hindus according to the Census of India. Several languages are recognized (now the number is 22) as official languages, a provision unheard of anywhere in the world. The motto of the Constitution is 'unity in diversity', and the advocacy of assimilation and integration championed by Ghurye is patently antithetical to India's Constitution. Ghurye (1968) is absolutely right in holding that society is not a mere aggregation of individuals, but an organic unity built through interpersonal and individual group relations. Thus viewed, India encapsulates several 'societies' within it and its organic unity can be established only through non-primordial, that is, civil ties.[15]

There are four broad visions which are in currency, but not clearly articulated, about the Indian republic which may be designated as cultural monism, cultural pluralism, cultural federalism, and cultural subalternism (see Oommen 2004c). According to cultural monists, the critical marker of Indian society is religion. Religious nationalism is central in this vision of India. As a part of Hindu consolidation, the traditionally underprivileged cultural subalterns—SCs and STs—are being incorporated into the Hindu mainstream. But to the critical thinkers among cultural subalternists, the values embedded in caste hierarchy, which legitimized and even sanctified by the Hindu scriptures, is the major obstacle to the socio-cultural consolidation of India (see, for example, Ilaiah 1996).

While cultural monism is flaunted by the traditionally privileged caste Hindus as the hope of India, cultural pluralists advocate secularism, that is, the dignified co-existence of all groups and communities, to be controlled by a strong centre. Cultural pluralism is considered a panacea for the ills of Indian society by the modernists. While cultural federalists too attest secularism, they insist on political decentralization given India's vast size and mind-boggling cultural diversity. The cultural subalternists believe that, in spite of the constitutional promises of equality, justice, and fraternity, the specificity of their needs, aspirations, and contributions of SCs and STs are ignored. The value orientations implied in Ghurye's advocacy of assimilation of SCs into Hindu society, Hinduization of STs of central India, and the political integration of STs of North East India for the consolidation of the 'Indian Nation' is clearly that of cultural monism. It falls in line with the European model of nation-state that coerced the weaker and smaller collectivities to abandon their identity to avail of equality, a model utterly unsuited for India.

NOTES

1. Ghurye authored 31 books and over 40 research papers. Except his first book *Caste and Race in India* published by Routledge in 1932 and the second book *Aborigines-so-Called* published by the Gokhale Institute of Economics and Politics, Pune in 1943, all his books were published by Popular Prakashan, Mumbai. Subsequent editions of the above two books were also published by Popular Prakashan.

2. *Caste and Race in India* had several incarnations, including *Caste and Class in India* and *Caste, Class and Occupation*. However, the reasons for the changes in its titles are not important for the present analysis.

3. The term Chandala was of Hindu textual origin. The term 'exterior caste' was introduced by British officials, and the term Harijan was coined by Narsinh Mehta and propagated by Mohandas Karamchand Gandhi. However, the term Dalit was coined by activists of SC background and has gained wider acceptance.

4. It was unlikely that a Sanskritist like Ghurye, who drew constantly and substantially on indology, would have been unaware of the distinction between Smritis and Shrutis and their differing positions on caste and untouchability. Therefore, Nadkarni's contention seems to be problematic.

5. Ghurye seems to be assuming that hygienic purity can mitigate the deficits of ritual purity. But the fact that Dr Baba Sahib Ambedkar could not hire a tonga in Baroda and Babu Jagjivan Ram was not allowed to enter the Puri temple contradict that assumption.

6. The idea of core institutional order of a society was initially suggested by Lockwood (1964). The core institutional order should not be mistaken for any kind of determinism, because it varies from society to society and in the same society over a period of time. But transformation from one type to another type of society can occur only if the core institutional orders changes.

7. This is precisely what Dr Baba Sahib Ambedkar did (see Ambedkar 1979).

8. I am not aware if Elwin was inspired by the 'reservations' that were established in the United States of America. The American aborigines numbered three million, that is, around 1 per cent of the national population in early twentieth century, half of whom were located in 260 reservations and the remaining were spatially dispersed. The Indian situation is quite different. Constituting 8 per cent of the national population, the tribes numbered 40 million in 1950s and lived mainly in their ancestral homelands. Elwin shifted his position and took a more moderate one later (see Elvin 1943). It is important to note here that: 'Reservations and reserves perpetuated racial segregation, administrative paternalism and lower-class status for Indian people' (Jarvenpa 1985: 29). For a comparison of the Indian and US situation, see Oommen (1989).

9. The implications of this position are substantial as it conceives tribes as 'nations'. But it disavows the ill-conceived West European idea that each nation should have its own sovereign state. It is a fact that most nations in South Asia have renounced sovereign states and settled for provincial states within a sovereign state (see Oommen 2004a). It is interesting to recall here that King Mutesa II of Baganda wondered:

'I have never been able to pin down precisely the difference between a tribe and a nation and see why one is thought so despicable and the other is so admired...the Baganda have a common language, tradition, history and cast of mind... We were accepted as the most civilised and powerful of the kingdoms' (1967a: 78–9). But he laments that colonialism changed all this!

10. The argument that India was the original homeland of the Aryans, but they migrated to Europe and a section of them returned to India has been in currency for some years. In a seminar held in the fourth week of November 2010 in New Delhi, several historians and archaeologists argued that there is no evidence to prove the Aryan invasion of India. These arguments need not detain us here, because Ghurye had endorsed the Aryan immigration into India. He wrote: 'It may be taken to be historical fact that people calling themselves "Aryan" poured into India through the North-West, somewhere about 2000 BC' (1979 [1932]: 117).

11. Incidentally, this seems to be true of all 'world religions'. There is a widely circulated remark attributed to an African tribal chieftain. On being asked to comment on the basic difference between the pre-colonial and colonial times, he remarked: 'When colonisation started they had the Bible and we had the land, but now we have the Bible and they have the land!'

12. Several tribes are vivisected and apportioned between bigger and stronger 'nations' of India. Thus, the Bhils are apportioned between Gujarat, Maharashtra, Madhya Pradesh, and Rajasthan; and the Santals, between Bihar, West Bengal, and Orissa. These and several other tribes, if kept together, can be formed into viable provincial states on the same basis as other states (see Oommen 2005b).

13. I have introduced the notion of culturocide to refer to the destruction and/or stigmatization of the cultures of weaker and smaller collectivities by the state and/or the dominant collectivities (see Oommen 1986a).

14. Ghurye writes: 'The constitution of India in its very preamble refers the country as the nation' (1974: 1). The first two chapters of the book *Whither India* have the same title: 'The Nation Implements its Constitution' (ibid.: 1–122). It is obvious that Ghurye is conflating state and nation, an inadmissible proposition in social science scholarship. Since I have discussed the issue at length elsewhere, I will not repeat them here. Interested readers may consult Oommen (1997b), particularly chapter 3.

15. Several commentators refer to Ghurye as a nationalist, and a Hindu nationalist at that (see, for example, Upadhya 2002). But, above all, he is a rigid statist, and his value orientation does not even accommodate the flexibilities evident in the Indian Constitution, a document he often praised in his writings.

References

Abdel-Malek, A. 1963. 'Orientalism in Crisis', *Diogenes*, 44 (1): 103–40.

Ahmed, A.S. 1987. *Towards Islamic Anthropology: Definitions, Dogma and Direction*. Lahore: Vanguard.

Albrow, Martin. 1990. *The Global Age*. Cambridge: Polity Press.

Ambedkar, B.R. 1979. *Castes in India: Their Mechanisms, Genesis and Development*. Bombay: Department of Education, Government of Maharashtra.

Appadurai, Arjun. 1997. *Modernity at Large: Cultural Dimensions of Globalization*. New Delhi: Oxford University Press.

Archer, M.S. 1991. 'Sociology for One World: Unity and Diversity', *International Sociology*, 6 (2): 131–47.

Asad, Talal. 1973. *Anthropology and the Colonial Encounter*. Ithaca, NY: Cornell University Press.

Aschroft, Richard. 1972. 'Leviathan Truimphant: Thomas Hobbes and the Politics of Wild Men', in Edward Dudley and Maximilian E. Novak (eds), *The Wildman Within: Western Thought from the Renaissance to Romanticism*. Pittsburg: University of Pittsburg, pp. 141–82.

Atal, Yogesh and Luca Dall Oglio (eds), 1987. *Migration of Talent: Causes and Consequences of Brain Drain*. Bangkok: UNESCO PRO for Asia and the Pacific.

Barker, Lee D. 1998. *From Savage to Negro: Anthropology and the Construction of Race*. Berkeley: University of California Press.

Barnes, J.A. 1959. 'Politics Without Parties', *Man*, 59: 15–16.

Barnett, M.R. 1976. *The Politics of Cultural Nationalism in South India*. Princeton: Princeton University Press.

Barton, A.H. 1955. 'The Concept of Property-Space in Social Research', in P.F. Lazersfeld and Morris Rosenberg (eds), *The Language of Social Research*. Glencoe: The Free Press, pp. 40–53.

Bauer, Yehuda. 1982. *A History of Holocaust.* New York: Franklin Watts.

Bauman, Zygmut. 1973. *Culture as Praxis.* London: Routledge and Kegan Paul.

Beattie, John. 1964. *Other Cultures.* London: Cohen and West.

Benton, Ted. 1977. *Philosophical Foundations of Three Sociologies.* London: Routledge and Kegan Paul.

Berreman, G.D. 1968. 'Is Anthropology Alive? Social Responsibility in Anthropology', *Current Anthropology,* 9 (5): 391–6.

Béteille, André. 1966. *Caste, Class and Power.* Bombay: Oxford University Press.

Béteille, André and T.N. Madan (eds). 1975. *Encounters and Experience: Personal Accounts of Field Work.* New Delhi: Vikas Publishing House.

Boas, F. 1938. *Mind of Primitive Man.* New York: MacMillan and Co.

Bottomore, T.B. 1962. 'Sociology in India', *British Journal of Sociology,* 13 (2): 98–106.

Chandra, Pratap. 1977. *The Hindu Hind.* Simla: Indian Institute of Advanced Study.

Chatterji, B.C. 1882. *Anandamath.* Calcutta: Bangadarshan.

Clinard, M.B. and J.W. Elder. 1965. 'Sociology in India: A Study in the Sociology of Knowledge', *American Journal of Sociology,* 30 (4): 581–7.

Collingwood, R.G. 1942. *The New Leviathan.* Oxford: Clarendon Press.

Connor, Walker. 1984. *The National Question in Marxist-Leninst Theory and Strategy.* Princeton: Princeton University Press.

Coomaraswamy, A.K. 1981. *Essays in National Idealism.* New Delhi: Munshiram Manohar Publishers.

Cox, R.W. 1992. 'Global Prerestroika', in R. Miliband (ed.), *New World Order, Socialist Register.* London: Merlin, pp. 30–45.

Damle Y.B. 1955. *Social Differentiation and Differentiation in Emoluments.* Pune: Deccan College Institute of Postgraduate Studies.

———. 1961. *A Review of Literature on Caste.* Pune: Deccan College.

———. 1965. 'For a Theory of Indian Sociology', in R.N. Saksena (ed.), *Sociology in India.* Agra: Institute of Social Sciences, pp. 32–52.

———. 1967. 'The School and College as a Social System', in M.S. Gore, I.P Desai, and Suma Chitnis (eds), *Papers in the Sociology of Education in India.* New Delhi: National Council of Educational Research and Training, pp. 250–80.

———. 1968. 'Reference Group Theory with Regard to Mobility in Caste', in J. Silverberg (ed.), *Social Mobility in the Caste System of India.* The Hague: Mouton and Co., pp. 95–102.

———. 1982. *Caste, Religion and Politics in India.* New Delhi: IBH Publishing Co.

———. 1985. 'Sociological Theory', in *Survey of Research in Sociology and Social Anthropology: 1969–79.* New Delhi: Indian Council of Social Science Research, pp. 51–72.

Damle Y.B. 1986. 'Sociology in India: Its Teaching and Status', in T.K. Oommen and P.N. Mukherji (eds), *Indian Sociology: Reflections and Introspections*. Bombay: Popular Prakashan, pp. 101–12.

———. 1989. 'Dialetics between Theory and Social Reality', *The Indian Journal of Social Science*, 2 (2): 145–57.

———. 1993. *Theory, Rhetoric and Social Reality*. Surat: Centre for Social Studies, pp. 1–27.

———. 1999. *Dr. B.R. Ambedkar: Critique and Reconstruction*. New Delhi: Centre for the Study of Social Systems, Jawaharlal Nehru University, pp. 7–39.

Daniel, Norman. 1966. *Islam, Europe and Empire*. Edinburgh: Edinburgh University Press.

Das, A.K. 1984. *The Artist in Chains: The Life of Bankimchandra Chatterji*. New Delhi: New Statesman Publishing Company.

Desai, A.R. 1948. *Social Background of Indian Nationalism*. Bombay: Popular Prakashan.

Desai, I.P. 1976. *Untouchability in Rural Gujarat*. Bombay: Popular Prakashan.

Dhanagare, D.N. 1980. 'Search for Identity: Symposium on Studying Our Society', *Seminar*, 254: 23–6.

Disraeli, Benjamin, 1945. *Sybil*. London: John Lane.

Dumont, Louis. 1957. 'For a Sociology of India', in L. Dumont and D. Pocock (eds), *Contributions to Indian Sociology*, I: 7–22.

———. 1964. 'Nationalism and Communalism', *Contributions to Indian Sociology*, VII: 30–70.

———. 1966. 'A Fundamental Problem in the Sociology of India', *Contributions to Indian Sociology*, IX: 17–32.

———. 1970. *Homo Hierarchicus: The Caste System and its Implications*. Chicago: University of Chicago Press.

Duster, Troy. 1990. *Backdoor to Eugenics*. New York: Routledge and Kegan Paul.

Duttagupta, Bela. 1972. *Sociology in India: An Enquiry into Sociological Thinking and Empirical Social Research in the 19th Century with Special Reference to Bengal*. Calcutta: Centre for Sociological Research.

Eisenstadt, S.N. 1965. *Essays on Comparative Institutions*. New York: John Wiley and Sons.

Elder, J.W. 1960. 'Caste and World Views: The Application of Survey Research Methods', in Milton Singer and Bernad Cohn (eds), *Structure and Change in Indian Society*. Chicago: Aldine Publishing Company, pp. 175–88.

Elias, Norbert. 1987. 'The Retreat of Sociologists in the Present', *Theory, Culture and Society*, 4 (2, 3): 223–48.

Elwin, Verrier. 1941. *The Loss of Nerve*. Bombay: Wagle Press.

———. 1943. *The Aboriginals*. Oxford: Oxford University Press.

Elwin, Verrier. 1957. *A Philosophy for North East Frontier Agency*. NEFA: Directorate of Information.

Erikson, K.T. 1967. 'A Comment on Disguised Observation in Sociology', *Social Problems*, 14 (4): 366–73.

Essed, Philomena. 1991. *Understanding Everyday Racism*. Newbury Park: Sage Publications.

Fabian, J. 1983. *Time and the Other: How Anthropology Makes its Object*. New York: Columbia University Press.

Fallding, Harold. 1968. *The Sociological Task*. New Jersey: Prentice Hall.

Fernandes, Florestan. 1969. *The Negro in Brazilian Society*. New York: Columbia University Press.

Feuer, L.S. 1969. *The Conflict of Generations*. London: Hineman.

Firth, Raymond. 1967. *Tikopia Ritual and Belief*. London: George Allen and Unwin.

Foster, G.M. 1953. 'What is Folk Culture?', *American Anthropologist*, 55 (2): 159–73.

Furnivall, J.S. 1948. *Colonial Policy and Practice*. Cambridge: Cambridge University Press.

Gandhi, M.K. 1938. *Hind Swaraj*. Ahmedabad: Navjivan Publishing House.

———. 1948. *India of My Dreams*. Ahmedabad: Navjivan Publishing House.

Gellner, Ernst. 1964. *Thought and Change*. London: Widenfield and Nicolson.

Genov, Nikolai (ed.). 1989. *National Traditions in Sociology*. London: Sage Publications.

Gerth, H. and C. Wright Mills (eds). 1948. *From Max Weber: Essays in Sociology*. London: Routledge and Kegan Paul.

Ghurye, G.S. 1959. *The Scheduled Tribes*. Bombay: Popular Prakashan.

———. 1963 [1943]. *The Aborigines 'So Called' and Their Future*. Pune: Gokhale Institute of Politics and Economics.

———. 1968. *Social Tensions in India*. Bombay: Popular Prakashan.

———. 1973. *I and Other Explorations*. Bombay: Popular Prakashan.

———. 1974. *Whither India*. Bombay: Popular Prakashan.

———. 1979 [1932]. *Caste and Race in India*. Bombay: Popular Prakashan.

———. 1980. *The Burning Caldron of North-East India*. Bombay: Popular Prakashan.

Giddens, Anthony. 1990. *The Consequences of Modernity*. Stanford: Stanford University Press.

Goffman, Erving. 1961. *Asylums*. New York: Doubleday Anchor.

Golwalkar, M.S. 1939. *We or Our Nationhood Defined*. Nagpur: Bharat Prakashan.

Gong, G.W. 1984. *The Standard of Civilization in International Society*. Oxford: Clarendon Press.

Goonatilake, Susantha. 2001. *Anthropologizing Sri Lanka: A Eurocentric Misadventure*. Bloomington: Indiana University Press.

Gough, Kathleen. 1968. 'New Proposals for Anthropologists', *Current Anthropology*, 9 (5): 403–7.

Guha, B.S. 1951. 'Indian Aborigines and Their Administration', *Journal of Asiatic Society*, 17 (1): 19–44.

Guha, Ranajit and Gayatri Chakravorty Spivak (eds). 1988. *Selected Subaltarn Studies*. New York: Oxford University Press.

Gupta, M.S. 1912. *Bharat Bharati*. Jhansi: Sahitya Sadan.

Gusfield, J.R. 1967. 'Tradition and Modernity: Misplaced Polarities in the Study of Social Change', *American Journal of Sociology*, 72 (4): 336–51.

Hadden, C. 1934. *History of Anthropology*. London: Watts and Co.

Hannerz, U. 1989. 'Notes on the Global Ecumene', *Public Culture*, 1 (2): 66–75.

Hardgrave, Jr. R.L. 1965. *The Dravidian Movement*. Bombay: Popular Prakashan.

Harris, M. 1968. *The Rise of Anthropological Theory: A History of Theories of Culture*. New York: Thomas Y. Crowell Co.

Hart, III, G.L. 1975 'Ancient Tamil Literature: Its Scholarly Past and Future', in B. Stein (ed.), *Essays on South India*. Hawai: The University Press, pp. 52–72.

Hays, S.P. 1989. 'The Devaluation of Place in Social Science', in J.A. Agnew and J.S. Duncan (eds), *The Power of Place: Bringing Together Geographical and Sociological Imagination*. Boston: Unwin Hyman, pp. 9–29.

Heller, Agnes. 1987. 'Sociology as Defetishisation of Modernity', *International Sociology*, 2 (4): 391–401.

Hetcher, Michael. 1975. *Internal Colonialism: The Celtic Fringe in British National Development, 1536–1966*. London: Routledge and Kegan Paul.

Hodgen, M.T. 1964. *Early Anthropology in the 16th and 17th Centuries*. Philadelphia: University of Pennsylvania Press.

Hoffman, D.P. 1961. *India's Social Miracle*. California: Naturegraph Co.

Homans, G.C. 1951. *The Human Group*. London: Routledge and Kegan Paul.

———. 1962. *Sentiments and Activities*. London: Routledge and Kegan Paul.

Howley, Amos. 1950. *Human Ecology*. New York: Ronald Press.

Huntington, Samuel. 1993. 'The Clash of Civilizations?', *Foreign Affairs*, 72 (1): 22–49.

Ilaiah, Kancha. 1996. *Why I am not a Hindu*. Kolkata: Samya.

Inayatullah. 1989. 'Social Science in Pakistan: An Evaluation', *International Social Science Journal*, 122: 617–33.

Indian Council of Social Science Research (ICSSR). 1973. *Report of the ICSSR Committee*. New Delhi.

———. 1974a, b, and c. *Survey of Research in Sociology and Social Anthropology*. Vols I, II, and III. New Delhi.

Indian Council of Social Science Research (ICSSR). 1985a and b. *Survey of Research in Sociology and Social Anthroplogy.* Vols I and II. New Delhi.
——. 1986. *Survey of Research in Sociology and Social Anthropology.* Vol. III. New Delhi.

Irschick, E.F. 1969. *Politics and Social Conflicts in South India: The Non-Brahmin Movement and Tamil Separatism, 1916–29.* Berkeley: University of California Press.

Jarvenpa, Robert. 1985. 'The Political Economy and Political Ethnicity of American Indian Adaptations and Identifies', in Richard D. Alba (ed.), *Ethnicity and Race in the USA: Towards the Twenty-First Century.* London: Routledge and Kegan Paul, pp. 29–48.

Jean-Philippe, Mathy. 1993. *Extreme Occident: French Intellectuals and America.* Chicago: University of Chicago Press.

Joshi, P.C. 1975. 'Reflections on Social Scier.ce Research in India', *Sociological Bulletin,* 24 (1): 139–62.

Kapadia, K.M. (ed.). 1954. *Professor Ghurye Felicitation Volume.* Bombay: Popular Prakashan.

Kuper, Adam. 1988. *The Invention of Primitive Society: Transformation of an Illusion.* London: Routledge.

Kymlicka, W. 1995. *Multicultural Citizenship: A Liberal Theory of Minority Rights.* Oxford: Clarendon Press.

Lanze, D.V. 1956. *Gandhi to Vinoba.* London: Rider and Co.

Leach, Edmund. 1961. *Rethinking Anthropology.* London: The Athlone Press.

Lévi-Strauss, C. 1961. *A World on the Wane.* London: Hutchinson.

——. 1966. 'The Scope of Anthropology', *Current Anthropology,* 7 (2): 112–23.

Levy, M.J. 1966. *Modernization and Structure of Societies, Vol. I.* Princeton: Princeton University Press.

Lockwood, David. 1964. 'Social Integration and System Integration', in G.K. Zollshan and W. Hirsch (eds), *Explorations in Social Change.* London: Routledge and Kegan Paul, pp. 244–57.

Long, C.H. 1978. 'Primitive/Civilized: The Locus of a Problem', *History of Religions,* 20: 401–12.

Luhman, Nicos. 1982. 'The World Society as a Social System', in R.F. Geyer and J. Vander Zouwen (eds), *Dependence and Inequality.* Oxford: Pergamon Press, pp. 295–306.

Madan, T.N. 1965. *Family and Kinship: A Study of the Pandits of Rural Kashmir.* Bombay: Asia Publishing House.

——. 1974. 'Research Methodology', *A Survey of Research in Sociology and Social Anthropology, Vol. III.* New Delhi: ICSSR, pp. 282–315.

Majumdar, D.N. 1939. 'Tribal Culture and Acculturation', *Man in India,* 19: 99–172.

Marcus, George E. 1995. 'Ethnography in/of the World System: the Emergence of Multi-sited Ethnography', *Annual Review of Anthropology*, 24: 95–117.

Marcus, G. and M. Fischer. 1986. *Anthropology as Cultural Critique: An Experimental Moment in the Human Sciences*. Chicago: Chicago University Press.

Marx, Karl and Frederich Engels. 1955. *On Colonialism*. Moscow: Foreign Language Publishers.

——. 1964. *German Ideology*. Moscow: Progress Publishers.

Merton, R.K. 1957. *Social Theory and Social Structure*. Illinois: The Free Press of Glenco.

Mintz, Sidney W. 1998. 'The Localisation of Anthropological Practice: From Area Studies to Transnationalism', *Current Anthropology*, 18 (2): 117–33.

Misra, B.B. 1961. *The Indian Middle Classes*. London: Oxford University Press.

Momin, A.R. (ed.). 1996. *The Legacy of G.S. Ghurye: A Centennial Festschrift*. Bombay: Popular Prakashan.

Motwani, Kewal. 1946. *India: A Conflict of Culture*. Nagpur: Nagpur University Press.

——. 1958. *Manu Dharma Sastra: A Sociological and Historical Study*. Madras: Ganesh.

Moynihan, D.P. 1993. *Pandemonium: Ethnicity in International Politics*. Oxford: Oxford University Press.

Mukerji, D.P. 1954. 'Social Research', in K.M. Kapadia (ed.), *Professor Ghurye Felicitation Volume*. Bombay: Popular Prakashan, pp. 234–7.

Mukherjee, Ramakrishna. 1979. *Sociology of Indian Sociology*. Bombay: Allied Publishers.

Mukherjee, R. and Haridas Majumdar. 1952. 'Sociology in India', in H. Becker and H.E. Barnes (eds), *Social Thought from Lore to Science, Vol. II*. Washington: Haven Press, pp. 1135–48.

Mukherji, D.P. 1945. 'Indian History and the Marxist Method', in D.P. Mukherji (ed.), *On Indian History: A Study of Method*. Bombay: Hind Kitabs, pp. 9–48.

——. 1958. 'Indian Tradition and Social Change', in D.P. Mukherji, *Diversities*. New Delhi: People's Publishing House, pp. 228–41.

——. 1961. 'Indian Sociology and Tradition', in R.N. Saksena (ed.), *Sociology, Social Research and Social Problems in India*. Bombay: Asia Publishing House, pp. 16–31.

Mukherji, P.N. 1980. 'Disciplined Eclecticism', *Seminar*, 254: 38–43.

Mukherji, Partha Nath and Chandan Sengupta (eds). 2004. *Indigeneity and Universality in Social Science: A South Asian Response*. New Delhi: Sage Publications.

Mutesa II. 1967. *The Desecration of my Kingdom.* London: Constable.

Myrdal, Gunnar. 1971. *Asian Drama: An Enquiry into the Poverty of Nations.* London: Allen Lane Penguin Press.

Nadkarni, M.V. 2003. 'Is Caste System Intrinsic to Hinduism? Demolishing a Myth', *Economic and Political Weekly*, 38 (45): 4783–93.

Nash, Y.D. 1974. *Red, White and Black: The Peoples' of Early America.* Englewood Cliff, NJ: Prentice Hall.

Nederveen Pieterse, Jan. 1994. 'Globalization as Hybridization', *International Sociology*, 9 (2): 161–84.

Needham, R.J. 1959. *Science and Civilization in China.* Cambridge: Cambridge University Press.

Nehru, Jawaharlal. 1956. *The Discovery of India.* London: Meridien Books.

Nisbet, R.A. 1966. *The Sociological Tradition.* London: Heineman.

Oommen, T.K. 1967a. 'The Rural Urban Continuum Re-examined in the Indian Context', *Sociologia Ruralis*, 7 (1): 30–48.

———. 1967b. 'Charisma, Social Structure and Social Change', *Comparative Studies in Society and History*, X (1): 85–99.

———. 1968. 'Strategy for Social Change: A Study of Untouchability', *Economic and Political Weekly*, 3 (25): 933–6.

———. 1969. 'Data Collection Techniques: The Case of Sociology and Social Anthropology', *Economic and Political Weekly*, 4 (19): 809–15 (reproduced with some additions as Chapter 2 in this volume).

———. 1970a. 'The Concept of Dominant Caste: Some Queries', *Contributions to Indian Sociology*, 4: 73–83.

———. 1970b. 'Rural Community Power Structure in India', *Social Forces*, 49 (2): 226–39.

———. 1971a. 'Green Revolution and Agrarian Conflict', *Economic and Political Weekly*, 6 (20): A. 95–A. 103.

———. 1971b. 'Agrarian Tension in a Kerala District: An Analysis', *Indian Journal of Industrial Relations*, 7 (2): 229–68.

———. 1972a. 'On the Distinction between Micro and Macro Studies', in Satish Saberwal (ed.), *Beyond the Village.* Simla: Indian Institute of Advanced Study, pp. 62–7.

———. 1972b. *Charisma, Stability and Change: An Analysis of Bhoodan-Gramdan Movement in India.* New Delhi: Thompson Press (India) Ltd.

———. 1976. 'Problems of Building Agrarian Organizations in Kerala', *Sociologia Ruralis*, XVI (2): 177–96.

———. 1977. 'Sociological Issues in the Analysis of Social Movements in Independent India', *Sociological Bulletin*, 26 (1): 14–37.

———. 1982. 'Foreigners, Refugees and Outsiders in the Indian Context', *Sociological Bulletin*, 31 (1): 41–64.

Oommen, T.K. 1983a. 'Towards Reconciling Traditional and Modern Values: The Indian Experiment', in J. Deppert (ed.), *India and the West*. New Delhi: Manohar, pp. 253–63.

———. 1983b. 'Sociology in India: A Plea for Contextualization', *Sociological Bulletin*, 32 (2): 111–36.

———. 1983c. 'Religious Pluralism in India: A Sociological Appraisal', in Ram Singh (ed.), *Christian Perspectives on Contemporary Indian Issues*. Madras: The Institute of Development Education, pp. 92–133.

———. 1985. *From Mobilization to Institutionalization: The Dynamics of Agrarian Movement in 20th Century Kerala*. Bombay: Popular Prakashan.

———. 1986a. 'Insiders and Outsiders in India: Primordial Collectivism and Cultural Pluralism in Nation-buildings', *International Sociology*, 1 (1): 53–74.

———. 1986b. 'Social Movements and Nation State in India: Towards Relegitimization of Cultural Nationalisms', *Journal of Social and Economic Studies (NS)*, 3 (2): 107–29.

———. 1987a. 'Theoretical Framework and Empirical Research: Their Interaction in the Analysis of Two Social Movements', *Sociological Bulletin*, 36 (2): 15–34 (reproduced as Chapter 3 in this volume).

———. 1987b. 'On the Craft of Studying Social Movements: Two Illustrations', *The Eastern Anthropologist*, 40 (3): 185–202 (reproduced as Chapter 4 in this volume).

———. 1988a. 'In Search of Qualitative Sociology in India', *Qualitative Sociology*, 11 (1, 2): 44–54.

———. 1988b. 'The Nature of Sociological Research and Practice Worldwide: A Perspective from India', *International Sociology*, 3 (3): 309–12.

———. 1989. 'Ethnicity, Immigration and Cultural Pluralism: India and the United States of America', in Melvin L. Kohn (ed.), *Cross-national Research in Sociology*. Newbury Park: Sage Publications, pp. 279–305.

———. 1990a. 'Movements and Institutions: Structural Opposition or Processual Linkage?', *International Sociology*, V (2): 145–56.

———. 1990b. 'Sociology for One World: A Plea for an Authentic Sociology', *Sociological Bulletin*, 39 (1, 2): 1–13 (reproduced as Chapter 7 in this volume.)

———. 1991. 'Internationalization of Sociology: A View from Developing Countries', *Current Sociology*, 39 (1): 67–84 (reproduced as Chapter 6 in this volume).

———. 1992. 'Restructuring Development through Technological Pluralism', *International Sociology*, 7 (2): 131–9.

———. 1995a. *Alien Concepts and South Asian Reality: Responses and Reformulations*. New Delhi: Sage Publications.

Oommen, T.K. 1995b. 'Contested Boundaries and Emerging Pluralism', *International Sociology*, 10 (3): 251–68 (reproduced in T.K. Oommen. 2002. *Pluralism, Equality, and Identity: Comparative Studies*. New Delhi: Oxford University Press).

———. 1996. 'Social Movements in a Comparative Perspective: Situating Alain Touraine', in J. Clark and M. Diani (eds), *Alain Touraine*. London: Falmer Press, pp. 111–25.

———. 1997a. 'From Plural Society to Pluralism: Towards a Just and Humane Social Order', *Social Action*, 47 (3): 259–71.

———. 1997b. *Citizenship, Nationality and Ethnicity: Reconciling Competing Identities*. Cambridge: Polity Press.

———. 1998. 'Society: Tradition and Autonomy', in Hirnmay Karlekar (ed.), *Independent India: The First Fifty Years*. New Delhi: Oxford University Press, pp. 229–40.

———. 2000. 'Changing Modes of Conceptualizing the World: Implications for Social Research', in P.N. Mukherji (ed.), *Methodology in Social Research: Dilemmas and Perspectives*. New Delhi: Sage Publications, pp. 153–70.

———. 2002. 'The Changing Trajectory of Constructing the Other: West Europe and South Asia', in T.K. Oommen, *Pluralism, Equality, and Identity: Comparative Studies*. New Delhi: Oxford University Press, pp. 111–26.

———. 2004a. *Nation, Civil Society and Social Movements: Essays in Political Sociology*. New Delhi: Sage Publications.

———. 2004b. 'New Nationalism and Collective Rights: The Case of South Asia', in Stephen May, Tariq Modood, and Judith Squires (eds), *Ethnicity, Nationalism and Minority Rights*. Cambridge: Cambridge University Press, pp. 121–43.

———. 2004c. 'Futures India: Society, Nation-state, Civilisation', *Futures*, 35 (61): 745–55.

———. 2005a. 'Challenges of Modernity in an Age of Globalisation', in Eliezer Ben-Rafael and Y. Sternberg (eds), *Comparing Modernities: Pluralism versus Homogeneity (Essays in Honour of S.N. Eisanstadt)*. Brill: Leiden, pp. 149–69.

———. 2005b. 'Re-organisation of Indian States: The Incomplete Agenda', in T.K. Oommen, *Crisis and Contention in Indian Society*. New Delhi: Sage Publications, pp. 142–52.

Pandian, Jacob. 1985. *Anthropology and the Western Tradition: Toward an Authentic Anthropology*. Illinois: Waveland Press.

Patel, Sujata (ed.). 2011. *Doing Sociology in India: Genealogies, Locations and Practices*. New Delhi: Oxford University Press.

Peterson, William. 1975. 'On the Subnations of Western Europe', in Nathan Glazer and D.P. Moynihan (eds), *Ethnicity: Theory and Experience*. Cambridge: Harvard University Press, pp. 177–208.

Pillai, S.D. (ed.). 1976. *Aspects of Changing India: Studies in Honour of Prof. G.S. Ghurye*. Bombay: Popular Prakashan.

Pletsch, C.E. 1981. 'The Three Worlds or the Division of the Social Scientific Labour Circa 1950–76', *Comparative Studies in Society and History*, 23 (1): 65–90.

Poliakov, Leon. 1974. *The Aryan Myth: A History of Racist and Nationalist Ideas in Europe*. London: Hienemann for Sussex University Press.

Pramanick, S.K. 2001. *Sociology of G.S. Ghurye*. Jaipur and New Delhi: Rawat Publications.

Radcliffe-Brown, A.R. 1952. 'Historical Note on British Social Anthropology', *American Anthropologist*, 54 (1): 275–8.

———. 1955 [1940]. 'Preface', in M. Fortes and E.E. Evans-Pritchard (eds), *African Political Systems*. London: Oxford University Press, pp. xi–xxii.

Rambhai, S.K. 1954. *Vinoba and His Mission*. Kashi: Akhil Sarva Seva Sangh.

———. 1958. *Progress of a Pilgrimage*. Kashi: Akhil Sarva Seva Sangh.

Redfield, Robert. 1955. *The Little Community*. Chicago: University of Chicago Press.

Roosens, E.H. 1989. *Creating Ethnicity*. Newbury Park: Sage Publications.

Rosenau, J.N. 1992. 'Governance, Order and Change in World Politics', in J.N. Rosenau and Ernst-Otto Czempiel (eds), *Governance without Government*. Cambridge: Cambridge University Press, pp. 1–22.

Rudolph, Lloyd and Susanne Rudolph. 1958. 'Surveys in India: Field Experiences in Madras State', *Public Opinion Quarterly*, 2 (2): 235–44.

Rush, G.R. and S. Denisoff. 1971. *Social and Political Movements*. New York: Meredith Corporation.

Saberwal, Satish. 1981. 'The Sociological Attitude', *Madras Development Seminar Series*, XI (12): 143–56.

———. 1982. 'Uncertain Transplants: Anthropology and Sociology in India', *Ethnos*, 47 (1, 2): 36–49.

Said, E.A. 1991. *Orientalism: Western Conceptions of the Orient*. Harmondsworth: Penguin Books.

Saksena, R.N. (ed.). 1961. *Sociology, Social Research and Social Problems in India*. New York: Asia Publishing House.

———. (ed.). 1965. *Sociology in India*. Agra: Institute of Social Sciences.

Sandholtz, W. and J. Zysman. 1999. '1992: Recasting the European Bargain', *World Politics*, 42 (1): 95–128.

Saran, A.K. 1958. 'India', in J.S. Rouceek (ed.), *Contemporary Sociology*. New York: Philosophical Library, pp. 122–35.

———. 1962. 'For a Sociology of India', *Eastern Anthropologist*, 15 (1), pp. 53–68.

Savarkar, V.D. 1929. *Hindutva*. Delhi: Bharti Sahitya Sadan.

Savur, Manorama. 2011. 'Sociology: The Genealogy of the Discipline in Bombay', in Sujata Patel (ed.), *Doing Sociology in India: Genealogies, Locations, and Practices*. New Delhi: Oxford University Press, pp. 3–28.

Schermerhorn, R.A. 1978. *Ethnic Plurality in India*. Tucson: University of Arizona Press.

Schumpeter, J.A. 1951. 'Imperialism and Social Classes'. London: Blackwell.

Sekhar, M.C. 1968. *Social Change in India: First Decade of Planning*. Poona: Deccan College Institute of Postgraduate and Research Institute.

Seminar. 1968. *Academic Colonialism*. p. 112.

Shah, G., S. Mander, S. Thorat, S. Deshpande, and A. Baviskar. 2006. *Untouchability in Rural India*. New Delhi: Sage Publications.

Shanklin, Eugenia. 2000. 'Representation of Race and Racism in American Anthropology', *Current Anthropology*, 41 (1): 99–103.

Shils, Edward. 1959. 'Social Inquiry and the Autonomy of the Individual', in Daniel Lerner, *The Human Meaning of Social Sciences*. Cleveland: Meridian Book Co.

Simmel, George. 1950. 'The Stranger', in K.H. Wolf (ed.), *The Sociology of George Simmel*. Glencoe, Illinois: The Fress Press, pp. 403–8.

Singh, Yogendra. 1973. 'The Role of Social Sciences in India: A Sociology of Knowledge', *Sociological Bulletin*, 22 (1): 14–28.

———. 1986. *Indian Sociology: Social Conditioning and Emerging Concerns*. New Delhi: Vistaar.

Smith, A. 1979. *Nationalism in the Twentieth Century*. Oxford: Oxford University Press.

Snipp, C.M. 1987. *The First of This Land*. New York: Basic Books.

Spratt, P. 1970. *DMK in Power*. Bombay: Nachiketa Publications.

Srinivas, M.N. 1942. *Family and Marriage in Mysore*. Bombay: New Book Company.

———. 1952. *Religion and Society Among the Coorgs of South India*. Oxford: Clarendon.

———. (ed.) 1955a. *India's Villages*. Bombay: Media Promoters and Publishers Pvt. Ltd.

———. 1955b. 'The Social Structure of a Mysore Village', in M.N. Srinivas (ed.), *India's Villages*. Bombay: Media Promoters and Publishers Pvt. Ltd., pp. 21–35.

———. 1956. 'A Note on Sanskritization and Westernization', *Far Eastern Quarterly*, XV (4): 481–96.

———. 1962. *Caste in Modern India and Other Essays*. Bombay: Media Promoters and Publishers Pvt. Ltd.

———. 1966. *Social Change in Modern India*. Bombay: Allied Publishers.

———. 1972. 'Some Thoughts on the Study of One's Own Society', in M.N. Srinivas. *Social Change in Modern India*. Bombay: Orient Longman, pp. 147–63.

Srinivas, M.N. 1975. 'Village Studies, Participant Observation and Social Science Research in India', *Economic and Political Weekly* (special number) X, 33, 34, & 35: 1387–94.

———. 1979. 'A Village in Karnataka,' in M.N. Srinivas, A.M. Shah, and E.A. Ramaswamy (eds), *The Fieldworker and the Field: Problems and Challenges in Sociological Investigation.* New Delhi: Oxford University Press, pp. 19–28.

———. 1980. *India: Social Structure.* Delhi: Hindustan Publishing Corporation.

———. 1994. 'Sociology in India and Its Future', *Sociological Bulletin*, 43 (1): 9–19.

———. 2002. *Collected Essays.* New Delhi: Oxford University Press.

Srinivas, M.N., S.C. Dube, N. Prasad, I.P. Desai, and P.J. Philip. 1961. *Sociology in Indian Universities* (Report of the University Grants Commission, Review Committee on Sociology). New Delhi: University Grants Commission.

Srinivas, M.N. and M.N. Panini. 1973. 'The Development of Sociology and Social Anthropology in India', *Sociological Bulletin*, 22 (2): 179–215.

Srinivas, M.N., A.M. Shah, and E.A. Ramaswamy (eds). 1979. *The Fieldworker and the Field.* New Delhi: Oxford University Press.

Stein, Burton (ed.), 1975. *Essays on South India.* Hawaii: The University Press, 52–72.

———. 1977. 'Circulation and Historical Geography of Tamil Country', *Journal of Asian Studies*, 37: 1–28.

Symcox, Geoffrey. 1972. 'The Wild Man's Return: The Enclosed Vision of Rousseau's Discourses', in Edward Dudley and Maximilian E. Novak (eds), *The Wild Man Within: Western Thought from the Renaissance to Romanticism.* Pittsburg: University of Pittsburg, pp. 223–47.

Tagore, Rabindranath. 1937. *Nationalism.* London: Macmillan and Co. (Indian edition).

Tennyson, Hallam. 1955. *Saint on March.* London: Victor Gollancz.

Thornton, R.J. 1983. 'Narrative Ethnography in Africa, 1850–1929: The Creation and Capture of an Appropriate Domain for Anthropology', *Man*, 18 (3): 502–20.

———. 1988. 'The Rhetoric of Ethnographic Holism', *Cultural Anthropology*, 3 (2): 285–303.

Tilly, Charles. 1990. *Coercion, Capital and European States: AD 990–1900.* Cambridge: Basil Blackwell.

———. 1994. 'States and Nationalism in Europe, 1492–1992', *Theory and Society*, 23 (1): 131–46.

Tinker, Hugh. 1974. *A New System of Slavery: The Export of Indian Labour Overseas, 1830–1920.* London: Oxford University Press.

Tiryakian, E.A. 1994. 'The New World and Sociology: An Overview', *International Sociology*, 9 (2): 131–48.

Tocqueville, Alexis de. 1956. *Democracy in America, Vol. I*. New York: Knopf.

Trouillot, Michel-Rolph. 2003. *Global Transformations: Anthropology and the Modern World*. New York: Palgrave Macmillan.

Unnithan, T.K.N., Yogendra Singh, Indra Deva, and Narendra Singhi. 1967. *Sociology for India*. New Delhi: Prentice Hall.

Upadhya, Carol. 2002. 'The Hindu Nationalist Sociology of G.S. Ghurye', *Sociological Bulletin*, 51 (1): 28–57.

Van der Berghe. 1983. 'Australia, Canada and the United States: Ethnic Melting Pots or Plural Societies', *Australia New Zealand Journal of Sociology*, 19 (2): 238–52.

Venugopal, C.N. 1977. 'Factor of Anti-pollution in the Ideology of Lingayat Movement', *Sociological Bulletin*, 26 (2): 227–41.

———. 1986. 'G.S. Ghurye's Ideology of Normative Hinduism', *Contributions to Indian Sociology*, 20 (2): 305–14.

———. 1993. 'G.S. Ghurye on Culture and Nation-building', *Sociological Bulletin*, 42 (1&2): 1–13.

———. 1996. 'G.S. Ghurye's Sociology of Religion: An Inquiry into Selected Aspects', in A.R. Momin (ed.), *The Legacy of G.S. Ghurye: A Centennial Festschrift*. Bombay: Popular Prakashan, pp. 47–60.

Wallerstein, Immanuel. 1979. *The Capitalist World Economy*. Cambridge: Cambridge University Press.

White, H. 1972. 'The Forms of Wildness: Archaeology of an Idea', in Edward Dudley and Maximilian E. Novak (eds), *The Wild Man Within: Western Thought from the Renaissance to Romanticism*. Pittsburg: University of Pittsburg, pp. 1–18.

Wissler, Clark. 1923. *Man and Culture*. New York: Thomas Y. Cromwell.

Worsley, Peter. 1984. *The Three Worlds: Culture and World Development*. Chicago: University of Chicago Press.

Wright, A.W. 1981. 'Socialism and Nationalism', in Leonard Tivey (ed.), *The Nation State*. Oxford: Martin Roberston, pp. 148–70.

Xaxa, Virginius. 2008. *State, Society and Tribes: Issues in Post-Colonial India*. New Delhi: Pearson Education.

Yinger, Milton (ed.). 1957. *Religion, Society and the Individual*. New York: Macmillan.

Zelditch, M., Jr. 1962. 'Some Methodological Issues of Field Studies', *American Journal of Sociology*, 67 (4): 566–76.

Name Index

Subject Index

❧